Dining in a Classical Context

Dining in a
Classical Context

Edited by William J. Slater

Ann Arbor

THE UNIVERSITY OF MICHIGAN PRESS

1994   1993   1992   1991   4   3   2   1

Library of Congress Cataloging-in-Publication Data

Dining in a classical context / edited by William J. Slater.
   p.   cm.
  Includes bibliographical references and index.
  ISBN 0-472-10194-3 (cloth.: alk.)
  1. Classical literature—History and criticism.   2. Dinners and
dining in literature.   3. Dinners and dining—Greece—History.
4. Dinners and dining—Rome—History.   5. Greece—Social life and
customs.   6. Rome—Social life and customs.   7. Civilization,
Classical.   I. Slater, William J.
PA3015.D56D56 1991
394.1' 2' 0938—dc20   90-27526
                                          CIP

For
Erika Simon

Preface

The chapters in this volume were delivered at a symposium at McMaster University in September of 1989 before a lively and appreciative audience. The initiative for the conference came largely from a chance suggestion by John D'Arms outside a pub in Oxford in 1981. Another debt is owed to Oswyn Murray for bringing some of us together at the first symposium on symposia at that time, an experience we enjoyed enough to wish to repeat. This one was smaller but the interest in the theme remains as great. We are more aware than ever of the amount that awaits exploration. The editor takes this opportunity to thank all the contributors once again and to express a special debt of gratitude to the Social Science and Humanities Research Council, for its support of the conference, and to the Arts Research Board of McMaster, for a subvention toward the cost of the indispensable illustrations.

Contents

Introduction

William J. Slater

In 1548 Gulielmus Philander of Castile, commenting on Vitruvius, could write that no one to his knowledge had investigated the ancient habit of lying down to dinner. By the end of the century, Girolamo Mercuriale, Pedro Chacon, and Johann Stucky had with vast philological learning effectively done so, their motive being largely to explain the historical circumstances of the New Testament. The chapters in this book represent a belated expansion of their researches, for their books had no adequate successors, especially for the earlier Greek period. Indeed the symposium will have to be rediscovered over again, not only because of the wealth of new information from art and archaeology, but also because of the new insights afforded by anthropology and social history. But as Stucky complained, the subject exceeded even then the formidable resources of a Renaissance polymath. No one can now hope to write a comprehensive study of the ancient symposium; and the chapters that follow—by their varied approaches—are designed to illustrate the diverse relations between the act of dining and the life of antiquity. In what follows readers should see an attempt to arouse scholars anew to consider the symposium as a living context for much of ancient culture and its literature.

Greeks and Romans lay down to eat and drink as they still sometimes do at outdoor picnics, by the sea or on the grass, sometimes on hallowed ground and sometimes not. That is not the immediate concern of this book. But at some point, for reasons largely unknown to us, they decided to transfer this habit indoors, and from that time onward the fashion for the reclining dinner party remained so firmly a symbol of classical culture that in its disappearance somewhere in France, fourteen centuries later, we can see with some justice the final extinguishing of the living society of antiquity, so final indeed that it was left to Renaissance scholars to discover that the ancients lay down at all. Those last symposiasts doubtless grimly determined to lie down in what they took to be the only civilized manner, in order to express as best they could their hostility to the barbarian fashions around them; but they also knew themselves to be part of a great and admirable tradition that extended back into the remote past, even if they must at the same time have known they were at its end. And it is that tradition that is the concern of this book.

It is easier to say why those French bishops were forced to give up their antique dinners than to explain why eastern Greeks began the fashion. We are told it was the manner of free men and not slaves to lie down for formal meals; it certainly appealed to aristocracies, and it was impossible without slaves. From early times the poets and philosophers concerned themselves with the symposium and mused on what it represented for their patrons and for themselves. Even Homer, officially the only poet who predates the arrival of the classical symposium, had set one of his epics largely at the dinner parties of the suitors of Penelope and of the happy dwellers in Phaeacia. He first expressed in canonical terms the atmosphere of the ideal symposium.

> Nothing is more graceful than when merriment possesses all the people, and banqueters listen in the halls to the singer, sitting in order, and the tables beside them are filled with bread and meat, and the wine pourer brings wine decanted from the bowl and pours it in the cups.

That early Greek poetry was largely meant for performance and presentation at symposia was first asserted nearly a hundred years ago by Richard Reitzenstein in *Skolion und Epigramm*, and, though objections were long voiced, he has now largely been vindicated. But one of the main preoccupations of this symposium poetry is its own context, the symposium itself: its atmosphere, its ethics, its virtues and dangers, and its meaning for those who participate in it. At its best it is held to represent everything that is finest in human congress, including poetry and music; at its worst everything that is barbaric. Not surprisingly the philosophers built their schools around dinner meetings and composed regulations for such gatherings, and no school entirely ignored their importance for social philosophy; yet their major contribution was in formulating a picture of the ideal symposiast, a task accomplished most effectively and unforgettably by the pupils of Socrates.

Under their influence a complete genre of literature was further developed describing the ideal symposium and its antithesis, doubtless primarily to recreate, exemplify, and celebrate their master's famous conversation in its best-known context. For civilized conversation was also a concern for the philosophers, and that its rules were observed can be seen both from the injunctions of Aristophanes in the *Wasps* or the discussions of Aristotle and Plutarch but also by contrast from the parodies of Petronius or Lucian. To go dining was to show by conversation and behavior that one knew and conformed to the ideals and traditions of a culture that remained a firm guide in an unstable world. Even the earliest symposium can be a place for the ostentatious display not just of gilded ceilings or inlaid floors, Ionian couches, exotic entertainment, or luxury vases, but also of the cultural quality of host and guests.

The ideals of the symposium are cultural ideals, and the well-organized and successful symposium is the vehicle for their expression. Greek uses many words in its attempts to express the objective of such a social ideal: *euphrosyne*, *charis* at first as in Homer, meaning roughly merriment and elegance. The poets add *eunomia*, good order, and other civic virtues, openly equating the ethics of the symposium with those of the *polis*. The philosophers add *koinonia* and *philanthropia* and much else. It is odd that the story of the ideals of the dining room in antiquity has yet to be written. That they existed and that the Renaissance inherited and understood them extraordinarily clearly—more clearly than classical scholars perhaps—has been recently illuminated by Michael Jeanneret's fascinating study of Rabelais: *Les Mets et les Mots*.

At the dinner table in the historical world politics were discussed, revolutions planned, and occasionally enemies eliminated in the manner of the Godfather. Here the epic poets related that Oedipus cursed his sons, and Alcaeus denounced his former friends. For theory held that at the symposium one declared what one hated and also what one loved, according to the principle that friendship required everyone to speak freely as equals and not to bear away with oneself grudges or gossip. Poets praised their friends and patrons and occasionally mocked them, for the spirit of good fellowship also entailed a display of that urbane wit upon which the elegant atmosphere of a dinner party tends to rest. As so often, the ideal was seen as the balance between two extremes, seriousness and frivolity, and it was the duty of the "leader of the symposium," the symposiarch, to preserve the balance between the two.

If, therefore, the dinner guest in imperial Rome was in danger between courses of having the latest news on Greek accents read to him by the house grammarian, he could at least cherish the hope that this indigestible material would be offset by lighter fare. All through antiquity the dining table was also a place of entertainment. Early black-figure vases show singers and dancers as a regular feature of the symposium, and Xenophon's symposium proves that such indoor entertainment was a professional product of international artists; even so it was left to the Roman world to privatize the entire culture of Greece for its dinner table. Comedy, tragedy, mime, and pantomime, suitably trimmed at times to fit the menu, alternated with musicians and those "travelling folk," jugglers, magicians, dwarfs, and the Spanish dancing girls whom Septicius Clarus preferred to Pliny's cultural offerings; and there were many more, whose odd skills are known to us now only from inscriptions and late glossaries. Perhaps it was to ward off too much frivolity that the baroque fantasies of wealthy Romans pushed the Horatian dialectic of "Eat, drink, and be merry; tomorrow you may be gone" to Fellini-like extremes, by stressing in drastic terms verbally and graphically the imminent prospect of death: the skeleton on the table or on the cup, as Dunbabin has shown elsewhere, accentuates the fragility of enjoyment. By such reasoning it was a heroic act, worthy of Sarpedon, to enjoy oneself in the face of mortality, surrounded by perfumes, flowers, and all the other delights of the senses. Dining is motivated not by mindless hedonism—so runs the argument—but by a philosophic awareness that the symposiast is defying death in celebrating life. The reward is not the future fame of the hero, but a profound certainty of the present.

Readers may be alarmed or delighted, according to their taste, by the relative absence of theory in these chapters. To be sure, the questions asked by the authors in this book are for the most part pragmatic. Where did one lie down? At what age? What did one wear? Why lie in a semicircle rather than a traditional triclinium? How did the symposium die out? Noel Robertson shows that from Greek myth also one might be able to extract some truth about the early history of the symposium, by inviting us to look further at the extraordinary behavior of Hippokleides, when he danced away his wedding. Oswyn Murray examines also with provocative parallels the underlying significance of the military symposium in early Greece, with its mixture of dining rituals and warlike ethics. Margaret Miller reminds us of the many odd fashions of the Attic symposium by illustrating in detail the wearing of "Persian" hats, and she considers the possible explanations.

Walter Burkert is concerned to shed light on the alleged origins of the symposium in the East, and Jeremy Rossiter on its last moments in the great villas of the classical world. From lying on the grass at a festival to meeting for drinks in the villa library is a long and complex path, but one that we can document. Alan Booth asks the interesting question: when was one old enough to lie down to dinner? John Yardley reviews some of the more eccentric activity that the Roman poet describes as part of the sympotic activity of his time. George Paul looks at what Plutarch makes of symposia in his biographies.

Katherine Dunbabin follows the architectural development of the dining room, especially as attested by the floor mosaics in the empire, and comes to some conclusions about the origins of the sigma couch. Christopher Jones reviews the evidence for the entertainment provided for these diners and extends the survey to include "theater-dinner." To a surprising degree the architectural development can be interpreted as favoring these performances. Finally John D'Arms offers a sobering essay on the position of the slaves, without whom this complex dining culture could never have functioned.

The editorial interference has been minimal, restricted to eliminating major anomalies of presentation as far as possible, and to the preparation of an index. All of the chapters have been rewritten, sometimes considerably, from their original form. The costs of publication have been substantially diminished by the absence of a Greek font. But by the same token this advantage was offset by the inevitable omission of the valuable contribution by Joachim Latacz on Greek sympotic literature; happily it will appear elsewhere in its proper format. Jeremy Rossiter and Margaret Miller both undertook much pictorial work at considerable expense to themselves. But it is hoped that the pictures in this volume will contribute substantially to its usefulness, and perhaps atone for the absence of Greek.

The editor is aware that throughout—and not only in the introduction—there is not always a clear division made between dining and symposium, *cena* and *comissatio*, *deipnon* and *potos*, though it is conventional wisdom so to distinguish. Such a division is impractical in a book covering over a thousand years of history, but it is in any event a distinction not always justified by the evidence. That is one of the many questions whose answer will not be found in this book. If the reader is disturbed by other incon-cinnities, these should sometimes be charitably attributed to the unavoidably different attitudes of scholars faced with a massively complex theme. On the whole it was the experience of the participants that each had learned something from the others in contemplating the communal dining of antiq-uity as a social phenomenon. It was the aim of the conference to promote a mutual illumination of literature and archaeology on a theme common to both, at a time when pressures exist to balkanize and impoverish classical studies. We like to think that this aim was achieved.

Oriental Symposia: Contrasts and Parallels

Walter Burkert

As soon as alcoholic beverages had been discovered and made readily available, the socializing functions of alcohol must have become apparent as well. Thus, some forms of drinking parties may be expected to occur everywhere, and feelings will have arisen such as are expressed in the oldest Sumerian drinking song that survives: "Our liver is happy, our heart is joyful . . . while I feel wonderful, I feel wonderful."[1] General human dispositions will nevertheless adapt themselves to differing cultural systems.

Thus the Greek symposium, which is in focus here, has quite specific characteristics. To recall its main features, following Oswyn Murray,[2] the symposium is an organization of all-male groups, aristocratic and egalitarian at the same time, which affirm their identity through ceremonialized drinking. Prolonged drinking is separate from the meal proper; there is wine mixed in a krater for equal distribution; the participants, adorned with wreaths, lie on couches. The symposium has private, political, and cultural dimensions: it is the place of *euphrosyne*, of music, poetry, and other forms of entertainment; it is bound up with sexuality, especially homosexuality; it guarantees the social control of the *polis* by the aristocrats. It is a dominating social form in Greek civilization from Homer onward, and well beyond the Hellenistic period.

Ceremonial drinking parties are in evidence in Minoan and Myceaean palaces, too, but these were of a different kind. At Knossos, a wall-painting from a room in the west wing, facing the west court, known as the "campstool fresco," has been reconstructed to present an extensive formal drinking party. Many pairs of seated men face each other, holding goblets and stemmed cups of well-known types, while servants serve wine; a few females of larger size are entering from the side—one of these is the woman of the famous Knossian painting known as *La Parisienne*. They seem to be guests of higher status—goddesses, or priestesses impersonating goddesses, who have been invited to join in.[3] At Pylos, more than 2,800 stemmed cups were found packed in one magazine of the southwest wing, and Gösta

7

Säflund has rightly suggested that huge drinking bouts must have gone on in the megaron, probably in connection with sacrificial banquets.[4] The numbers of revellers suggested by these finds correspond to palace organization, but they would never fit the frame of a later Greek symposium.

Oriental, to be contrasted with *Greek*, is quite a questionable and vague term. In the following discussion, it is meant to include Mesopotamia, Anatolia, Syria, Palestine, and Egypt, with a certain preponderance on Mesopotamia and Palestine—this may be a personal limitation. There are two types of alcoholic beverages competing in these regions, beer and wine, as against the complete dominance of wine in classical Greece. Beer is much more common in Mesopotamia and in Egypt,[5] whereas wine is in the foreground in Syria and Palestine;[6] it is designated by the same word as in Greek: Aramaic *wain*, Western Semitic *jain*, identical with *woinos*. At the time of Herodotus (3.6), there was a considerable export of wine from Syria to Egypt. An important difference, besides taste, would have been that beer could be produced at any time of the year (although it would require more complex preparation) whereas the supply of wine would be dependent on the seasonal cycle. Vintage festivals are more closely prescribed by nature than beer festivals.

It is to be said in advance that, from the "oriental" side, we shall find more contrasts than parallels with the Greek symposium. Let us begin with the earliest evidence, the ceremonial drinking party in old Mesopotamian tradition. A well-established iconographic type from the third millennium B.C. shows a seated couple, one male, one female, drinking together, usually drawing the beverage from a vessel with a tube. This is evidently beer; Xenophon still witnessed such a form of drinking in Armenia (*Anab.* 4.5.26ff., 32). According to Selz, who has presented a recent survey with careful discussion of earlier interpretations,[7] the scene should refer to a ceremonial evening meal (KIN SIS or SUBUN) at a temple, held by the royal couple representing the gods at the occasion of a harvest festival.[8] This means that this form of "drinking together," of ceremonialized drinking, is in many respects the very opposite of a Greek symposium: there is a couple instead of an all-male society, there is a monarchic representation instead of an egalitarian group. Nevertheless, we find common drinking as the essence of a festival already by this point, and it constitutes some form of social control, since it demonstrates the established hierarchy by bringing the rulers, in a state of bliss, close to the gods and by creating distance from the waiters and other groups of people who watch from afar. Specialists find that this type of representation seems to lose its function in

Mesopotamia already in the third millennium B.C. It nevertheless persists as an iconographic type, which reaches as far as Syria[9] and finally even to Cyprus.[10] One Syrian seal dated ca. 1700–1500 presents a seated goddess together with a worshipper who is introduced by a priest, drawing beer from the vessel.[11] This seems to be a strange yet memorable form of communion with a divinity.

As to Syria and Palestine, there is more direct evidence from written sources since the Late Bronze Age. It centers on the term *marza'u* (Ugaritic) or *marzeah* (Hebrew). This word had always been known from the Old Testament, and the Septuagint gives the translation *thiasos* in one case.[12] But it was only through new evidence—mainly from Palmyra and then from Ugarit—that its real meaning and implications became apparent.[13] The Ugaritic testimonies are most important because they clearly antedate the formation and influence of Greek civilization.[14] A *marza'u* at Ugarit is an important social organization, an exclusive club consisting of the "men of the *marza'u*," headed by a president (*rb*), owning a "house" and other property; in one instance there is a mention of vineyards. The men meet for ceremonial feasts, including heavy drinking, in the worship of a specific god. Membership may be hereditary.

The *marza'u* has made its entrance into a mythological text:[15] the god El/Ilu was "giving a banquet in his palace. He called in the gods for the carving: 'Eat, gods, and drink, drink wine unto satiety, must unto drunkenness!'" Yet it turns out that El himself gets too much of it: sitting "in his *marza'u*," "he drinks wine unto satiety, must unto drunkenness . . . He has fallen into his own dung and urine! Ilu is like a dead man . . . " So his daughters ᶜAnatu and ᶜAthtartu took care of him, and with a certain herb "they restored the strength of his hands, when they had healed him, look, he awoke!" This strange myth is in fact, as the concluding lines show, part of a practical recipe against the consequences of drunkenness. Thus the god's experience is to influence the real world of men, which it is seen to mirror. Some details remain unclear,[16] but we get a vivid impression of what may happen at the reunions in a *marza'u*.

An additional illustration comes from another mythological text from Ugarit.[17] In Aqhat there is Danel, a pious man, who has no son—the gods are to help him in due course. Among the deprivations he must endure in this sad family situation, besides the lack of future funeral cult, there is no one "who takes him by the hand when he is drunk, carries him when he is sated with wine." The next verse is not quite clear, and so we are left to wonder where this heavy yet regular drinking should occur—in his *marza'u?* It definitely happens at some distance from the bedroom. Interpreters have long compared a passage in Isaiah (51.17ff.) where the prophet tells Jerusalem: "Get up. . . . You have drunk the chalice of wrath from the hand of Jahweh . . . and no guide was left for her from all the sons that she had borne, none to hold her hand from all the sons she had raised." Drunkenness has become a metaphor for catastrophe in the prophetic text— but this applies only if the young generation is not available to help. In the El text the daughters were seen to take care of their father, and so this is a prime reason why men must have offspring. We may well doubt whether this is a way to instil respect for parents, but probably the adolescents were quite eager to take part in adult pleasures even if this meant menial duties.[18]

The most interesting, and most discussed, testimony for *marzeah* is a passage of Amos that at the same time is the first attestation of lying on couches for a feast.[19] The prophet threatens people who are lying on couches of ivory, eating choice lambs from the herd, drinking, singing, and anointing themselves: "The *marzeah* of the recliners will disappear." The picture is not too different from what the Ugaritic sources suggest, i.e., conspicuous consumption within a closed circle of well-to-do revellers. The organization of *marzeah* is also attested in two Phoenician inscriptions, one from Marseille/Carthage, where it seems to be an organization parallel to clan and family, the other from Piraeus, where it designates a yearly feast.[20] More abundant, if much later, evidence comes from Palmyra.[21]

There is no doubt that with the *marzeah* institution we come quite close to Greek social organizations that are connected with the symposium, to *thiasoi* or *hetairiai* in which sacrifice and feasting are central activities. The equivalence as stated by the Septuagint translators seems to make sense. We must still remain aware that the Semitic evidence is lacunose, variegated, spread over centuries, and hardly suffices to pronounce a verdict of either identity or derivation with regard to the Greek symposium. There remains a remarkable case of parallelism. The couches of the "recliners" are a special problem to which we shall come back.

Further aspects are known of oriental drinking in myth and in reality: gods feasting among themselves with ceremonial yet heavy drinking are a familiar concept wherever a divine pantheon is described.[22] There are more texts from Ugarit that introduce the gods feasting and consuming huge amounts of wine at the time. Thus Baal makes a festival in his new house, and "Radmanu served Baꜥclu, the Almighty. . . . He took a thousand pitchers of foaming wine, ten thousand he mixed in his mixture. . . ."[23] As for Babylon, when Marduk has vanquished Tiamat, built the universe, and created man, he causes the sanctuaries of Babylon to be established.

The gods, his fathers, at his banquet he seated: "This is Babylon, the place that is your home! Make merry in its precincts, occupy its joys!" The great gods took their seats, they set up the beer mug, sat down to the banquet. After they had made merry within it, in Esagila, the splendid, they performed their rites. Fixed were the norms and all their portents; the stations of heaven and earth the gods divided. . . .

So they finally decreed the fates and proclaimed the fifty names of Marduk.[24] The word for "banquet" is *qeretu,* which properly means "invitation." It is interesting to note that the final ceremony does presuppose communal drinking—"merrymaking" first of all—reflecting probably some practice among men. It is in a mood of happiness produced by the beer mug that the gods set out to make their final decrees; it is in consequence of this mood that the poem about the foundation of Marduk's power comes to its conclusion.

Egyptian gods indulge in revelling, too; they do it together with their worshippers at the great festivals. Thus the "Calendar of Efu" speaks about the gods who have arrived for the celebration from distant towns: "They sit down and drink and celebrate a festival before this venerable god [the god of Edfu]: they drink and anoint themselves and celebrate very loudly, together with the inhabitants of the city."[25] The joys of gods and of men are parallel and mirror each other in the festival.

Myth nevertheless may also tell about serious dangers lurking in the consumption of alcohol. In the Aqhat text, Pughat, the sister of the murdered hero, invites the murderer, Yattupanu, and pours huge amounts of wine for him—no doubt this is to prove fatal for him, but the preserved text breaks off here.[26] In the Hittite myth of Illuyankas the Dragon and the Weather God, this is the method used to overcome the adversary: the goddess Inaras prepares a great festival, with three kinds of intoxicating drinks, and all the amphoras filled to the brim.

Inaras put on her finery and lured the Dragon Illuyankas up from his lair: "See. I am holding a celebration. Come you to eat and to drink." The Dragon Illuyankas came up with his children and they ate and drank. They drank every amphora dry and quenched their thirst. Thereupon they are no longer able to descend to their lair.

And thus they are caught and bound.[27] Such an effect was to be foreseen, especially with strange and uncivilized guests. "Wine also ruined the centaur, well-famed Eurytion," the *Odyssey* says (21.295f.), and we remember what happened to the Cyclops. How to deal with alcohol is part of cultivated manners, so it can be used to trick nature demons, including dragons and their kin.[28]

As to real life, it is not surprising to find in Mesopotamia and Israel the common, even banal form of drinking that is conspicuously absent from reputable archaic Greek society: the inn, the innkeeper, the selling of alcoholic beverages, the commercialized form of drinking beer. In Mesopotamia, this goes together with the craft of brewing beer. The brewer is *sabu* in Akkadian, or *sirasu,* but more often it is a female, *sabitu,* who is offering the beverage—and somewhat more—to clients who are able to pay. The traditional rendering in English has become "ale-wife." The word for *inn* is "house of the brewer" or "house of the ale-wife," *bit sabi* or *bit sabiti.* Another Akkadian word for inn is *astammu.* Payment is usually in grain; clients may have drinks on credit. But when Assurbanipal's plunderings brought affluence to Niniveh, "camels were sold for 1½ shekels of silver in the gate of sale, and the Ale-Wife received camels and slaves as a present."[29]

The institution of inns and ale-wives goes far back at least in imagination: according to the Sumerian king-list, the founder of the fourth dynasty of Kish, Ku-Baba, was an "ale-wife."[30] The best-known appearance of a *sabitu* is in *Gilgamesh,* tablet X: Siduri the Ale-Wife receives Gilgamesh beyond the cosmic mountain and helps him to pursue his way to Utnapishtim, the hero of the Flood. Why she dwells there, and in what function, remains enigmatic: "They made a jug for her, they made a mashing bowl of gold for her"—this line seems to allude to some myth or ritual that is lost to us.[31] Her role in relation to Gilgamesh has been compared to that of Circe in the *Odyssey,* who receives Odysseus in her house and gives advice about his further journey to the Beyond. There is nothing in the lacunose text of *Gilgamesh,* though, to hint at intimacies such as those that happen on the bed of Homer's Circe, although it would perhaps not be too far off the point.

In real life the inns seem to have been brothels, by common understanding;[32] the combination of alcohol and sex is not a Greek prerogative. Heinrich Zimmern has published a text that he called *Schenkenliebeszauber,* "the love charm of the inn"; it is an incantation to make a female attractive "to bring profit to the inn."[33] There could be more special forms of service. In a text pertinently included in Lambert's edition of Babylonian Wisdom Literature, there is the joke of an "effeminate man" *(sinnisanu),* evidently a eunuch, entering an inn *(astammu)* and praying to Ishtar, the love goddess.

To this should be compared the girl in the *Schenkenliebeszauber:* "You are plenty—I am half"; in Akkadian this is a play on words.[34] This would take us right to the sphere of Hellenistic *kinaidoi, delicati* as passive homosexuals. No wonder a more serious text of Babylonian Wisdom Literature warns: "Do not hasten to a banquet in the inn, and you will not be bound with a halter."[35]

In the *Codex Hammurabi* there are some regulations about payments and credits in relation to the ale-wife, which are difficult to understand. A more interesting paragraph is #109: "If outlaws have congregated in the establishment of a woman wine seller and she has not arrested those outlaws and has not taken them to the palace, that wine seller shall be put to death."[36] The designation of "outlaws" *(sarrutum)* is, of course, from the perspective of the ruler and his ideas about law and order. But that inns should be the place where *mafiosi* tend to meet is a notion not unknown to moderns. The word translated "congregated" in *ANET* basically means "to bind."[37] Thus it is "being bound together" that may occur in a tavern, as the authorities suspect; hence the ferocious punishment for the innkeeper who does not call the police, or indeed assume police functions herself. We may set a classical Greek text right beside this; it comes from Timaeus and refers to Empedocles.[38] Empedocles, invited to a symposium at Akragas, noticed strange proceedings which, as he recognized, meant "a beginning of tyranny"; thus "the next day he brought to court and secured a death sentence for both the host and the symposiarch," the unlawful fellows who had "bound together" at the drinking party. What could happen at a Greek symposium was already suspected by the royal authority of Babylon. But evidently inns and ale-wives went on to flourish, in spite of professional risks, down to the time of Assurbanipal, as mentioned above. The "houses of drinking" appear in the Hebrew Bible as well, and there is many a warning about them in the texts of wisdom. Even the double function of inn and brothel seems to recur. The house of Rahab the whore at Jericho, where the Hebrew spies find shelter, is turned into an inn by Josephus.[39]

In the Old Testament there is more about communal drinking at festivals. The main word normally translated "festival" or "banquet" means just "drinking": *mishtäh*, from *shatah:* "to drink"; the Septuagint appropriately translates it as *potos.* The real essence of a festival is drinking.[40] A "banquet" is "made" upon invitation by a lord, a king; sometimes all the people of the village or "city" are invited *(Gen. 29.22)*; an appropriate occasion may be the birth of a child *(Gen. 21.8)*. Of course this results in "merrymaking," i.e., heavy drinking; more serious affairs therefore will have to wait for the next morning *(I Sam. 25.36)*. In these cases it is always clear who is the host, and who is invited: the banquet is a gesture of a grand seigneur. The communal aspect that is so important for the Greek symposium hardly comes to the surface. It is wine that is common in everyday life and is integrated into religious ritual. Priests, however, are forbidden to drink wine before officiating *(Lev.* 10.9), and there is the special status of the *Nazir,* the man "devoted" to Jahweh, which includes rejection of everything connected with the vine *(Num.* 6, etc.). Likewise Jeremiah (16.8) is forbidden to enter a "house of drinking" *(bet mishtäh).* Beer is normally ignored in the Hebrew text, although the Akkadian word *sikaru* is there as a loan-word, *shekar* (Septuagint *sikera),* and it is usually translated just "alcoholic beverage," *Rauschtrank.*

Let us have a closer look at a very late text from Esther and at a very early text about Sampson. The most prominent role of banquets occurs in one of the latest books of Scripture and not even in an Israelite context, in the book of Esther. Its date is still controversial, and opinions differ accordingly as to how much real information about the Persian court and its customs can be expected to come from this text.[41] Such are the habits at the Persian court as seen by the author: King Ahasuerus/Xerxes is giving a great banquet for all his princes and his servants, which is to last 180 days, and seven days for all the people in the enclosed garden of his palace. "And for drinking there was the ordinance that nobody should be stopped." At the same time the queen is giving a banquet for the women in the palace. This implies separation of sexes; the main banquet was to be an all-male affair. Hence, when the king wishes his queen, Vashti, to appear before his companions, the queen understandably refuses to do so. The queen is divorced in consequence, and Esther gets her chance. Incidentally, what is presupposed in this little drama seems to be more Hellenistic than Persian, at least to judge by Herodotus. Herodotus has the story—a highly novelistic story, no doubt—that the Persians of Darius asked the women to take part in the symposium (5.18–20). On another occasion Herodotus has the Persian king present a feast to his friends, but he puts "sacrifice," i.e., the amount of meat made available for consumption, in the first place (1.126). On the other hand Herodotus describes it as a Persian custom to discuss problems during heavy drinking together in a closed room (with a *stegarchos,* 1.133.4), and to make the final decisions next morning in a state of soberness. All this is different from the proceedings in the book of Esther. To go on with the story: for Esther's marriage another big banquet is organized, for all the princes and officials, and taxes are reduced and grain is distributed (2.18); a typical Hellenistic usage, or so it would seem. Later, when Esther has decided to intervene for the sake of her people and induces the king to grant her a favor, it is she who provides a banquet of her own, to which she invites the king and Haman the chamberlain (5.4). She is granted a wish by the king, but she postpones this to a second banquet to be held on the next day; there, after more or less heavy drinking in the "room of drinking wine" (7.8), she finally says what she wants the king to do, and ensures the execution of the wicked Haman (7.1–10). The whole story is to be read at the Israelite festival of Purim, days of "drinking and merrymaking" for all the Jews (9.17–19), the well-known combination. This evidently is why banquets play such a prominent role in the whole book of Esther.

Much more interesting is an incident in the story of Samson, which takes us back to the age of the Philistines—in our chronology, this would be the twelfth century. Samson meets a girl from the Philistines of Timnath and arranges to marry her (*Judges* 14). The marriage ceremony consists of a seven days' banquet (*mishtäh*) "for this was the use with the young in those days." The Philistines provide thirty "friends" (*mere'im*) to attend the bridegroom during his banquet. It is to them that Samson tells his riddle about the lion and the bees. If they cannot solve it, they are to provide thirty linen garments and thirty sets of clothes to Samson; if they solve it, Samson has to give the same amount to them. Samson is tricked by his cunning wife into giving away the solution; he finally provides the garments through pillage from Askalon, while his marriage has come to an abrupt end.

This is not the place to analyze the Samson stories as to either their mythical content or their historical background. It is only the custom of ceremonial drinking that is introduced in the text that must be in focus here. The author evidently looks back at a remote custom, which he does not know from his own experience. This "use" was intended to celebrate a marriage by a symposium seven days in length, in which apparently only young men participated, and in which a group of thirty "friends" from the bride's kin met and challenged the bridegroom. Exogamous marriage is presented here as a deal the suitor has to make with the young men of the girl's village; they are acting as a collective. The deal is acted out at a protracted symposium that in fact takes the form of an *agon*, a ritualized duel through riddles, with sizable prizes at stake. Samson, however, has been overdoing the game, the "friends" threaten collective action against the bride's father (14.15), and Samson finally turns to violence.

I think it is clear that this tale in many respects comes very close to what we understand a Greek symposium to have been: a group of young men similar in age who find their identity in communal drinking, and the ritualized agon in the form of language play. The use of riddles in the Greek symposium is well attested.[42]

Two observations make this all the more interesting. Specialists do not agree at all as to the date of Old Testament books, but there seems to be some consensus that *Judges* is relatively early and at any rate contains very old material, not far in time from the twelfth-century Philistines.[43] The testimony here thus antedates everything known about Greek symposia by centuries. The other observation is that, according to the author, we are in fact dealing with a custom of the Philistines, not of the Jews. The material relics of the Philistines that have come to light in more recent excavations have confirmed what had already been gathered from the name: the Philistines are the most distinctive group among those "people from the sea" who devastated Mycenaean Greece and the Levant about 1200 B.C.; they carried with them what looks like a barbarized version of Mycenaean civilization.[44] They will have been very close to the Greeks, or at least to certain Greeks, of the early Dark Age. So if, in all the "oriental" evidence, we get the closest analog to the Greek symposium here, is this because the information is not even "oriental" in content, but belongs to another, in fact to a "western" or "northern" tradition? This conclusion, however, is not compelling. One remarkable feature of *Judges* is the introduction of nonmonarchic societies with their archaic habits. Greek symposia too are characterized by their nonmonarchic, aristocratic environment. The similarity thus may as well be interpreted in terms of social structure as through "Nordic" kinship.

As to Israelite customs, there is still a remarkable chapter in *Jeremiah* (35): on the command of Jahweh, Jeremiah invites the "Sons of Rechab," members of a special clan, to the Temple of Jerusalem. He invites them to one of the several banquet halls, exactly specified, which are built there in the precinct; Jeremiah sets up cups full of wine and invites them to drink. They sternly refuse, because this has been a rule of their house, never to drink any wine. The whole action of the prophet is to contrast this kind of pious behavior by one family—according to *nomos,* the Greeks would say—with Judah's unlawfulness against the Lord. Without being addicted to structuralism we may still affirm that taboos presuppose forms of normal behavior that they contradict. In Greece, e.g., normal people will tear out thistles wherever they can, but there is one family, the Ioxidai, who never do this, and they have a special myth explaining this peculiarity.[45] Normal people, in contrast to the Rechabites, will invite each other to a feast in one of the banquet halls built at the temple, and drink wine there. The cups and goblets mentioned in the Jeremiah text evidently were stored in such a building. It was in such a hall at the sanctuary of Shiloh that the future parents of Samuel held their feast, and when the priest saw the woman praying in a most emotional way, he naturally thought she was drunk *(I Sam.* 1.9; 13). One may recall the situation of the Ugaritic *pater familias* who, after ceremonialized drinking, needed his children in order to return home.

There are special halls in the sacred precinct for the purpose of drinking, named after their private donors, even if they may be used by others as well. In Ezekiel's idealized vision there are thirty such halls at the temple *(Ez.* 40.17). These banquet halls in the sanctuaries, well known also from the archaeological evidence, are called *lishkah* in Hebrew, and this evidently equals *lesche* in Greek. One immediately thinks of the so-called Knidian Lesche at Delphi. The association was made a long time ago and appeared already in Robertson Smith's *Religion of the Semites.*[46] This is one of the most intriguing Semitic-Greek parallels: we get a correspondence of topography, architectural design, function, and name. But since *lesche* belongs to the root *legh-*, "to lie down,"[47] the whole problem of reclining on couches for the banquet seems to arise again.

This would call for another chapter. I rapidly will give the reasons why I think this is not a problem of the period with which we are concerned— the eighth century onward—but rather of the Bronze Age. Not only does the archaeological evidence for structures of this kind go back to the Bronze Age,[48] *lishkah* is also prominent in the older strata of the Bible,[49] and from the Greek side there is the month name *Leschanorios,* occurring in Thessaly, Achaia Phthiotis, and Gortyn.[50] Further, there is Apollo *Leschanorios,* and especially there is the month *Leschanasios* attested for Tegea in a comparatively old inscription, a name that seems to be downright Mycenaean.[51] The month's name implies a festival in which a "lord of the *lescha*" or "man of the *lescha*" was prominent, possibly in a festival of *theoxenia* type. In fact a festival *lechestroteria* is attested at Pylos.[52] All this points to a pre-Iron Age setting. Semitic borrowing from Mycenaean would remain a possibility. It follows that the word *lescha* has nothing to do with the problem of how old the reclining symposium may be and whether it can be considered an orientalizing import of the seventh century. Note that a couch for reclining at a meal is never called *lechos* in Greek, but *kline*.

The oldest literary testimony for couches at symposia seems to remain the *Amos* passage (6.7) from the eighth century; the oldest, and decisive, pictorial document from the oriental side is "Assurbanipal's garden party," in the midst of the seventh;[53] in Greek, we get both the Corinthian Eurytos krater[54] and Alcman[55] about 600. It has generally been assumed that the custom of lying down for the feast, instead of sitting on chairs, has come from a more primitive, "nomadic" life-style, either from an Iranian[56] or rather from a Syrian-Aramaean background.[57] Von der Mühll had speculated about Lydian influence on the Greeks, associating Lydians and Etruscans with the *lectisternium*.[58] What has been unduly neglected in this discussion is the primitive use of *stibades*.

In fact lying down for a meal must have been an old and natural custom. In connection with inviting gods as guests, there is every chance that it is an Indo-European ritual. It is hardly a coincidence that the horse-brothers, the Dioscuri—called by a Mycenaean title *Anakes* in Attica and elsewhere—were especially involved with *theoxenia*. The oldest way to do things was to prepare a couch of twigs and grass, called *stibas* in Greek.[59] Whenever a sacrifice was held outdoors, one would not normally transport chairs to the sacred place. It was different of course for the ceremonial meals for the dead, which were held indoors. We cannot expect to get direct evidence, either literary or archaeological, for *stibades* from the Dark Centuries; but we may confidently assume sacrifices both indoors, in the houses especially of the chieftains, and outdoors, at sacred places more or less distant from the settlement. There people would naturally lie down on *stibades*.

With the establishment of communal temples in the eighth century, the spatial categories changed: there was a new form of "space" for the sacred, outside the private house yet within a "house" of the god. In the new situation, and with the new oriental luxuries introduced, lying on couches within the temple may have partly replaced the *stibades*. A transitional stage could have been the *Herdhaus-Tempel*, although there has been controversy about this concept.[60] Later the dining-halls—*hestiatoria*—were separate from the *naos;* they were regularly equipped with couches. Thus, we should consider seriously the possibility that dining on couches was introduced not in connection with the symposium proper but with the ritual feast at the sanctuary, with *stibades* supplying the temple space. The appropriate halls are in evidence at least from the sixth century.[61] They could be called by an old term, *leschai*.

This would also have had its effect on the symposium proper: as communal sacrifice with the extensive meat courses moved from private homes to the temple, the "feast" in the private house was mainly confined to drinking. The symposium as the ritual that constituted the closed club of *hetairoi* was in fact in opposition to the public sacrificial feast at the temple of the *polis*. It is interesting to note that in Euboea of the eighth and seventh centuries, the banquet, as shown in funerary practice, still concentrated on the *lebes;* but Book 24 of the *Odyssey* has an "amphora of Dionysus" instead.[62]

A last problem: whereas for the Greek symposium mixing wine with water was basic, indeed the epitome of civilized drinking in contrast to what barbarians did,[63] there seems not to be much evidence about this procedure in the oriental sources. In the Hebrew texts there are references to "mixing" wine *(msk)*, and there is even the designation of a "mixed drink" *(mimsak, Isa.* 65.11, *Prov.* 23.30), but this refers to mixing wine with other ingredients to make it more sweet or savory.[64] Mixing wine with water is even considered degradation by Isaiah: "Your fine wine has been mixed with water" (1.22). In the Ugaritic texts, on the other hand, the same word "to mix" *(msk)* is found so regularly in the formulaic description of banquet scenes[65] that its function must have been different: to serve wine is "to mix" the drink. Mixing wine occurs in the *Iliad,* in a much-discussed passage (9.203), and in what may be the earliest description of a symposium *(Od.* 9.5–11): people are seated and wait for wine from the krater. An archaeological history of the krater might bring out more details in the complex prehistory of the Greek symposium; but in this regard the aim of this essay has been not to offer a theory of derivation, but rather to provide some illumination by various Lights from the East.

NOTES

The following abbreviations are used:

AHw: W. v. Soden, *Akkadisches Handwörterbuch* (Wiesbaden 1965–81).

ANET: J.B. Pritchard, ed., *Ancient Near Eastern Texts Relating to the Old Testament* (Princeton 1974³).

BWL: W.G. Lambert, *Babylonian Wisdom Literature* (Oxford 1960).

Doc.: M. Ventris, J. Chadwick, *Documents in Mycenaean Greek* (Cambridge 1972²).

IG: Inscriptiones Graecae.

KAI: H. Donner, W. Röllig, *Kanaanäische und aramäische Inschriften* (Weisbaden 1966²).

KTU: M. Dietrich, O. Loretz, J. Sanmartin, *Die keilalphabetischen Texte aus Ugarit* (Neukirchen-Vluyn 1976).

LS: F. Sokolowski, *Lois sacrées des cités grecques* (Paris 1969).

1. Civil 1964, 74.

2. Murray 1983 (bis); see also Schmitt-Pantel 1982; 1985; Vetta 1983; Levine 1985; Lissarague 1987. Among earlier studies, Von der Mühll (originally 1924) retains its value.

3. Cameron 1987, 324ff.

4. Säflund 1980.

5. Cf. Meissner 1920, I 241ff.; 419; Hartman-Oppenheim 1950; Salonen 1970.

6. Dommershausen 1977 with lit.

7. Selz 1983; see also Weber 1920, figs. 415–22; Fehr 1971, 9–14.

8. Weber 1920, 107–9 spoke of "Totenmahl."

9. It occurs on a painted mug from the "house of the magician-priest" at Ugarit, *Syria* 43, 1966, 3ff. with pls. 1, 2; A. Caquot and M. Sznycer, *Ugaritic Religion, Iconography of Religions* XV, 8 (Leiden 1980), pl. XXII, p. 26: "undoubtedly the banquet of the god El."

10. "Hubbard amphora," eighth cent., V. Karageorghis, *Cyprus Museum* (Athens 1975), 38.

11. A. Furtwängler, *Die antiken Gemmen* (Leipzig 1900), I pl. I 4; Moortgat 1940 nr. 526, cf. p. 52.

12. *Jer.* 16.5; at *Amos* 6.7 *LXX* has, through a strange misunderstanding, *chremetismos hippon* instead.

13. For the attestations of the word see Jean-Hoftijzer 1965, 167ff.; Koehler-Baumgartner 1974, II 599: "Kultfeier mit Gelage."

14. See Greenfield 1974; Barstad 1984, 126–45; Barnett 1985.

15. *KTU* 1, 114, first edited in *Ugaritica* V (Paris 1968) 545–51; Pope 1972; de Moor 1987, 134–37, whose translation is given in the text. In Ugaritic texts specialists tend to disagree in certain points—this cannot be discussed here.

16. The problem is how to correlate El feasting "in his palace" or "in his *marza'u*," and finally going "to his house," cf. Pope 194; de Moor 136 has "sitting with his society" for *marza'u*.

17. *KTU* 1.17, i 30, ii 5, ii 19; translation in *ANET* 150; de Moor 1987, 228, 230ff.

18. The role of the sons in particular is reminiscent of the Greek symposium, where corresponding duties of *paides* are mentioned more than once, and regularly appear in the iconography. In myth, Heracles kills a *pais* inadvertently by boxing his ears, Athen. 410F = Hellanicus *FGrH* 4 F 2, Herodorus *FGrH* 31 F 3, Nicander fr. 17 G-S; Apollod. *Bibl.* 2.150; Paus. 2.13.8.

19. *Amos* 6.4–7, cf. Dentzer 1982, 54; Barstad 1984. I have not yet seen King 1988.

20. *KAI* 69, 16, the sacrificial calendar of Marseille, usually attributed to Carthage; bilingual inscription from Piraeus, *KAI* 60 = *IG* II/III² 2946 (dated 3d/2d cent. B.C. in *IG*).

21. It has been discussed, among others, by H. Gressmann *ZNTW* 20, 1921, 228–30; H. Ingholt *Syria* 7, 1926, 128–41; Hoftijzer 1968, 28ff.

22. Adapa, though admitted to Heaven, is only offered water and bread, *ANET* 101ff.

23. *KTU* 1.3 i 8–21; de Moor 1987, 2–4.

24. *Enuma elish* VI 71–9, *ANET* 69.

25. A. Erman, *Die Religion der Aegypter* (Berlin 1934), 376. The text is Hellenistic, but is taken to reflect New Kingdom tradition.

26. *KTU* 1.19, iv 50ff., de Moor 1987, 264ff.

27. *ANET* 125ff.

28. On overcoming a nature demon by wine as a folktale motif, see Meuli 1975, 641–44.

29. Cyl. A IX 50, cf. *AHw* 85 *astammu;* wrong reading *(sinnistu) sutammu* instead of *(sinnist) astammi* ("women of the inn") in Streck 1916, II 76 and Luckenbill 1927, #827.

30. Jacobsen 1939; D.O. Edzard, *Reallex. d. Ass.* VI 299 s.v. *Ku(g)-Baba.*

31. X i,3, *ANET* 90.

32. Th. Jacobsen, *JNES* 12, 1953, 184ff. n. 68; A. Falkenstein, *ZA* 56, 1964, 118–20.

33. Zimmern 1918/19.

34. *mesru/meslu, BWL* 219, 3–5.

35. *BWL* 256 a 8–12.

36. *ANET* 170; cf. Driver-Miles 1952, I 205; *AHw* 1030: s.v. *sarru.*

37. *rakasu* N, *AHw* 947.

38. *FGrH* 566 F 134 = Diog. Laert. 8.64.

39. *Josh.* 2.1–22; Josephus *A.J.* 5.1, *katagogion.*

40. This is not to deny that there are invitations for eating, e.g., *Gen.* 31.54. See in general Amadasi Guzzo 1988.

41. Bickermann (1967, 202; 207) thought the main text of this "strange book" was written at Susa in the second century, whereas others would still assign the work to the Persian epoch (Baldwin 1984).

42. See esp. Athen. 448Bff., 457C, partly following Clearchus *Peri griphon,* fr. 84–95 Wehrli.

43. Cf. Soggin 1981. For an interpretation as to narrative strategy and folktale motifs, see Crenshaw 1974.

44. Dothan 1982; Gitin-Dothan 1987.

45. Plut. *Thes.* 8.6.

46. Smith 1889, 236, 6; 1894, 254, 6.

47. Chantraine s.v.; the association with *legein* made by the Greeks later is impossible, because *legein* acquired the meaning "to speak" only in the historical period; so Horovitz 1978. *Lesche* first occurs in Hesiod, *Erga* (493, 501), and in the *Odyssey* (18.328ff.) as a public building, where one might warm up, or where a beggar might stay overnight. The Knidian Lesche is mentioned by Plutarch and Pausanias. There is no Semitic etymology for *lishkah;* the derivation from Greek is routinely noted as a possibility in Hebrew lexica. There is one dubious instance in one Phoenician inscription, broken, without context (Koehler-Baumgartner II 509ff.).

48. Starcky 1949; Ottoson 1987.

49. See *I Sam.* 1.9; 13; 9.22.

50. See Samuel 1972, Index.

51. *IG* V 2.3 = *LS* 67.29ff., beginning of fourth cent. B.C.; the name evidently is to be analyzed as *lescha-wanaktios*. For another Mycenaean month-name surviving in Arcadia, *Lapatos* (KN Fp 13, *Doc.* 305) is the notable example.

52. PY Fr 343; *Doc.* 579.

53. Meissner 1920, I Tafel-Abb. 46; Fehr 1971, 7–18; Barnett 1985.

54. Schefold 1964, 66, pl. III.

55. 19 *PMG* = 11 Calame.

56. Fehr 1971, 16–18.

57. Tentatively suggested by Dentzer 1982, 56ff.

58. Von der Mühll 1975, 485.

59. Cf. Burkert 1979, 44.

60. Drerup 1969, esp. 123–28; Martini 1986; criticism of the concept "Herdhaus-Tempel" in favor of *hestiatorion* in Bergquist 1973, 60–62.

61. See Börker 1983.

62. See Mele 1982.

63. The Scythians nevertheless made use of the krater, according to Herodotus (4.66), but this may be a misnomer for a beer bowl.

64. It had been suggested that the Hebrew word for "mixing" comes from the Akkadian designation of the raisin, *muziqu,* before the Ugaritic evidence turned up.

65. *KTU* 1.3 i 8–21, de Moor 1987, 31ff.; 1.5 i 21, de Moor 71; 1.16 ii 16, de Moor 215; 1.19 iv 62, de Moor 265.

BIBLIOGRAPHY

M.G. Amadasi Guzzo, "Sacrifici e banchetti: Bibbia ebraica e iscrizioni puniche," in C. Grottanelli and N.F. Parise, eds., *Sacrificio e società nel mondo antico* (Bari 1988), 97–122.

J.G. Baldwin, *Esther. An Introduction and Commentary* (Leicester 1984).

R.D. Barnett, "Assurbanipal's Feast," *Eretz Israel* 18, 1985, 2–6.

H.M. Barstad, *The Religious Polemics of Amos* (Leiden 1984).

B. Bergquist, *Heracles on Thasos* (Uppsala 1973).

E. Bickermann, *Four Strange Books of the Bible* (New York 1967).

Ch. Börker, *Festbankett und griechische Architektur* (Konstanz 1983).

W. Burkert, *Structure and History in Greek Mythology and Ritual* (Berkeley 1979).

M.A.S. Cameron, "The 'palatial' Thematic System in the Knossos Murals," in R. Hägg and N. Marinatos, eds., *The Function of the Minoan Palaces* (Stockholm 1987), 320–28.

P. Chantraine, *Dictionnaire Étymologique de la lange grecque* (Paris 1968–80).

M. Civil, "A Hymn to the Beer Goddess and a Drinking Song," in *Studies Presented to* A. *Leo Oppenheim* (Chicago 1964), 67–89.

J.L. Crenshaw, "The Samson Saga: Filial Devotion or Erotic Attachment," *ZAW* 86, 1974, 420–504.

J.M. Dentzer, *Le Motif du Banquet couché dans le Proche Orient et le Monde Grec du VIIe au IVe siecle* (Paris 1982).

W. Dommershausen, "jajin," in G.J. Botterweck and H. Ringgren, eds., *Theologisches Wörterbuch zum Alten Testament* III (Stuttgart 1977), 614–20.

T. Dothan, *The Philistines and Their Material Culture* (New Haven and London 1982).

H. Drerup, *Griechische Baukunst in geometrischer Zeit: Archaeologia Homerica* II O (Göttingen 1969).

G.R. Driver, J.C. Miles, *The Babylonian Laws* I/II (Oxford 1952).

B. Fehr, *Orientalische und griechische Gelage* (Bonn 1971).

D. Flückiger-Guggenheim, *Göttliche Gäste. Die Einkehr von Göttern und Heroen in der griechischen Mythologie* (Bern 1984).

S. Gitin and T. Dothan, "The Rise and Fall of Ekron of the Philistines," *Biblical Archaeologist* 50, 1987, 197–222.

J.C. Greenfield, "The Marzeah as a Social Institution," *Acta Antiqua Academiae Scientiarum Hungaricae* 22, 1974, 432–35.

L.F. Hartman and A.L. Oppenheim, *On Beer and Brewing Techniques in Ancient Mesopotamia* (Baltimore 1950).

J. Hoftijzer, *Religio Aramaica* (Leiden 1968).

Th. Horovitz, *Vom Logos zur Analogie* (Zürich 1978).

Th. Jacobsen, *The Sumerian King List* (Chicago 1939).

C.F. Jean and J. Hoftijzer, *Dictionnaire des inscriptions sémitiques de l'ouest* (Leiden 1965).

P.J. King, *Amos Hoseah Micah: An Archaeological Commentary* (Philadelphia 1988).

L. Koehler and W. Baumgartner, *Hebräisches und aramäisches Lexikon zum Alten Testament³*, fasc. I-III (Leiden 1961, 1974, 1983).

D.B. Levine, "Symposium and the Polis," in Th. J. Figueira and G. Nagy, eds., *Theognis of Megara: Poetry and the Polis* (Baltimore 1985), 176–96.

F. Lissarague, *Un Flot d'Images. Une Esthétique du Banquet Grec* (Paris 1987).

D.D. Luckenbill, *Ancient Records of Assyria and Babylonia* (Chicago 1926–27).

W. Martini, "Vom Herdhaus zum Peripteros," *AM* 101, 1986, 23–36.

B. Meissner, *Babylonien und Assyrien* I/II (Heidelberg 1920–25).

N.V. Mele, "Da Micene a Omero: Dalla Phiala al Lebete," *AION* 4, 1982, 97–133.

K. Meuli, *Gesammelte Schriften* (Basel 1975).

J.C. de Moor, *An Anthology of Religious Texts from Ugarit* (Leiden 1987).

A. Moortgat, *Vorderasiatische Rollsiegel* (Berlin 1940, repr. 1966).

O. Murray, "The Greek Symposium in History," in E. Gabba, ed., *Tria Corda. Scritti in onore di Arnaldo Momigliano* (Como 1983), 257–72.

———. "The Symposium as Social Organisation," in R. Hägg and N. Marinatos, eds., *The Greek Renaissance of the Eighth Century* B.C.: *Tradition and Innovation* (Stockholm 1983), 195–99.

M. Ottoson, "Sacrifice and Sacred Meals in Ancient Israel," in T. Linders and G. Nordquist, eds., *Gifts to the Gods* (Uppsala 1987), 133–36.

M.H. Pope, "A Divine Banquet at Ugarit," in J.M. Efird, ed., *The Use of the Old Testament in the New and Other Essays: Studies in Honor of W.F. Stinespring* (Durham 1972), 170–203.

G. Säflund, "Sacrificial Banquets in the Palace of Nestor," *Opuscula Atheniensia* 13,6, 1980, 237–46.

E. Salonen, "Ueber das Erwerbsleben im alten Mesopotamien I," *Studia Orientalia* 41, 1970, 186–206: "Die Bierbrauer"; 206–9: "Die Weinkelterer."

A.E. Samuel, *Greek and Roman Chronology* (München 1972).

K. Schefold, *Frühgriechische Sagenbilder* (München 1964).

P. Schmitt Pantel, "Image et société en Grèce ancienne: Les représentations de la chasse et du banquet," *RA* 1982, 57–74.

————. "Banquet et cité grecque. Quelques questions suscitées par les recherches récentes," *MEFRA* 97, 1985, 135–58.

G. Selz, *Die Bankettszene. Die Entwicklung eines 'überzeitlichen' Bildmotivs in Mesopotamien, von der frühdynastischen bis zur Akkad-Zeit* (Wiesbaden 1983).

W.R. Smith, *Lectures on the Religion of the Semites* (Edinburgh 1889, 1894²).

J.A. Soggin, *Judges: A Commentary* (London 1981).

J. Starcky, "Salles de banquets rituels dans les sanctuaires orientaux," *Syria* 26, 1949, 62–85.

M. Streck, *Assurbanipal und die letzten assyrischen Könige bis zum Untergange Ninivehs* (Leipzig 1916).

M. Vetta, *Poesia e Simposio nella Grecia antica* (Rome 1983).

P. Von der Mühll, "Das Griechische Symposion," in *Ausgewählte Kleine Schriften* (Basel 1975, originally 1926), 483–505.

O. Weber, *Altorientalische Siegelbilder* (Leipzig 1920).

H. Zimmern, "Der Schenkenliebeszauber," *ZA* 32, 1918–19, 164–84.

The Betrothal Symposium in Early Greece

Noel Robertson

The betrothal symposium is a custom of early Greece that is not directly reported. It is, however, presupposed by a good many old myths and even by a few later stories. By "betrothal symposium" I mean a drinking party at which eligible bachelors ask for the girls of their choice and are accepted or rejected by the fathers or brothers who have charge of the girls. In the historical period the girls themselves are not as a rule present at the drinking party, but they have been highly visible for a day or two beforehand, dancing and sporting and parading. The occasion is a festival, which also allows the young men to compete in various games, to bring offerings to the sacrifice, and, in general, to show just how eligible they are.

Whenever the story provides sufficient detail, the festival is seen to be the same in any part of Greece: a spring festival of Apollo. Sometimes the festival can be named; it is a Pythian festival, or the *Delia*, or the *Thargelia*. Apollo is often joined by Artemis (goddess of the hunt, and therefore of the moonlit night, and therefore of the opening of navigation in the springtime); the girls and their mothers resort to the sanctuary of Artemis. With or without Artemis, Apollo's festival in May is a large formal reunion, whether of a single community and its visitors, or of many communities together, as on the island of Delos. After the games, the sacrifices, and the feasting comes the drinking party at which suitors are chosen and girls are betrothed. In earlier periods the drinkers gathered in some great house; later the symposium was sometimes a public affair, and facilities might be provided in a sanctuary.

The betrothal symposium is a natural conclusion to the festivities. Young men have come from far and wide to throw and run and wrestle before admiring crowds. Marriageable girls have come from far and wide to dance and sing before admiring crowds. In early days the banquet and the drinking that followed gave girls and youths a chance to mingle: a girl could be seen to advantage while pouring wine or washing someone's hands or feet. Her prototype in myth is Hebe or Harmonia, a beautiful cupbearer who becomes an ideal wife. The whole custom is bound up with the love of contest and display that typifies aristocratic society.

Broadly speaking, the myths are of two kinds. Some, among them a few very early and very famous stories, take us back to the Heroic Age and to the days when the custom was familiar to everyone. Other myths are later aetiologies that point to interesting vestiges of the Archaic custom. All these stories focus attention, as a story will, on just one woman, on the princess or the beauty who is wooed by the hero or by contending heroes. But the festival setting makes it clear that this was indeed a general custom.

The symposium is not always mentioned; we may only glimpse the festival and perhaps the bride-contest, or in the earlier period a hunt. A few stories, however, include interesting symposiac details: tongues of sacrificial victims offered with the libations; a cake or loaf tendered by the suitor to the girl's father or brother; a betrothal oath pledged with wine; garlands and other festive gear discarded on the day after so as to make an end of jealousy and rancor.

We shall take the instances in geographic order. First the homeland: three Dorian cities of the northeast Peloponnesus, Sicyon and Argos and Megara; Schoenus in Boeotia; Oechalia and Iolcus and other places in Thessaly; and last, Aetolia. Then three Ionian islands, Delos and Ceos and Naxos; and Miletus. Finally, the wooing of Penelope.

Cleisthenes and Adrastus at Sicyon

Before turning to the myths, we should consider a clear historical instance, the bride-contests and the betrothal symposium arranged by Cleisthenes of Sicyon and described by Herodotus. Though Cleisthenes is said to have tested his daughter's suitors for a whole year, the appointed day for the announcement of the marriage was a day of festival: Cleisthenes sacrificed a full hundred oxen and fêted not only the suitors but all the people of Sicyon.[1] The festival can be identified. Literal "hecatombs" are distinctive of Apollo.[2] Moreover, Cleisthenes wanted a festival that would bring foreigners from far and wide to hear the announcement (the invitation to the suitors had been issued at the Olympic Games). These considerations point to the Sicyonian *Pythia*, an agonistic festival founded by Cleisthenes himself, after the model of the Delphic *Pythia* founded not long before.[3] The festival has very likely helped to shape the story. Herodotus begins by saying that Cleisthenes constructed both a racecourse and a wrestling-ground for the suitors.[4] These details have the look of aetiology: it is as if Sicyon previously had no racecourse and no wrestling-ground that could accommodate a dozen suitors. The facilities in question must be those that Cleisthenes constructed for the Pythian festival; observers said that these mighty works were in fact designed for the tyrant's bride-contests.

One would like to know the time of year when this festival took place and also the years in which it fell.[5] Herodotus fixes the proceedings with reference to the Olympic celebration at which Cleisthenes won the four-horse chariot race. On this occasion suitors were invited to come to Sicyon within sixty days and to remain for a year, *eniautos*; whereafter, the banquet and the announcement.[6] Sixty days after the Olympic Games brings us to mid-October, but if we reckon a year forward to the next October, this is not a likely season for an agonistic festival that drew competition from abroad. By insisting on the year's interval, Herodotus surely does not mean that twelve whole months elapsed, but rather that another year was well advanced. Thus the Sicyonian festival came in the year following an Olympic celebration, which was also the year preceding a Pythian celebration at Delphi: a natural choice. The time of year was probably the spring, to judge from other Pythian festivals outside Delphi. We shall come to the *Pythia* of Megara and Ceos below, in search of the betrothal symposium; both are celebrated in the spring. Athens had no Pythian festival, but here the Pythian Apollo was honored by the festival *Thargelia*, celebrated about the end of spring.[7] This example suggests that the "Pythian" festivals are sometimes the older Apolline festivals but with new names. When Cleisthenes betrothed his daughter during that festival of Sicyon, at a symposium after the sacrifice, he may have followed an age-old custom.

Or rather, he must have; for one of our mythical instances comes from just the same milieu. Adrastus king of Argos betroths his two daughters to two heroes just arrived from abroad; as we shall see below, the setting is a symposium at a festival of Apollo, the Pythian festival of Argos. Now it is a remarkable feature of Adrastus' story, for which no proper explanation has yet been found, that he is said to have ruled as king first at Sicyon, then at Argos. Only his reign at Argos brings him fame, when he musters the great expedition against Thebes and returns from its defeat; his reign at Sicyon is an obscure interlude that is somehow justified by genealogy.[8] So it is all the stranger that even our earliest authorities insist upon this interlude. In the *Catalog of Ships* Sicyon is the place "where Adrastus first bore rule"; and when the tyrant Cleisthenes inquired of the Delphic Oracle, he was told that Adrastus, unlike himself, was truly king of Sicyon.[9]

Almost the only substantive detail of Adrastus' reign at Sicyon is supplied by Pindar, apropos of a victory at the Sicyonian *Pythia*: this agonistic festival was founded by Adrastus while he was king of Sicyon.[10] The report is dismissed out of hand by the scholia, and after them by modern commentators, as a manifest invention designed to glorify the festival and perhaps to slight the tyrant's achievement.[11] If, however, Cleisthenes did no more than to rename and refurbish an older festival of Apollo, the mythical origin asserted by Pindar was no doubt traditional at Sicyon. This becomes a certainty when we find that at Argos too Adrastus is associated with the cult and festival of Apollo Pythius, and that he is credited with establishing a certain usage, the monthly consultation of Apollo's oracle, of which more below.

It is reasonable to conclude that the hero Adrastus is a projection of Apolline ritual. Since the ritual and its nomenclature are the same at Argos and at Sicyon, the hero is at home at both places. Against this background the transparent name *a-drastos* (or *a-drêstos*) is easily explained: "doer-in-common," *alpha athroistikon* and the agent noun *drastês* (or *drêstês*), i.e., one who assembles the people at the spring festival of Apollo, and one who musters an army to march against Thebes.[12] Apollo's festival is also implicated in that innovation of Cleisthenes that Herodotus quite chimerically interprets as an attempt to expel Adrastus as an Argive hero. In Pindar's day the Pythian festival of Sicyon was renowned for its athletic and equestrian contests.[13] What we miss in this description are musical contests, elsewhere a prominent feature of Pythian festivals, as also of the festival *Thargelia*, a feature that gives Apollo his reputation as god of music. They had once existed at Sicyon too. "The Sicyonians were accustomed to honor Adrastus greatly," says Herodotus, "and with reference to his sufferings they paid him the tribute of tragic choruses"; yet these were now transferred to Dionysus.[14] The "tragic choruses," whether dithyrambs or something else, must have formerly belonged to the festival of Apollo, like the other honors for Adrastus (as Herodotus conceives them); for Adrastus himself belongs to the festival of Apollo.[15] Cleisthenes dropped them from the program to make room for more athletic and equestrian contests. Delphi, asked to sanction the change, rebuffed him—the priests were presumably jealous of their own Pythian festival.

The topography of Sicyon is so obscure that the shrine of Pythian Apollo can only be located in general terms. Ampelius describes a temple of Apollo in the agora of Sicyon that was said to be full of antiquarian treasures, including a chest left by Adrastus, its contents unknown.[16] The same temple, with still other reputed treasures, was seen by Pausanias "in the present agora"; the ritual at the temple he traces to the time when Apollo came to Sicyon to be purified after slaying the serpent,[17] so this is Pythian Apollo. In Pausanias' time and for long before, the agora was on the lower level of the plateau to which Demetrius moved the city; an excavated temple here is sometimes thought to be Apollo's, but this is quite uncertain.[18] This plateau has a spur at the southeast, isolated from the rest, which formed the acropolis of the earlier city—on another reckoning the whole plateau was the acropolis—and on this spur was a temple of Hera Alea founded by Adrastus on the very site of his palace.[19] In sum, whereas the early city mostly lay in the plain northeast of the plateau, the shrine of Pythian Apollo was on high ground near the acropolis.[20] The settings are similar at Argos and Megara.

Adrastus at Argos

The myth of Adrastus is like the story of Cleisthenes. Adrastus too welcomes certain suitors from abroad, entertains them at a feast and a symposium, and betroths his daughters. To be sure, the suitors acquire this role unexpectedly; they are the exiled heroes Tydeus of Aetolia and Polyneices of Thebes. Arriving at Argos on the same night from different quarters, they meet and wrestle. Though this is not a professed bride-contest, the result is that the two contenders are recognized by Adrastus as the destined husbands for his daughters—Apollo has predicted the emblems they will wear. Apollo Pythaeus, god of prophecy, is worshipped on the northern acropolis of Argos.

The fullest surviving account is by Statius in the *Thebaid*, drawing on Greek sources whose identity escapes us. When Tydeus and Polyneices are admitted to the palace of Adrastus, Statius explains at length that the celebration that is under way is a festival of Apollo, a festival founded by an earlier king of Argos.[21] Even though the festival is mentioned nowhere else, it is plainly a traditional element of the story. The ritual background can be indicated by other means. In Statius the quarrel between Tydeus and Polyneices breaks out in the porch of the palace, but Mnaseas told how the heroes fought beside a temple of Apollo.[22]

From other details in Statius we can identify the shrine and the festival that are in view. When Adrastus perceives the fulfillment of Apollo's prophecy, he invokes the goddess Night and promises a sacrifice of black sheep every month of the year.[23] It has not been noticed that this is the *aition* of a prophetic ritual described by Pausanias. The priestess of Apollo Pythaeus prophesies at night, once a month, after drinking the blood of a newly sacrificed lamb.[24] Thus, the festivities in Statius take place at or near the shrine of Apollo Pythaeus on the ascent to the acropolis.[25] Perhaps Apollo's temple was sometimes equated with Adrastus' palace, for, as we saw, the quarrel between the heroes is located now here, now there. Near Apollo

Pythaeus was a shrine of Hera Akraia;[26] we recall that at Sicyon Adrastus was associated with both Apollo Pythius and Hera Alea.

As for the season, the palace folk in Statius are all wearing laurel crowns.[27] It is Apollo's spring festival, when worshippers everywhere either wear or carry laurel in honor of the god. We should note too that Polyneices and Tydeus journey to Argos during a terrible storm.[28] In Statius' account it comes on at nightfall, as Polyneices passes Corinth. The winds tear branches from the trees, and rain swells the rivers until they overflow; rocks tumble down from the hills, and houses are swept away. It is the storm that makes the heroes fight for shelter in the forecourt of the palace; or, in Mnaseas' version, that makes them fight for the hides of boar and lion that have been dedicated in Apollo's temple as trophies of the hunt. This is a storm of late winter or early spring. We shall find just the same seasonal indication in the story of Odysseus. Odysseus sails to Phaeacia during a terrible storm, and once ashore he huddles up to keep off the cold; when he arrives on Ithaca soon after, the first night is one of cold and wind and rain. Ithaca's festival of Apollo, with its contest of the bow, is again a festival of spring, on the twentieth anniversary of Odysseus' departure.

In Statius, Apollo's festival consists of a meal followed by a symposium.[29] When the meal is over, Adrastus pours libation to all the gods, but especially to Apollo; after the final libation, a hymn goes up to this god. The literary tradition is matched by the symposium scene on a Chalcidian skyphos, with names inscribed: Adrastus reclines on his couch, his two daughters stand before him, and the two heroes sit as suppliants on the floor.[30] It has been argued lately that the same episode is depicted on a black-figure hydria by the Antimenes Painter, but this is doubtful.[31]

Alcathous at Megara

Another myth associates our custom with Apollo's spring festival at Megara. The setting is much the same as at Sicyon and Argos: a shrine on the acropolis, the western acropolis called Alcathous. The ritual conducted at the shrine includes a symposium at which betrothals are announced. We shall consider first the aetiological myth that reflects the symposium, then the other evidence that identifies the shrine and the festival.

The myth was recounted by Dieuchidas the local historian of Megara, writing probably in the second half of the fourth century, and after him by Pausanias.[32] The king of Megara has lost his son to the lion of Cithaeron; he promises his daughter's hand to the man who kills the lion; young men come from afar to join the hunt and woo the princess. Hunting, no less than games, provides an opportunity for competition and display. The successful hunter and chosen suitor is Alcathous son of Pelops.

A betrothal symposium is implied by the circumstances in which Alcathous is adjudged the winner. He declares that he has killed the lion, but the claim is disputed by his rivals; he then produces the lion's tongue, which he has cut out and placed in his wallet. This is a widespread motif—the tongue or other bit that has been secretly kept as proof of the kill.[33] But now it becomes a ritual *aition,* and the ritual belongs to a symposium. Dieuchidas is thus paraphrased by a scholiast. "After sacrificing to the gods, the king at the very last placed the tongue [i.e., the lion's tongue] upon the altar; and since then this custom has held at Megara." In Dieuchidas' time the ceremony in question was still concluded by this act of placing a tongue upon the altar.

To throw the tongues of animal victims into the altar fire is a custom that poets attribute to the Heroic Age. We find it twice described: in the *Odyssey,* at the festival of Poseidon that Nestor celebrates on the shore at Pylos; and in Apollonius' *Argonautica,* at the sacrifice to Apollo that the Argonauts conduct on the shore at Iolcus.[34] These descriptions reveal that the tongues were burnt up at the very last, just as in the story of Alcathous, after the sacrifice and the feasting, after most of the drinking, at the last round of wine. The identity of the gods who are honored seems of little consequence. In the *Odyssey* the libations are made to Poseidon and "to the other gods" as well; in the *Argonautica* the sacrifice to Apollo is concluded by a libation to Zeus.

The custom of burning up the tongues has always puzzled commentators. The question is rehearsed at length in the scholia to Homer and Apollonius, but all the various answers are patently inadequate.[35] The difficulty arose because the custom itself was abandoned; it is not attested anywhere in historical times, except at Megara. Modern scholars point to epigraphic *leges sacrae* in which the victim's tongue is specified as either a priestly perquisite or a table-offering. It is a priestly perquisite in more than a dozen documents, mostly Ionian.[36] Yet in almost every case the priest receives other portions as well; they might be organs, feet, head, hide, or particular joints of meat; so the tongue has no significance of its own, or none that we can discern.[37] Less commonly it is a table-offering,[38] and here too it serves only as a modest portion. These are workaday uses for the victim's tongue, unrelated to that early custom.

Attic comedy is more revealing. The victim's tongue, though claimed as usual by the officiating priest, is singled out for attention at a certain stage of the ceremony. In the sacrificial scene of Aristophanes' *Peace* it is just as

Trygaeus prepares to make a libation that the priest, admittedly an unwelcome priest, calls for the tongue to be cut out. And it is just as the libations are being poured that the priest calls for the tongue to be presented as his due. In Menander's *Flatterer* a cook who is performing sacrifice likewise pauses in the middle of his libation to ask for the tongue.[39] The sacrifice to Poseidon in the *Odyssey* takes a similar course. It is just as the wine is being mixed for the libation that the victims' tongues are cut out. And it is just as the libations are being poured that the tongues are thrown in the fire. The ritual is the same in Attica as in Homer, save that the tongues are no longer burnt up but kept for the priest. The separate treatment of the victim's tongue was distinctive of Attica, as Aristophanes intimates.[40] One of the antiquarian comments in the *Odyssey* scholia is that the Homeric practice continued as an Attic custom; this turns out to be substantially right.

This connection between tongues and libation discloses the purpose of the rite. The general purpose of animal "sacrifice" is magical, to strengthen or invigorate the gods. Different victims, or different parts of victims, are subjected to different operations, burning or burying or immersion or the like, so as to impart different kinds of strength. In the present instance the tongues that are burnt up with the wine enhance the gods' power to taste and enjoy the wine. The custom, whether viewed as quaint or crude, was afterwards discarded, surviving only at Megara and, in a faded form, in Attica. At Megara it survived as a conspicuous public rite that Dieuchidas traces back to the time when Alcathous won the king's daughter. The rite was therefore an occasion for announcing betrothals.

We should consider the shrine and festival at which this rite took place. Alcathous is closely linked with Apollo, the chief god of Megara. Having killed the lion, Alcathous founded a shrine of Artemis Agrotera and Apollo Agraios, Artemis and Apollo of the hunt; this lay somewhere in the lower town.[41] Now a shrine that Alcathous reputedly founded is not the setting in which he was reputedly received as a newcomer by the ruling king.[42] The principal shrine of Apollo, with the title Pythaeus, was on the acropolis called Alcathous.[43] The spot was shown nearby where Apollo laid down his lyre while he helped Alcathous to build the city walls; Apollo Pythaeus is patron of music. In later life Alcathous was sacrificing to Apollo on the acropolis when news came that his elder son had been killed by the Calydonian boar. This event duplicates the misadventure that brought Alcathous to Megara in the first place, the killing of the king's son by the Cithaeronian lion. The acropolis is also the place for the king's palace, and hence for the festivity that followed the lion hunt.

The festival of Apollo Pythaeus is known from a poem handed down in the *Theognidea,* composed just after the Persian invasion, and plainly intended for recitation at the festival.[44] It evokes the Persian invasion and the walls built by Alcathous and Apollo. The festival, we learn, was celebrated in the spring; there was singing and dancing round the altar, and a great feast. This was the festival that included the rite of burning the victim's tongues.

Two Old Customs at Schoenus

At Sicyon and Megara the betrothal symposium lasted into historical times. Another survival can be detected at Schoenus, a small town a few miles north of Thebes. Schoenus is chiefly known for the myth of Atalanta, the fleet-foot beauty whose suitors were matched against her in a footrace and put to death when she outran them. It is not the myth, however, but a later document that illustrates our custom. A Hellenistic epigram by one Phaedimus is almost the sole surviving record of Schoenus in the historical period. The epigram takes the form of a fictitious dedication to Apollo, one of the town's presiding deities (as we now learn).[45]

The dedicator asks Apollo the archer-god to help Schoenus in time of war. Instead of wielding the mighty bow that destroys giants and wolves, let him turn the darts of love toward young men so that they will fight bravely for their homeland. According to the commentators, the love matches that the poet has in mind are homosexual pairings such as we hear of in Thebes' Sacred Band. But Greeks could also be inspired to fight for home and country by the love of wives, as we see from Hector's example. The language of the epigram points unmistakably to conjugal love. The young men who need Apollo's prompting are *êïtheoi,* "young bachelors." Afterward they are made bold *philotêti kourôn,* "by love of young brides" (*kourôn* with perispomenon accent). The phrase cannot mean "by love of young men" (*kourôn* paroxytone), i.e., other young men, since the preferred homosexual attachments are between older and younger men. Marriage is in view. Apollo is not as a rule a god of love and marriage, but Phaedimus as a learned poet refers to a local custom of arranging marriages at the festival of Apollo.

Schoenus was a small town with a slender existence. During the Peloponnesian War the inhabitants moved in a body to Thebes, like the inhabitants of some other towns that lacked walls. Later they returned, but by the time of Strabo and Pausanias the settlement seems to have disappeared.[46] It may be thought surprising that such a custom as ours was kept up for so long. But the myth of Atalanta, who was the daughter of the eponym Schoeneus, testifies to another strange old custom observed at Schoenus. This custom also has to do with marriageable youths and maidens, and we should pause to consider it.

The myth of Atalanta, like some other Boeotian myths, derives from the cult of Aphrodite.[47] The cult at Schoenus was distinctive enough for Lycophron to evoke the goddess as *Schoinêis*.[48] Atalanta is beaten by the suitor Hippomenes when Aphrodite gives him three golden apples. In the earliest source, the Hesiodic *Catalog*, the apples are styled the "gifts of Aphrodite"; in the next, a red-figure krater of the late fifth century, the goddess approaches Hippomenes just before the race.[49] We therefore ask, what is the cult practice that gives rise to the myth?

Atalanta's name, a feminine form of *atalantos*, provides an obvious clue: she is a woman who is "equal" or "equivalent" to a man. We are reminded that it is precisely in the cult of Aphrodite that men and women exchange roles. Men put on women's dress, even veils, or a young man pretends to be a woman in labor. Women put on men's dress or men's armor, or they sometimes wear false beards. Such ritual is depicted by statues of Aphrodite that show her dressed as a man, or armed as a man, or sporting beard or phallus. Cult legends tell how women once fought as men, or how some hero once posed as a woman, or how a girl or boy once underwent a change of sex. This material has often been studied, but the best account by far is Nilsson's, apropos of festivals of Aphrodite.[50] From a careful sifting of the evidence he demonstrated that the purpose is magical. Men and women promote their respective roles by exchanging them, for either sex has a fund of power that can be used on behalf of the other. Men enact the woman's role to make women bear children; women enact the man's role to make men strong in their exertions.

At Schoenus the magic procedure reciprocally employed by men and women is not to exchange dress but to go naked. The same procedure can be inferred for a cult at Phaestus, a cult of Leto, to be sure; but as others have remarked, Leto here resembles Aphrodite.[51] The aetiological myth tells of a girl changed into a boy in answer to her mother's prayer; the event was commemorated by the festival *Ekdysia*, "Disrobing," "because the child put off her robe." Returning to the myth of Atalanta, we find that the nakedness of both Hippomenes and Atalanta is insisted upon.

Hesiod, said Aristarchus, described Hippomenes as running naked.[52] It is wrong to infer from this, as Aristarchus did, that "Hesiod" is later than "Homer," or later than the time when the fashion first arose of competing naked at Olympia and elsewhere. But Aristarchus' remark is important nonetheless: though we can only guess what words "Hesiod" actually used, they were words that set this race apart from all the other races and games described in epic poetry.[53] Hippomenes' nakedness was thus an essential feature of the myth. Now "Hesiod" did not say that Atalanta ran naked. A papyrus passage tells how all the spectators were lost in admiration as the West Wind caught the tunic round her breast.[54] This description makes a contrast with Hippomenes' nakedness. It is, however, a case of epic euprepeia, which conceals the full truth about the race, for on the red-figure krater already mentioned, both Atalanta and Hippomenes are quite naked. In Ovid, moreover—the only extended treatment we have after the Catalog—Atalanta's nakedness is very much before the eye.[55] Ovid relished this aspect of the race, but it must have been perfectly familiar from the previous versions that he knew; why she ran naked he does not trouble to explain. It is also significant that Ovid and the red-figure krater agree in one curious item: Atalanta wears bands round her ankles, evidently to prevent a sprain.[56] The tradition dwelt on the details of Atalanta's nakedness.

Schoenus' festival of Aphrodite doubtless included a footrace. Dionysius of Halicarnassus, describing a cult of Aphrodite on Zacynthus that was linked with Aeneas, mentions a footrace of ephebes, called for whatever reason "the footrace of Aeneas and Aphrodite."[57] It need not be supposed that at Schoenus girls raced with youths, or that girls raced at all. The myth of Atalanta is well accounted for if we posit both an ordinary footrace of naked youths and the public appearance of a naked girl, or girls.

Since no treatment of the myth survives from classical or Hellenistic times, we cannot trace any further the interplay between the myth and the rite. It is likely nonetheless that the festival of Aphrodite continued at Schoenus as of old, like the festival of Apollo that stands behind Phaedimus' epigram.

Heracles at Oechalia

In all the mythical cases that we examined above, the hero wins the bride-contest and is praised and rewarded at the drinking party. Heracles' wooing of Iole gives us a burlesque variation in which Heracles does not in fact prevail. Eurytus of Oechalia promises his daughter to the man who can outshoot him with the bow. The contest between Eurytus and Heracles is not described by our sources, and perhaps the outcome was ambiguous. As we might expect, Heracles claims the girl, but the symposium brings only humiliation. The hero is insolently mocked by Eurytus and his sons and then trounced in a brawl and thrust out-of-doors. This inhospitable conduct is recounted in Sophocles' *Trachiniae* and depicted on a red-figure cup of ca. 500 B.C.[58] A much earlier vase, a Corinthian amphora of ca. 600, shows the ominous beginning of the symposium.[59] Heracles, Eurytus, and the four sons are all reclining; Iole stands beside Heracles' couch. But her face is turned away from Heracles, and whereas the other symposiasts are all attending to their wine, Heracles is in the act of carving food with a knife, evidently another instance of his gluttony. It may be that Iole herself remarked on his offensive manners, for elsewhere, in other versions, we find her resisting Heracles, and she is threatened or punished by him.[60] At all events, Heracles' discomfiture was once a favorite scene in literature and art; it provides some relief from the lengthy pageant of triumphant heroes.

The story of Iole gives no hint that the contest or the symposium belongs to a festival of Apollo. But we should remember that Eurytus of Oechalia is a close congener of the archer-god, either his rival or his favorite. It is Apollo who slays Eurytus for his presumption as an archer or else bestows on him a famous bow and skill in using it; it is Apollo who first begets Melas or Melaneus, the father of Eurytus, upon a mountain nymph, and then abducts a lady revelling on Parnassus to be Melas' wife; the very names Eurytus and Melaneus are redolent of Apolline worship.[61] So it is probable that a festival of Apollo is the starting point for the story of Iole.

Admetus and Other Suitors in Thessaly and Aetolia

Although Oechalia was later sought and found in different parts of Greece, there can be no doubt that a site in Thessaly was the locus of the original story,[62] so that the betrothal ceremony existed here too. Thessaly gives us other old myths in which Apollo is concerned with wooing and betrothal, as when he helps Admetus win Alcestis (more of this in a moment). It is striking that in other stories the god himself appears as the suitor of a mortal woman, with a mortal suitor as his rival. Several stories of this kind are mentioned in the Pythian suite of the *Homeric Hymn to Apollo*. Searching for a theme, the poet thinks first not of Apollo's oracles, but of Apollo's wooing.[63]

> How then shall I hymn you, who deserve to be hymned in every way? Shall I sing of you among wooers and love, how you came a-wooing to the Azantid [?] girl, together with god-like Ischys, the equestrian son of Elatus? Or with Phorbas of the stock of Triopas? Or with

Ereuthes? Or with Leucippus and the wife of Leucippus [?]? You were
on foot, the other was in a chariot; yet he did not leave you behind.

In these stories Apollo woos a mortal woman and competes in a bride-race
with a mortal suitor. In yet another story Apollo woos Marpessa daughter
of Evenus, but the mortal suitor Idas outdraws him with the bow.

This passage of the *Homeric Hymn* has suffered in transmission. This
is not the place to expound the difficulties, only to gather the prima facie
indications. Of the four stories alluded to, none but the first is known from
other sources. Apollo and Ischys, "Strength," are rivals for the hand of
Coronis, "Crow," daughter of Phlegyas the eponym of a people in Thessaly.
"Crow" is a teasing or endearing name for any girl, used in a common
wedding chant.[64] Apollo saw her as she bathed her feet in Lake Boebeis,
and they were united at once. But afterwards "Crow" preferred "Strength,"
and Apollo in a rage killed them both. In this form the story was also
known to pseudo-Hesiod.[65] Afterwards it was given a new twist, in which
the healing god Asclepius is born from the brief love match of Apollo and
"Crow." As to the other rivals, Phorbas and Leucippus are at least familiar
as heroes of Thessaly, and it is not surprising that stories were told of them
that have not survived. It may be relevant that in a myth of Elis or there-
abouts the girl Daphne is loved now by a youth Leucippus, now by Apollo,
and their rivalry causes the death of Leucippus; a good many mythical
names and families are common to Thessaly and the western
Peloponnesus.[66]

Idas and Marpessa are at home in Aetolia, outside the purview of the
Hymn. In this story, already known to Homer, the mortal suitor confronts
Apollo and wins the girl by his prowess; or she chooses him from prudent
calculation.[67] Apollo spies Marpessa as she dances in a sanctuary of Artemis. The same setting is mentioned in several Ionian stories to be considered
below; it belongs to a spring festival that honors Apollo and Artemis
together.

Returning to the story of Admetus and Alcestis, we find many details
that recur elsewhere. Alcestis is the daughter of Pelias king of Iolcus; he
and his twin brother Neleus king of Pylos are among the most venerable
figures of Greek myth. Neleus too is known for his marriageable daughter
Pero and for testing her suitors. That story, however, is best deferred until
we come to Ionia and to Neleus of Miletus; the two bearers of the name
Neleus are strangely alike. As for Pelias, the chief episodes of his career
are the marriage of his daughter and his own funeral, the occasion of
famous funeral games. Pelias and his reign were later subsumed in the cycle

of the Argonauts, but he was once renowned in his own right.[68] Those two early myths, about the marriage and the funeral, are aetiologies that exhibit the splendor of a royal household.

Both Apollo and Artemis take a hand in the marriage of Alcestis.[69] Pelias promises Alcestis to the suitor who can yoke a lion and a boar to the wedding chariot. To deal thus with a lion and a boar is to capture them in the hunt, a form of bride-contest we have met at Argos and Megara. Lion and boar appear in the story of Tydeus and Polyneices, now as hides and now as shield emblems, but evoking a bride-contest in either case. They also appear in the story of Alcathous and his son, for Alcathous kills the lion of Cithaeron, and his son is killed by the boar of Calydon. At Argos and Megara a festival of Apollo is in the background. At Iolcus Apollo helps Admetus in his task.

At the wedding ceremony Admetus forgets to sacrifice to Artemis, and her anger threatens death. So it does in two Ionian stories, about Cydippe of Naxos and Ctesylla of Ceos, which we shall examine below. As these examples show, and as we should expect, Artemis visits her anger on the bride, not the groom. But the story of Admetus and Alcestis continues with a folktale motif, the husband whose life is forfeit and the wife who takes his place. So the story feigns that Admetus must die; then the substitution gives the right ending, the death of Alcestis.

Love Matches on Delos and Ceos

Still other tales that reflect the betrothal ceremony come from the Ionian domain, and most of them are not myths of the Heroic Age but love stories of later times. In such stories the ritual background emerges much more clearly. Another element of the ritual is the betrothal oath, which the father or brother solemnly swears at the betrothal of a daughter or sister. The practice is reflected in these love stories, and it also appears in a very old myth. First the love stories.

Callimachus tells the story of Acontius and Cydippe, a youth and maiden from different islands, Ceos and Naxos, who have both come to Delos to attend a festival of Apollo and Artemis.[70] Acontius falls in love with Cydippe and gains her hand by a trick. He inscribes an oath—it is a promise to marry Acontius—upon an apple that he then puts in Cydippe's way. Cydippe betroths herself inadvertently by reading the oath aloud. As befits a woman's oath, the deity adjured is Artemis rather than Apollo. And because the incident takes place in Artemis' sanctuary, the goddess overhears the oath and enforces it in the further course of the story: whenever Cydippe is about to be married to another, she sickens and nearly dies. At last the father inquires of Apollo at Delphi and learns the truth; Acontius and Cydippe are wed on Naxos. The story is rather early, as such stories go, for Callimachus had it from Xenomedes of Ceos, writing in the fifth century,[71] and as we shall see, the conditions it reflects are those of the Archaic period.

Antoninus Liberalis records a later variation, cited from Book 3 of Nicander's *Heteroeumena*, which is set on the island of Ceos, again at a festival of Apollo. The two principals are now Ctesylla of Ceos and Hermochares of Athens. Ctesylla, like Cydippe, betroths herself inadvertently by reading the inscribed apple, but Hermochares is a more prudent lover than Acontius. He goes to the father as well, and makes him swear another oath while holding Apollo's laurel branch. In real life the father, not the daughter, arranges the marriage, so that in this respect the later variation is more veristic. The story continues with a second encounter in a sanctuary of Artemis, the elopement of the lovers to Athens, Ctesylla's death after childbirth, and finally the founding of a commemorative cult on Ceos.

We should examine the ritual details in both stories. In the story of Acontius and Cydippe, the festival on Delos is one of Apollo and Artemis together, and worshippers come from abroad to offer sacrifice and perform choral dances.[72] This festival must be the *Delia* (as it is called from the fifth century onward), not the *Apollonia*, for the latter is only a local festival and honors Apollo alone.[73] The calendar date of the *Delia* is undoubtedly *Thargelion* 6–7, the notional birthdays of Artemis and Apollo;[74] in other cities the festival *Thargelia* is associated with Delian Apollo.[75]

On Ceos Acontius is the progenitor of the family Acontiadae, who were prominent in the time of Xenomedes and perhaps of Callimachus too.[76] If the Acontiadae are glorified by an alliance with Naxos that is formed at Apollo's festival on Delos,[77] the story probably goes back to the time when Naxos was powerful and displayed its power on Delos, i.e., to the mid-Archaic period. In any case it is an *aition* pertaining to the Delian festival in those early days when Ionians gathered there from afar and intermarried.[78] Although Xenomedes and the Acontiadae are Ceans, the story does not draw on any custom of Ceos, so far we can see.

The story of Hermochares and Ctesylla is a doublet of the other, and it takes place mainly on Ceos and refers to several cults of Carthaea and Iulis. The ultimate source can hardly be Xenomedes,[79] for the celebrity of Acontius and Cydippe is presupposed, and on the evidence of Callimachus Xenomedes was the first to tell their story. The Aristotelian *Constitution of Ceos* is a more likely candidate.

Hermochares first sees Ctesylla at the Pythian festival of *Carthaea*, but not in a sanctuary of Artemis; she is dancing round the altar of Apollo.[80] Thereafter the father lays hold of Apollo's laurel as he swears, thereby disclosing a festival of spring. In these circumstances Artemis is hardly needed in addition to Apollo, but she appears nonetheless. Ctesylla too discovers the apple in Artemis' sanctuary and reads out the oath, which includes the goddess' name; Acontius and Cydippe are expressly mentioned as a precedent. After the Pythian festival is over and the father forgets his oath, Ctesylla happens to be sacrificing again in Artemis' sanctuary, where Hermochares now confronts her openly. It must be a different sanctuary, however, not a sanctuary at Carthaea, but a sanctuary at Iulis, which is Ctesylla's home.

The story ends when the girl, dying in childbirth, is transformed into a dove, to be commemorated at Iulis by a cult of Aphrodite Ctesylla, elsewhere by a cult of Ctesylla Hecaerge. These are names for an old deity of women's fertility and childbirth who was widely worshipped on the Ionian islands and coast.[81] Thus we see that the *aition* of this cult, about a girl who dies in childbirth, has been spliced together with the story-type of Acontius and Cydippe. The latter was at first an *aition* of betrothals on Delos, but is now an *aition* of betrothals at the Pythian festival of *Carthaea*.[82] The encounters in a sanctuary of Artemis are merely an unthinking repetition of the earlier story.[83]

Love Matches at Miletus

To these stories of Delos and Ceos we can add two others of Miletus, in which a girl comes from abroad to a festival of Artemis and is admired and wooed, or accosted by Apollo. In Book 3 of Callimachus' *Aetia* the story of Acontius and Cydippe was followed almost at once by the story of Phrygius and Pieria.[84] Phrygius king of Miletus falls in love with Pieria of Myus when he sees her at the festival of Artemis. He promises anything, and Pieria asks for peace between their cities, which are at war. Apollonius the rival of Callimachus told a rival story in his work *On the Foundation of Naucratis*.[85] The Samian nymph Ocyrrhoe comes to the festival of Artemis at Miletus and is almost seized by Apollo, but a seaman named Pompilus undertakes to convey her home. Apollo, however, changes the ship to a stone and Pompilus to a pilot fish, and he then has his way with Ocyrrhoe. Even though Apollonius' story is about Apollo and a nymph, the festival setting at Miletus is realistic; Pompilus is described as a friend of Ocyrrhoe's father, i.e., a guest-friend.[86]

We have then a Milesian festival of Artemis that is attended by marriageable girls from other cities. In the story of Phrygius and Pieria, Artemis has the curious title *Nêlêis*, formed from "Neleus" as the name of Miletus' founder.[87] Phrygius himself, the king of Miletus, is a scion of the Neleid family.[88] Callimachus alludes to this ancestry by saying that Pieria as an advocate of peace was as eloquent as Nestor of old.[89] Elsewhere, in Callimachus' *Hymn to Artemis*, we learn that it was Artemis Chitônê who guided Neleus across the sea to found Miletus.[90] The cult epithet *Kithônê*— as it is spelled in a document—was distinctive of Miletus though used at other places too.[91] Artemis is here named from the dress of her worshippers, girls who wore only chitons.[92] The custom is alluded to by Callimachus. When Pieria is allowed to choose whatever she desires, she rejects, as we are elaborately told, all feminine adornments,[93] i.e., she typifies girls who are plainly dressed, in nothing more than a chiton. Since Artemis Chitônê is also concerned with seafaring, as we see from these stories,[94] her festival will fall in spring, when the sailing season opens, or soon thereafter.

Why is Artemis associated with Neleus, and called *Nêlêis* after him? We infer that the name "Neleus" is somehow significant for the ritual of Artemis. Now, there are two bearers of the name, the ancient king of Pylos and his much later descendant, the founder of Miletus. Yet they are oddly similar, and the similarity consists in the betrothal of a daughter. The elder Neleus had a daughter Pero who was wooed by many, including the brother of the great Melampus, and who was finally betrothed to him on payment of an extravagant bride-price; the story goes back to Homer,[95] and there is little else to tell of Neleus of Pylos.[96] The younger Neleus had a daughter Elegeis, in one account also called Pero, who was most impatient to be wed; her lewd behavior produced an omen that caused her father to sail from Athens to Miletus, and either here or there she found a mate.[97] Thus the story of "Neleus," whether elder or younger, turns upon a marriageable daughter "Pero."

The names of father and daughter are both transparent. The father's name occurs in two forms, *Nêleus* and *Neileôs*.[98] The first element is the asseverative particle *nê* or *nei*, with the same variant spellings; the second is the expressive sound *-l-* denoting a repeated utterance, as in *lalein*, Latin *lallare*, and many other words. Neleus is "*nê*-sayer," i.e., either one who assents or one who promises on oath (for the particle is commonly used in adjuring the gods). In either case the term denotes a father who accepts a suitor. The name *Pêrô* is plainly related to *pêos, paos*, "kinsman by marriage," and to *paôthênai*, "to be related by marriage to," and denotes a girl who is given in marriage.[99] So the betrothal ceremony is already imprinted in the old myth of Neleus of Pylos.

A Love Match on Naxos

It is time to examine a more complicated story. We have seen that Delos, Ceos, and Miletus each had its own tradition of festive wooing and betrothal. So did Naxos, which has already figured as Cydippe's homeland. A Naxian girl named Polycrite, "Much-chosen," finds herself in the *Delium*, an extramural shrine of Apollo and Artemis, as Naxos town is besieged by an army from Miletus and Erythrae. There she is observed by Diognetus the Erythraean commander; he falls in love and swears by Artemis to give her anything she wishes. Polycrite then contrives to save Naxos: while the Milesians celebrate the festival *Thargelia*, she summons a surprise attack against them. The story resembles that of Phrygius and Pieria insofar as the girl saves her city in time of war; it resembles that of Hermochares and Ctesylla insofar as the girl is observed in her home sanctuary by an outsider; it resembles nearly all the others insofar as the love match is sealed by an oath.

This was a popular story, told by pseudo-Aristotle and Theophrastus and by more than one chronicler of Naxos.[100] The derivative versions that survive, in Parthenius and Plutarch, are full enough so that the ritual can be reconstructed in some detail. It is therefore surprising that the story-type has been completely misconceived by modern interpreters: Polycrite is said to be a virtual traitress or *pharmakos* who is dispatched at the end by a virtual stoning.[101]

We must begin by distinguishing a common narrative motif. The story unfolds in time of danger, during a siege by powerful enemies; it is likely that different sources gave different reasons for the siege.[102] Any festival in which women are busy outside the city walls is likely to inspire a tale of enemy invasion. The *Thesmophoria* did so at several places, as did the *Nonae Caprotinae* at Rome.[103] Sometimes the motif is evoked by nothing more than a procession that goes out from the city. Nowhere is it evident that the ritual in question is itself a means of combatting danger, as the *pharmakos* rite is often supposed to be.

Turning to the ritual details, we note that much of the action takes place in the *Delium*, just outside the city walls. It is in the *Delium* that Diognetus first sees Polycrite and approaches her as a respectful suitor, not as a brutal conqueror. It is in the *Delium* that the Milesians celebrate the *Thargelia* with feasting and drinking, for the *Delium* is the very place that Diognetus engages to deliver up to the Naxians and that is then taken by a surprise attack at night.[104] The Milesian celebration in the story corresponds to the Naxian celebration in real life.

The *Delium* on Naxos has not been found, but it must have been very like the excavated *Delium* on neighboring Paros: a large, nearly square precinct on a hill, enclosed by a wall with one gate; within, a temple, dining room, and kitchen, and plenty of open ground for temporary lodging.[105] It would suit the action of the story very well.

So far we have witnessed two stages of the Naxian *Thargelia*. Girls like Polycrite resorted to the *Delium* and were admired and perhaps approached by suitors like Diognetus. Later, and into the night, there was feasting and drinking. Since Polycrite and Diognetus are together throughout, we may wonder whether girls and suitors continued to enjoy each other's company at the banquet; but it is not safe to press the story on this point.

The next step reveals a peculiar Naxian custom. Polycrite and Diognetus send a cake or a loaf into the city to Polycrite's brothers, evidently a token of their attachment. For the sake of the story a secret message is concealed within, a lead tablet inviting the Naxians to seize the opportunity and attack. But although the hidden message is a narrative fiction, the presentation of a cake or loaf must be true to life. During the festival banquet a suitor would send a cake or loaf to the father or brother of the girl he wished to marry. To accept the present was to accept the suit and betroth the girl.

The conclusion of the story gives us yet another piece of ritual. The grateful citizens of Naxos meet Polycrite at the city gate, and fling festive objects upon her, garlands and headbands and belts. She expires from joy or suffocation, and is buried on the spot. It is called "the tomb of envy," and it serves to commemorate Polycrite. Some scholars are reminded of the stoning of a *pharmakos* or of the punishment of Tarpeia,[106] but they have failed to ask themselves what was actually done each year at "the tomb of envy." It is obvious that the Naxians did not pelt anyone with these festive objects; they simply threw them in a heap. It is this gesture, and the name "tomb of envy," that suggest the manner of Polycrite's death.

The true sense of the gesture and the name is not hard to grasp. The garlands, headbands, and belts are the festive gear that was used at the banquet of the night before; the story cannot say so, for it has feigned that the banquet was conducted by the Milesians, not the Naxians. To discard the festive gear at a "tomb" is to signal that the banquet is past and forgotten.

We should reflect that the betrothal rites brought disappointment to many (as once to Heracles). Many a suitor, after intense rivalry, found himself cheated out of his hopes. "The tomb of envy" was meant to dispel those inflamed feelings of the night before.

The Golden Bowl

These Ionian stories have acquainted us with other usages of the betrothal symposium. On Naxos the suitor's petition is accompanied by a token gift, a cake or loaf; since a cake or loaf is an elementary form of sustenance, he thereby indicates his readiness to support a household. In accepting a suitor the father swears an oath, and on Ceos he takes hold of Apollo's laurel as he does so. No doubt the oath was pledged with wine. Pindar shows us yet another custom that arises from the pledge.

The poet's tribute to Diagoras of Rhodes and his family is likened to a golden bowl, brimming with wine, which a bride's father presents as a gift to his new son-in-law, after first toasting the alliance.[107] The occasion is a betrothal rather than a wedding feast.[108] Pindar implies that the gift is the first announcement of the marriage: "Therein, while friends are gathered round, he [the bride's father] has made him [the young man] admired for a congenial marriage" (lines 5–6). This form of gift-giving, by the bride's father to the groom, is less appropriate to a wedding feast. For it was just then, when the men were joined in the dining room by the bride and the other women of the family, that another kind of gift was presented *by* the groom to the bride—the "unveiling gifts," *anakalyptêria*.[109]

The custom described by Pindar may remind us of a folktale gesture that appears in two parallel tales of Athenaeus.[110] A king summons his daughter's suitors to a feast and allows her to choose among them; she does so by tendering a bowl of wine. In the first tale, from Chares of Mytilene, a Sarmatian princess mixes the wine in a golden bowl and presents it to an unexpected suitor from afar, Zariadres the Mede. In the second, pseudo-Aristotle's version of the founding of Massalia, we have again a native princess, and again an unexpected suitor from afar, the Phocaean colonizer, and again a bowl of wine that she presents to him. In Pompeius Trogus' version of the same event, she offers water instead, whether for washing or for mixing.

Chares says that the tale of Zariadres was cherished by the barbarians of Asia, and was both set down in writing and depicted in shrines and palaces and private houses. Zariadres is in fact identifiable with a figure of Iranian legend, Zairiwairi (later Zarer) brother of Vishtaspa the patron of Zarathustra;[111] here too the romantic adventure unfolds as it does in Chares, save that the princess' gesture is to throw a goblet. It is often assumed that Chares' and pseudo-Aristotle's tales are related, and then it is disputed which comes first, and whether the story-type originates in Ionia or the East.[112] We might rather suppose that storytellers in different quarters came independently to the same result, when they wished to feign that a marriageable princess somehow made her own surprising choice.[113] The gesture that signifies the choice will vary from place to place; the water fetching in Pompeius Trogus may well be an authentic practice of either Massalia or Gaul. On this reckoning, the same Greek custom is reflected both in Chares' version of the Zariadres story and in pseudo-Aristotle's version of the founding of Massalia: the bowl of wine presented by the father to the groom.

The Wooing of Penelope

Let our last example be the most famous wooing in the world, the wooing of Penelope by fifty suitors. The choice is finally decided by the contest of the bow, which takes place at a festival of Apollo in early spring. The festival is referred to quite offhandedly in the *Odyssey*, and the offhandedness makes these references all the more significant. The festival setting was so bound up with the traditional story that Homer could not dispense with it entirely, even though it had become superfluous. In Homer's rendering of the story, the contest appears to be dictated rather suddenly by the intolerable circumstances in the palace.

The traditional story, which has often been told with other names than Odysseus and Penelope, is about a man who leaves home for distant adventures and charges his dear wife to be steadfast in awaiting his return.[114] To be steadfast, that is, until all hope is lost; the story fixes the term for hope, in this case twenty years. All through the story we await the day that follows the completion of twenty years. On that day the wife must choose another husband.

Different methods may be used for measuring a year. The Greek cities all used a lunisolar calendar in which the year was made coterminous with twelve lunations, the lunations being named after festivals. The civic years mostly began with the lunation nearest the winter or the summer solstice, but there is no reason to assume that the years of Odysseus' absence were reckoned from either of these points.[115] On the contrary, they were reckoned from the moment he left, and the time to set forth upon a long sea voyage was the spring, soon after the sailing season opened. Thus, the twenty

years expired in spring. Homer indicates that the last stages of Odysseus'
travels took place in winter; the journey to Phaeacia was made in storm
and cold, and the first night in Ithaca was bitter cold.[116] Yet we do not
find that the time of Odysseus' return is described as a change of season,
from winter to spring.[117] As we shall see in a moment, the time is given
more precisely, in terms of the dark of the moon and of Apollo's festal day.
The *Odyssey* provides the earliest direct evidence for the Greek lunisolar
calendar, though we cannot doubt that it was in use for centuries before
Homer.

Odysseus in disguise predicts about himself, first to Eumaeus and then
to Penelope, that he will return "within this same *lykabas,* as one moon
wanes and the next begins."[118] The statement about the moon is often taken
to mean precisely the day of the conjunction, a day that the Athenians
called "the old and the new."[119] But the statement seems to explain, not to
qualify, the longer period already indicated as "this same *lykabas.*" It must
be the period of several days when the nights are virtually moonless; they
are reckoned by an agricultural writer as the twenty-ninth through the
second and a similar computation now appears in a papyrus commentary
on the *Odyssey.*[120] The old word *lykabas,* which occurs only here, will
signify "the passing of the light," i.e., the dark of the moon.[121] The first
night after Odysseus' return, a night of wind and rain, is described as "a
bad one, in the dark of the moon."[122] It is two or three days later that
Odysseus makes his prediction to Penelope.

It is three or four days later—four or five days after Odysseus' return—
that the festival of Apollo comes round.[123] To be sure, Homer hardly
expected his readers, or his listeners, to be keeping count; yet he did expect
them to be aware of a lapse of time. On the festal day heralds drive a
hecatomb of oxen to sacrifice, and the people gather in Apollo's sacred
grove.[124] The scholia say that this was a festival of the new moon, with
Apollo as the presiding deity.[125] Modern commentators accept this, and
they envisage an ideal time scheme in which Odysseus returns on the last
day of the old year and takes vengeance on the first day of the new.[126] This
reckoning, as we have seen, is quite impossible. Moreover, the festival of
Apollo was surely thought of as falling on the statutory day for his festivals,
the seventh of the month.[127] The reason for this preference is not so much
that seven is a magic number[128] as that by the seventh the moon has reached
the first quarter, i.e., has become a half-moon. This is the earliest phase
that is plain to everyone, for the first sighting of the crescent is often difficult.
Since the whole community must assemble for Apollo's festival, a reliable
sign is needed: the half-moon. For a like reason the early Romans did not

conduct any festival before the *Nones,* the fifth or seventh of the month.[129] The first quarter is sacred to Apollo because his worship brings the community together just at that time, the earliest feasible date in each month. As a further consequence Apollo is sometimes associated with the day of the new moon; but this association was not nearly so common or so important.[130]

Thus, the story of Penelope's wooing, as it was told in the days before Homer, reached its climax at the spring festival of Apollo. In the *Odyssey,* however, we are too intent upon the scandal in the palace to be distracted by any public celebration. Antinous complacently declares that Apollo's festival is not the time for bending bows; he proposes to defer the contest until the next day, and to make a new start then by sacrificing goats to Apollo.[131]

NOTES

The following abbreviations are used:

   LS: F. Sokolowski, *Lois sacrées des cités grecques* (Paris 1969).

   LSS: F. Sokolowski, *Lois sacrées des cités grecques: Supplément* (Paris 1962).

   LSAM: F. Sokolowski, *Lois sacrées de l'Asie Mineure* (Paris 1955).

   1. Hdt. 6.129.1. The announcement will be made at *hê kataklisis tou gamou,* "the wedding feast": here, as in two stories examined below—those of Zariadres and of the founding of Massalia—the betrothal symposium and the wedding feast are spoken of as one, obviously for the sake of effect.

   2. M.P. Nilsson, *Griechische Feste* (Leipzig 1906), 174.

   3. Schol. Pind. *Nem.* 9 inscr., 20, 25b.

   4. Hdt. 6.126.3.

   5. U. v. Wilamowitz-Moellendorff, *Pindaros* (Berlin 1922), 257 n. 1, leaves the question undecided. Inscriptions are no help: L. Moretti, *Iscrizioni agonistiche greche* (Rome 1953), 30.

   6. Hdt. 6.126.2; 6.128.1.

   7. *AthMitt* 66, 1941, 181–95 no. 2 (*LSS* 14), an Athenian decree of 129/8 B.C.; *BCH* 87, 1963, 603–34 B 45–51 (*LS* 18), the Erchia calendar.

   8. Cf. C. Robert, *Die griechische Heldensage* (Berlin 1920–26), 911–13.

   9. *Il.* 2.572; Hdt. 5.67.2.

   10. *Nem.* 9.9–12.

   11. Schol. *Nem.* 9.20, 25b; Wilamowitz, *Pindaros* 258.

   12. The name is usually derived from *alpha sterêtikon* and *didraskein,* but the suggested meanings are all unsatisfactory. The meaning "who cannot be evaded" was only credible in the days when Adrastus was deemed a faded god, perhaps of

the underworld; it is strikingly inappropriate to the hero as we know him. The meaning recently preferred is "who does not run away"; E. Maass, *Byz.-Neugr. Jbb.* 5, 1926/27, 180–81, compares Adeistos, Adeimantos, Atrestos, Aphobêtos, Atromêtos—parallels enough in respect of both form and meaning. But while this meaning is plausible in itself, it hardly fits the hero, who *does* run away, and becomes a paradigm for indecent flight, e.g., *A.P.* 7.431.

13. Pind. *Nem.* 9.9, 12.

14. Hdt. 5.67.5.

15. Schol. *Nem.* 9 inscr. begins, "Concerning the *Pythia* at Sicyon the Halicarnassian writes thus," and then there is a lacuna. Herodotus has no express mention of the festival; perhaps the scholiast quoted the account of "tragic choruses" (at 30a he quotes other remarks of Herodotus on Adrastus) and referred it to Apollo's festival.

16. Ampel. *Lib. Mem.* 8.5 (*FGrH* 551 *Anhang* F 3a).

17. Paus. 2.7.7–9.

18. A. Griffin, *Sikyon* (Oxford 1982), 10–11, 17.

19. Schol. Pind. *Nem.* 9.30 (Menaechmus *FGrH* 131 F 10); Paus. 2.11.2, cf. 2.5.6.

20. On the other hand the "hero shrine" of Adrastus known to Herodotus was "in the very agora of Sicyon" (5.67.1), i.e., in the earlier agora, somewhere in the plain. This was doubtless a secondary monument. Another such was the tomb of Iphinoe, likewise in the agora (*SEG* 15.195).

21. Stat. *Theb.* 1.557–668.

22. Schol. Eur. *Phoen.* 409 (Mnaseas fr. 48 Müller).

23. Stat. *Theb.* 1.498–510.

24. Paus. 2.24.1 Pausanias speaks of a single ewe-lamb; Statius of several black sheep, male. Statius may be inaccurate, or his source may be faithful to an earlier period. For a general discussion of the rite, see E. Kadletz, *TAPA* 108, 1978, 93–101.

25. The excavated remains are described by R.A. Tomlinson, *Argos and the Argolid* (London 1972), 247–49.

26. Paus. 2.24.1

27. Stat. *Theb.* 1.554–55.

28. Stat. *Theb.* 1.342–89, 403–7, 454–56; schol. Eur. *Phoen.* 409 (Mnaseas fr. 48 Müller). In the early lyric poem of *PLille* 76, tentatively assigned to Stesichorus, the stages of Polyneices' journey are as in Statius, but the papyrus breaks off after Corinth and Cleonae; no doubt the storm was described next. Cf. P.J. Parsons, *ZPE* 26, 1977, 33–34.

29. Stat. *Theb.* 1.512–29, 539–43, 552–56, 694–95.

30. Copenhagen, Nat. Mus. VIII 496 (*LIMC* 1, pl. 171, Adrastos 1).

31. Berlin 1890 = *ABV* 269.34; M. Robertson in E. Böhr and W. Martini, eds., *Studien zur Mythologie und Vasenmalerei: K. Schauenburg zum 65 Geburtstag* (Mainz 1986), 47–51, pl. 9.

32. Dieuchidas *FGrH* 485 F 10 (L. Piccirilli, *Megarika* 2 F 8); Paus. 1.41.3–4,

6. On Dieuchidas' date, Piccirilli (pp. 14–15) hesitates between the fourth century and the second.

33. Frazer on Paus. 1.41.3; Robert, *Griechische Heldensage*, 73 n. 3; Thompson, *Motif Index* H 105, "Parts of slain animal as token of slaying," including, e.g., H 105.1, "Dragon-tongue proof."

34. *Od.* 3.332–34, 341; Apoll. Rhod. *Arg.* 1.516–18.

35. Schol. *Od.* 3.341, citing several authorities; schol. Apoll. Rhod. 1.516/18c, citing Dieuchidas and Philochorus; cf. Athen. 1.28, 16B-C. For modern discussion, see P. Stengel, *Opferbräuche der Griechen* (Leipzig 1910), 172–77; F. Puttkammer, *Quomodo Graeci victimarum carnes distribuerint* (Königsberg 1912), 13; Jacoby on Philochorus *FGrH* 328 F 80; E. Kadletz, *HThR* 74, 1981, 21–29.

36. *IG* 1³ 246 C 24 (*LS* 2 A 7), a doubtful restoration, Athens, ca. 470–60; *IosPE* 1005.8 (*LS* 89), another doubtful restoration, Phanagoria, s. II; *SIG*³ 1024.8, 31–34 (*LSS* 96), Myconus, ca. 200 B.C.; *Chiaca Meletemata* 1, 1958, 26.2–3 (*LSS* 129), Chios, s. V; *SIG*³ 1013.3, 7 (*LS* 119), Chios, s. IV; *Athena* 20, 1908, 222.7 (*LSS* 77), Chios, s. IV; *LS* 120.7, a supplement *in vacuo*, Chios, s. IV; *Athena* 20, 1908, 220.7 (*LSS* 78), Chios, s. II; *ASAtene* 33/34, 1955/56, 164.2 (*LSS* 93), Ialysus, s. II; *AnzWien* 1959, 39.20 (*LSS* 121), Ephesus, s. III p.; *SIG*³ 1003.9 (*LSAM* 37), Priene, s. II; *SIG*³ 1002.7–8 (*LSAM* 44), Miletus, ca. 400; *SIG*³ 1037.2, 3, 5–6 (*LSAM* 46), Miletus, ca. 300; *AbhBerl* (1908) 22.17 (*LSAM* 48), Miletus, ca. 276/5; *SIG*³ 1017.7 (*LSAM* 1), Sinope, s. III.

37. Thus in the calendar of Myconos a priest often gets tongue and shoulder together; when, however, sheep are sacrificed in numbers by boys or ephebes, they share the tongues with the priests.

38. *IG* 1³ 255 B 8 (*LS* 11 B 7), Attica, ca. 430; *SIG*³ 1047.7 (*LS* 103 B 7), Minoa on Amorgos, ca. 100. In the latter, the tongue is accompanied by other offerings; in the former, a lacuna leaves room for other offerings. Since the priest generally took the table offerings for himself, they are virtual perquisites.

39. Ar. *Pax* 1059, 1109; Men. *Kolax* fr. 1.4–5 Sandbach (292 Kock). Cf. Ar. *Plut.* 1110, "This herald gets a tongue cut out," an alarming equivocation.

40. Ar. *Av.* 1704–5.

41. Paus. 1.41.3, 6. A. Muller, *BCH* 105, 1981, 209, suggests a location at the north foot of the Alcathous.

42. Jacoby, n. 8 to Philochorus F 80, errs on this point.

43. Paus. 1.42.2, 5–6.

44. Theogn. 773–88; cf. schol. Pind. *Nem.* 3.147. For other details of the festival, see K.J. Rigsby, *GRBS* 28, 1987, 93–102.

45. *A.P.* 13.22 (A.S.F. Gow and D.L. Page, *Hellenistic Epigrams* [Cambridge 1965] 1, 158: Phaedimus 3, with commentary in 2, 455).

46. *Hell. Oxy.* 17.3; Str. 9.2.22, p. 408; Paus. 8.35.10.

47. Cf. Argynnus and Agamemnon at Argynnium (Aristophanes *FGrH* 379 F 9, etc.); Harmonia and Cadmus at Thebes.

48. Lyc. *Alex.* 831. The epithet is one of three in the same line, and it is hard to guess why the paraphrase speaks of "Aphrodite on Samos."

49. [Hes.] *Cat.* fr. 76.6, 10 M-W, where the phrase "the gifts [of golden Aphrodite]" is twice restored with near certainty; calyx krater of the Dinos Painter (formerly called "the Atalanta Painter"), Bologna 300 = *ARV*² 1152.7. Cf. Theogn. 1293–94: Atalanta seeks to evade marriage, "the gifts of golden Aphrodite."

50. Nilsson, *Griechische Feste*, 369–74. According to Nilsson, the rites in question properly belong to wedding ceremonies and are transferred to public festivals at a later stage (p. 372); yet, this assumption is not required. In the first case, he thinks of a magic means of deceiving evil spirits (p. 372), in the second, of "an act of sympathetic magic" to promote (e.g.) childbirth (p. 373). Either kind of magic is appropriate to the public domain.

51. Ant. Lib. *Met.* 17, purportedly from Nicander. Cf. Nilsson, *Griechische Feste* 370–71; F. Wehrli, *RE Suppl.* 5 (1931) 558–59 s.v. *Leto*.

52. [Hes.] *Cat.* fr. 74 M-W.

53. "We cannot be sure that [the passage] said unambiguously that Hippomenes wore nothing": M.L. West, *The Hesiodic Catalogue of Women* (Oxford 1985), 135. But the point is rather that the passage differed from any other account of a hero preparing himself for a race.

54. [Hes.] *Cat.* fr. 75.8–10 M-W.

55. Ov. *Met.* 10.578–80, 591, 593.

56. Cf. Wilamowitz, *Kleine Schriften* 5.2 (Berlin 1938), 95 n. 1.

57. D. H. *Ant. Rom.* 1.50.3.

58. Soph. *Trach.* 262–69, 281; cup of Onesimus, New York 12.231.2 = *ARV*² 319.6. In Sophocles the speaker makes no mention of Iole, so as to spare Deianeira's feelings, and as a result the treatment of Heracles is altogether mystifying. On the cup the drunken Heracles is trading blows with Eurytus and the four boys.

59. Early Corinthian column krater, Louvre E 635. A passage of Ion's *Eurytidae*, *TrGF* 19 F 10, addresses the servants as they ladle wine from jars into pitchers.

60. An amphora by the Sappho Painter, Madrid 10916 = *ABV* 508.0, presents a sequel to the archery contest that is not recorded in literary sources: Heracles has just shot two sons of Eurytus and takes aim at Iole. Cf. R. Olmos Romera, *MadrMitt* 18, 1977, 130–51. Some accounts dwell on Iole's reluctance and Heracles' coercion: Robert, *Griechische Heldensage* 584 n. 2; [Hes.] *Cat.* 229.5 M-W. Serv.; *Aen.* 8.291 says that after taking Oechalia, Heracles killed Iole too.

61. Eurytus, Melas, and Apollo: Robert, *Griechische Heldensage* 581–82; [Hes.] *Cat.* 26.22–28 M-W. Eurytus son of Melaneus at Andania: Robertson, *GRBS* 29, 1988, 250 note.

62. See A. Severyns, *Le cycle épique dans l'école d'Aristarque* (Liège 1928), 188–91; Y. Béquignon, *La vallée du Spercheios* (Paris 1937), 142–43, 228–30.

63. *H.Ap.* 208–13. For the text, see Wilamowitz, *Isyllos von Epidauros* (Berlin 1884), 80–81. In the last line I translate an emendation of Buecheler that is unlikely to be right (despite Wilamowitz), but serves to round off the sense.

64. *Ekkorei korikorônên;* cf. L. Deubner, *Hermes* 48, 1913, 299–304 = *Kleine*

Schriften (Königstein 1982), 171–76. In the "Crow Song" of Phoenix of Colophon (fr. 2 Powell) children carry round a crow that brings luck to marriageable girls. The myth of "Crow" as a faithless bride is fittingly concluded by the raven's tattling ([Hes.] fr. 60 M-W).

65. West, *Hesiodic Catalogue of Women*, 69–72, has argued forcefully that the *Catalog* did not represent Coronis as mother of Asclepius. He also observes that fr. 60 (about the raven) seems not to be part of an *Ehoiê*, but only a passing reference, which may not even come from the *Catalog*. As to fr. 59, the beginning of an *ehoiê* about a girl at Lake Boebeis, he suggests that it was either a quite different story about Coronis or a story about some other heroine of the district. Both suggestions are unsatisfactory, and we need only suppose that the story of Coronis was told without the birth of Asclepius as a sequel. West finds difficulty in placing Coronis and Phlegyas within the genealogies of Book 1. Yet the details of Phlegyas' parentage that we find in late sources are not likely to be exhaustive; it seems quite conceivable that in the *Catalog* Phlegyas was counted among the Aeolids.

66. Note too that the name Ereuthes (or Ereutheus) in line 211 has no match anywhere but in the warrior Ereuthus who dwelt by the Alpheius and followed Nestor to Troy (Q.S. *Posthom.* 2.239). The rivalry between Leucippus and Apollo is reported by Parthenius, *Narr. Amat.* 15 (Diodorus Elaita, *Suppl. Hellen.* fr. 380; Phylarchus *FGrH* 81 F 39a), Plut. *Agis* 9.3 (Phylarchus F 37b), and Paus. 8.20.4. Admittedly the manner of Leucippus' death, being pierced by the spears of girl huntresses, is typical of youths who offend the goddess Artemis, and is therefore the *aition* of a ritual bloodletting in her cult, such as we hear of directly at Halae in Attica and at Spartan Limnae.

67. *Il.* 9.557–64; other versions in Robert, *Griechische Heldensage*, 311–13.

68. Cf. Robert, *Griechische Heldensage*, 37, 766, 865–66.

69. For the story of Alcestis, see A. Lesky, *SBWien* 203.2 (1925); G. Megas, *ARW* 30, 1933, 1–33; L. Weber, *RhM* n.s. 85, 1936, 117–64; M. Gaster, *Byz.-Neugr. Jbb.* 15, 1939, 66–90. The folktale elements do not explain the origin of the story.

70. Call. *Aet.* Bk. 3, frs. 67–75, with Pfeiffer's addenda at Call. 1.500–1, 2.113; *Suppl. Hell.* fr. 301; cf. Aristaenetus *Ep.* 1.10; Ov. *Her.* 20, 21.

71. *FGrH* 442; for the date see Jacoby *ad loc.*

72. The occasion, says Callimachus, is Apollo's "cattle slaughter," *bouphoniê*, on Delos (fr. 67.5–6), but Artemis is present too (fr. 75.26); there was some mention of a chorus that came to Delos (fr. 71). In Ovid Cydippe and her mother sacrifice to both Apollo and Artemis (*Her.* 21.93–96), though it is precisely in the temple of Artemis that Cydippe encounters the apple and swears the oath (*Her.* 20.7, 182, 205–8; 21.107–10).

73. P. Bruneau, *Recherches sur les cultes de Délos à lépoque hellénistique* (Paris 1970), 65–66, identifies the festival as the *Apollonia*, presumably because the *Delia*

were no longer celebrated in Callimachus' day. But the *Delia* flourished in the time of Xenomedes, whom Callimachus professes to follow faithfully. The *Apollonia* come too early in the year, in *Hierus = Anthesterion,* to draw worshippers from overseas.

74. Bruneau, *Recherches,* 87–91, sets out the evidence—chiefly the legends of Plato's and Socrates' birthdays—which expressly indicates *Thargelion* 6–7, but he refuses to believe it. Cf. Robertson, *TAPA* 113, 1983, 152.

75. Theophrastus said that the *Thargelia* of Phyla honored Delian Apollo (Athen. 10.24, 424F). We shall see below, apropos of the story of Polycrite, that the *Thargelia* of Naxos are linked with a shrine of Delian Apollo.

76. Call. fr. 75.50–52. Acontius in turn was descended from the Euxantidae (frs. 67.7, 75.32–37, 67–69).

77. Callimachus, doubtless after Xenomedes, provides some curious details of the Naxian background (frs. 67.11–14, 75.1–4).

78. P.M. Fraser, *Ptolemaic Alexandria* (Oxford 1972), 1.727, 2.1017 n. 77–79, takes it as established that our story has no aetiological reference. Since it was told at great length in Callimachus' *Aetia,* this is an intolerable paradox.

79. Jacoby, *FGrH* 442 [*Dritter Teil b, Kommentar,* p. 178] n. 6 on Xenomedes, thinks this a possibility.

80. The "Pythian" festival agrees with the legendary ties between Ceos and Delphi, attested by Xenomedes: the Corycian nymphs were in the island first of all; afterwards Ceos son of Apollo came from Naupactus. Cf. Jacoby on Xenomedes *FGrH* 442 F 1 line 63.

81. Robertson, *TAPA* 113, 1983, 144–53.

82. According to Plutarch (*Mul. Virt.* 12, 249D), wooing on Ceos was done with old-fashioned decorum. During the day marriageable girls danced and sported in "public sanctuaries," doubtless those of Artemis; this was an opportunity for suitors to admire them. At evening the girls went to each other's houses and performed such domestic chores as washing the men's feet. Though several suitors might fix on the same girl, their love was so restrained that when one was chosen, the others straightway retired. All this is a moralizing comment on ceremonies like the one at Carthaea.

83. It is quite possible that the Cean story was first told without Artemis, and that she was added by either Nicander or Antoninus to drive home the analogy with Acontius and Cydippe.

84. Call. *Aet.* Bk. 3, frs. 80–83, with Pfeiffer's addenda at Call. 1.501, 2.113–14; cf. Aristaenetus *Ep.* 1.15; Plut. *Mul. Virt.* 16, 253F–254A; Polyaenus 8.35.

85. Ath. 7.19, 283D–284A (Apollonius frs. 7–9 Powell); Ael. *Nat. Anim.* 15.23.

86. Since Ocyrrhoe's parents are the river Imbrasus and the nymph Chesias, and since Apollo's pursuit begins on Samos, it is clear that this is a tale of Samos that Apollonius has embroidered with an episode at Miletus. Apollo *Nymphêgetês* and the Nymphs had a shrine near the source of the Imbrasus; G. Shipley, *A History of Samos* (Oxford 1987), 261.

87. Call. fr. 80.18 (see Call. 2.113 for the improved text of this passage, after Barber and Maas); Plut. *Mul. Virt.* 16, 254A; Polyaenus 8.35. Polyaenus took Plutarch to say that the festival, not the goddess, was called *Nêlêis;* but Callimachus shows that the goddess is meant.

88. Plut. *Mul. Virt.* 16, 253F; Polyaenus 8.35.

89. Call. fr. 82 (again, see Call. 2.113); Aristaenetus *Ep.* 1.15.

90. Call. *Dian.* 225–27. Cf. schol. *Jov.* 77b, recording that Neleus brought with him a statue of Artemis Chitônê.

91. *Milet 1.7, Der Sudmarkt und die benachbarten Bauanlagen* 202 (*LSAM* 51) has *kithônê;* A. Rehm, *Didyma II: Inschriften* (Berlin 1958) no. 315 has *chitônê.* Cf. Hsch. s.v. *kithônea.*

92. The custom was very common: schol. Eur. *Hec.* 934 says that Dorian girls came to dance in Artemis' sanctuary "with just one chiton," and the ritual scenes on vases from Attic shrines of Artemis show younger girls in chitons, older girls quite naked. The iconography of Artemis, as well as the title *kithônê,* is projected from her worshippers; at Call. *Dian.* 11–12 Artemis asks her father for a knee-length chiton. It is odd that scholars have ignored or resisted this understanding of *kithônê.* Nilsson, *Geschichte der griechischen Religion*[2/3] (Munich 1967), 1.494 n. 3, thinks of the practice of dedicating clothes, especially chitons, after childbirth; but Artemis could not be assimilated to a woman just delivered, as this explanation implies.

93. Call. fr. 80.5–9; Aristaenetus *Ep.* 1.

94. At Call. *Jov.* 77 Artemis Chitônê is patron of fishermen, if *epaktêres* meant the same to Callimachus as to Apollonius (*Arg.* 1.625). Neleus, Pieria, Ocyrrhoe all reach Miletus by sea. We may conjecture that a Naxian festival of Artemis has inspired a story in Aelian (*V.H.* 8.5). When Neleus sailed from Athens, the winds blew him to Naxos and kept him there until he managed to identify those of his company who were tainted by blood crimes; he left them to settle Naxos.

95. *Od.* 11.287–97, 15.231–38.

96. Cf. Robert, *Griechische Heldensage,* 36, 195.

97. Lyc. *Alex.* 1385–88, schol. 1378, 1385; *Etym. Magn.* s.vv. *aselgainein, Elegêis;* cf. Robertson, *GRBS* 29, 1988, 243–45.

98. Etymologies ancient and modern are canvassed by van der Kolf, *RE* 16.2 (1935) 2278–79 s.v. *Neleus* 1; the general favorite is "unpitying," from *nê-* and *eleos,* cf. epic *nêlês,* supposed to signify a god of the underworld. Yet another has been advanced by L.R. Palmer and is widely accepted by Mycenologists: Palmer, *The Interpretation of Mycenaean Greek Texts* (Oxford 1963), 79–80, and *The Greek Language* (London 1980), 34–35; H. Mühlestein, *MH* 22, 1965, 155–65; M. Durante, *Studi Micenei ed Egeo-Anatolici* 3, 1967, 33–46; C.J. Ruijgh, *Études sur la grammaire et le vocabulaire du grec mycénien* (Amsterdam 1967), 369–70; Ruijgh in A. Morpurgo Davies and Y. Duhoux, eds., *Linear B: A 1984 Survey* (Louvain-La-Neuve 1985), 164. The form *ne-e-ra-wo,* a man's name in the dative (PY Fn 79), is taken to represent *Nehelawos,* i.e., **Nese-lawos,* "saving-the-folk,"

from the root *nes-* "save." Neileos and Neleus are shortened forms in Ionic and Aeolic respectively; Nestor is an agent noun from the same root. Morphology aside, one asks why the name "saving-the-folk" was given to a king of Pylos who ended by losing his twelve sons, his kingdom, and his life.

99. The root is *paso-*, seen also in Latin *parricida*, "slayer of a kinsman."

100. Plut. *Mul. Virt.* 17, 254B-F (*FGrH* 501 F 2, Naxos, *Anhang;* [Arist.] fr. 559 Rose³ = 567 Gigon); Parthenius, *Narr. Amat. 9* (Andriscus *FGrH* 500 F 1; Theophrastus); Gellius 3.15.1.

101. A.H. Krappe, *RhM* 78, 1929, 253–54; Mielentz, *RE* 4A.2 (1932) 2337–38, s.v. *Tarpeia;* G. Radke, *RE* 21.2 (1952) 1753–59 s.v. *Polykrite* 1; U. Hetzner, *Andromeda und Tarpeia* (Meisenheim 1963), 62–67; P. Pinotti, *GIF* 26, 1974, 18–32; W. Burkert, *Structure and History in Greek Mythology and Ritual* (Berkeley 1979), 72–77.

102. The Milesian attack was provoked by a woman's baseness, just as it was repulsed by a woman's gallantry, says Plutarch (*Mul. Virt.* 17, 254C). The version that he takes from the "Naxian chroniclers" tells of an adulterous woman of Miletus who fled to Naxos with her lover. A *casus belli* so sensational and so banal may have been introduced at any time; whether it was endorsed by [Aristotle], whom Plutarch cites for variant details about Polycrite, we cannot tell, but the Naxian chronicler Andriscus appears to have given only a chronological indication for the siege: "At that time the Milesians came against Naxos with their allies," etc. Perhaps Andriscus meant the famous siege of ca. 500 B.C. that lasted four months; it would be natural for the Naxians to embroider this event with a ritual myth.

103. We are told that Megarian invaders landed at Eleusis or Cape Colias and that fugitives from Lade put in at Ephesus, while local women were conducting the *Thesmophoria.* At Rome the *Nonae Caprotinae* are said to commemorate various attacks by Latins and Gauls and Etruscans.

104. Andriscus mentions the *Delium* as the spot where Polycrite was separated from her countrymen and admired by Diognetus. Subsequently the target of the attack is described as a seeming stronghold, a place with a wall and a gate; this suits an extramural sanctuary. It is [Aristotle] who explains that the contested area was precisely the *Delium.*

105. O. Rubensohn, *Das Delion von Paros* (Wiesbaden 1962); N.M. Kontoleon, *Gnomon* 38, 1966, 202–11.

106. See note 101 above.

107. *Ol.* 7.1–6.

108. Pindar's commentators have generally spoken of a wedding feast, but a betrothal is rightly preferred by B.K. Braswell, *Mnemosyne*⁴ 29, 1976, 241, and C. Brown in D.E. Gerber, ed., *Greek Poetry and Philosophy: Studies in Honour of L. Woodbury* (Chico 1984) 38. W.J. Verdenius, *Commentaries on Pindar* 1 (Leiden 1987) 45, disputes this on the ground that a betrothal as "a preliminary agreement" is insufficient to sustain the comparison: a most unconvincing objection.

109. Cf. L. Deubner, *JdI* 15, 1900, 148–51 = *Kleine Schriften* (Königstein 1982) 5–8; Heckenbach, *RE* 8.2 (1913) 2130, s.v. *Hochzeit.*

110. Athen. 13.35–36, 575A–576B (Chares *FGrH* 125 F 5; [Arist.] fr. 549 Rose[3] = 560 Gigon); cf. Justin 43.3.8–11.

111. Cf. W. Hinz, *RE* 9A.2 (1967) 2325, s.v. *Zariadres;* P. Calmeyer, *Iran,* 18, 1980, 60–61.

112. Cf. E. Schwartz, *RE* 3.2 (1899) 2129, s.v. *Chares* 13; E. Rohde, *Der griechische Roman*[3] (Leipzig 1914), 47–55; Jacoby on Chares F 5; G. Nenci, *Riv. di Studi Liguri* 24, 1958, 51–53.

113. Cf. Thompson, *Motif Index* T 55.7, "Princess elects herself husband from the young men present"; T 55.8, "Princess declares love by presenting cup of drink at feast"; T 131.01, "Princess has unrestricted choice of husband."

114. Cf. Wilamowitz, *Die Ilias und Homer* (Berlin 1920), 482–85.

115. Apollo's festival is commonly equated with a "new year's festival" falling at the winter solstice or the spring equinox. Wilamowitz, *Ilias und Homer,* 433, 485, and *Der Glaube der Hellenen* (1931–32, reprint Darmstadt 1959[3]) 2.29 n. 2, makes it the winter solstice, and compares the Samian *eiresiônê*-festival in the *Vita Homeri.* This, however, was assuredly not a festival of the solstice but of the beginning of spring, when Apollo himself returns. E. Schwartz, *Die Odyssee* (Munich 1924), 187, makes it the spring equinox ("as on Chios," he says; but nowadays it is admitted that the new-year season on Chios is unknown). G. Thomson, *JHS* 63, 1943, 57 n. 40, identifies the festival as the *Hecatombaea,* and compares the Athenian festival of *Hecatombaeon* 7, which he perhaps thought of as marking the summer solstice (cf. his p. 55).

116. The stormy passage to Phaeacia: *Od.* 5.291–332, 365–70, 391–92. Cold winds ashore: 5.465–87. Cold weather at Eumaeus' hut: 14.457–533. Note too that the nights are long (15.392), and that the braziers at the palace give warmth as well as light (19.64). As we saw before, Polyneices and Tydeus come to Argos in storm and cold.

117. Or at least it is not literally so described. J.N. Austin, *Archery at the Dark of the Moon* (Berkeley 1975), 238–53, argues that Odysseus' return is the coming of spring in a symbolic sense, for spring is mentioned in a couple of similes, and Athena takes the form of a swallow, elsewhere the harbinger of spring. This exegesis is too selective to be convincing.

118. *Od.* 14.161–62, 19.306–7.

119. So Plut. *Sol.* 25.4. Modern exponents include Wilamowitz, *Homerische Untersuchungen* (Berlin 1884), 54–55, and *Die Heimkehr des Odysseus* (Berlin 1927), 92; E. Meyer, *Hermes* 27, 1892, 376–77; Nilsson, *RE* 17.2 (1937) 1292–93, s.v. *Noumênia* 1, and *Die Entstehung und religiöse Bedeutung des griechischen Kalenders*[2] (Lund 1962), 15; E. Gjerstad, *OpAth* 1, 1953, 191. It is only the Athenian phrase *enê kai nea* that gives any color at all to this interpretation of Homer. The phrase is usually taken as "old and new day," i.e., on the day when the old moon is invisible at sunrise and the new moon appears at sunset. If we supply *selene* instead, as West does on Hes. *Op.* 770, the same sequence may be in view; but West has a more ingenious explanation—"the old moon in the new moon's arms," a faint disk and a bright crescent. It does not really matter for our understanding

of the phrase whether the evening of the new moon was counted as the next day in the calendar (so Nilsson, West, and others) or as the same day (so W.K. Pritchett, *ZPE* 49, 1982, 260–66).

120. Sotion, *Geopon.* 1.13.2, 5.10.3. Professor W.J. Slater drew my attention to the commentary on *Od.* 20 preserved in *OxyPap* 3710 (M.W. Haslam, *OxyPap* 53 [London 1986] 89–112). On line 156, Penelope's announcement of the festival, there is a long discussion of the interlunium (col. ii 34–52) and of the new crescent (col. iii 1–18). Heracleitus seems to be quoted as saying that the moon may not appear for two or more days (col. ii 43–47); and a very fragmentary passage seems to say that the new moon may not be sighted until "the third day" (col. iii 7–9, 17). The gist of the discussion is perhaps to equate the interlunium with the period of several days between Odysseus' return and the festival of Apollo; cf. Haslam on col. iii 18f.

121. The meanings usually alleged for *lykabas* are either "year" or "month" or "day" or "season." But if the following line is explanatory—"as one moon wanes and the next begins"—then the meaning is precisely "interlunium," "dark of the moon." And if the word is formed, as it seems to be, from *luk* - "light" and *ban-* "go," the second element must be used in a sense appropriate to a celestial phenomenon, and this we find in the aorist forms of *bainein:* "to have gone away" (LSJ s.v. A I 3). Hence "the passing of the light."

122. *Od.* 14.457. The solar eclipse that Theoclymenus sees with the mind's eye (20.356–57) can occur only at the *interlunium*.

123. Odysseus spends at least three nights at Eumaeus' hut (*Od.* 14.457, 15.494, 16.481); four, if Telemachus' journey to Pherae occupies another day (15.188). He spends the last night at the palace (20.1).

124. *Od.* 20.276–78, cf. 20.156, 21.258–59. Other intimations of the festival appear at 17.600, 20.162–63, 173–75, 185–86, 250–51; cf. Wilamowitz, *Heimkehr,* 91–93.

125. Schol. *Od.* 20.156 (Philochorus *FGrH* 328 F 88b). Cf. schol. Pind. *Nem.* 3.4; schol. Ar. *Plut.* 1126; *Oxy.Pap.* 3710 (n. 120 above) col. ii 34–35, citing Aristonicus.

126. See notes 115 and 119 above.

127. Cf. W. Schmidt, *Geburtstag im Altertum* (Giessen 1908), 86–87, 89–92.

128. So Nilsson, *Griechische Kalender* 48–51; West on Hes. *Op.* 770. Nilsson supposed that the seventh as a holy day was adopted from Babylon in the Archaic period, together with the calendar of months. West rightly says that the calendar of months goes much further back; yet he thinks that the seventh as a holy day may still have been borrowed from the East in the Archaic period, and then attached to Apollo. This is to forget that the calendar of months takes a large part of its nomenclature from festivals of Apollo that fall on the seventh.

129. Cf. Robertson, *MH* 44, 1987, 19–20.

130. The observances attested for the *noumênia* are various and often are private

rather than public; Apollo's role is modest. The *Vita Homeri* should not be cited for the association of Apollo and the *noumênia*. On Samos, we are told, Homer would go begging at the *noumêniai*, and he had some success with the *eiresiônê*-song that he recited as the children led him round. This sequence does not imply that the *noumêniai* are the occasion of the *eiresiônê*-song, for the song itself shows that it was sung once a year; the children are said to commemorate Homer by singing it "at the festival of Apollo."

131. *Od.* 21.256–68. Soon after, Odysseus invokes Apollo to direct his shot against Antinous (22.7).

Foreigners at the Greek Symposium?

Margaret Miller

A symposiast plays the double pipes for his fellows (no. 3, fig. 3); a komast balances his cup through the steps of his dance (no. 7, fig. 11); a *kottabos*-player prepares for his cast (no. 8, fig. 14).[1] All three figures engage in activities typical of symposium and *komos* in late Archaic Attic red-figured painting, but exceptionally they wear a floppy Oriental hat that Beazley termed the *kidaris*.[2] Attic sympotic vessels so often illuminate the milieu of lyric poetry that we frequently expect close levels of correspondence between images and texts. Yet occasionally, as here, a knowledge of Greek literature does not help. No text explains the significance of adding a *kidaris* to otherwise unremarkable symposiasts.

The wearers of the *kidaris* include nine symposiasts (nos. 3–6, 8–10, 12) and three komasts (nos. 2, 7, 11) on eleven drinking vessels and wine containers (figs. 2–24). Though few in number, they are persistent, spanning three generations of vase-painters, ca. 510–450 B.C. The greatest concentration occurs ca. 500–480 B.C. and the three pieces from the following decades are all in some sense archaising. In addition, some fifty cups of and near the Pithos Painter share the formulaic tondo decoration of a symposiast wearing a *kidaris* (no. 1, fig. 1). The best-known vessel, Douris' cup in Florence (no. 8, fig. 14), gives a full symposium with seven men reclining on *klinai* throughout exterior and interior. Other depictions abbreviate the scene; the Nausikaa Painter's column krater has only two symposiasts (no. 12, fig. 24). In each instance, with the exception of the Leipzig cup (no. 4, figs. 5–6) and possibly the Berlin cup (no. 5, figs. 7–8), only one figure sports the *kidaris*.

When Paul Jacobsthal first grouped the *kidaris*-wearers in his work *Symposiaka*, he aired a number of possible explanations. They may be read literally: either they are some form of *barbaroi* (possibly Scythians) or they are Greeks and the cap signifies the office of *symposiarchos*. Alternatively, the images may not denote reality, being either meaningless jokes on the part of the painters or a metaphor for excessive drinking. More recently Lissarrague has pursued the latter line of interpretation, viewing the *kidaris* as a sign of the Dionysiac escape from social constraint. The wide range of modern attempts at explanation betrays a fundamental problem of ambiguity. It is no easy task to choose between these alternatives nor even to decide whether the multiplicity of choices stems from the painters' own attempt at ambiguity and multivalence or from our ignorance of the requisite codes and context.[3] Yet even at the outset we may note that Wegner's attempt to deny any significance whatsoever to the *kidaris*, as if it were a whim of the moment, is a facile and inadequate solution to the problem.[4] Whims, too, have motives and meanings and this "whim" merits attention, for it affected a variety of painters over a considerable period of time.

Much of the discussion of the appearance of the *kidaris* on symposiasts and komasts has taken the form of either *obiter dicta* or statements *ex cathedra*. One of the tasks of this chapter is to weed and sort. At the end, I will propose a new but simple solution, which relates the material to a current in Athenian social history. Almost all previous scholarship takes one of two different approaches to interpreting the *kidaris*; my own approach is yet a third.

These three approaches to the interpretation of the *kidaris*-wearing symposiasts can be described in terms of the assumed relationship between the painted hat (as signifier) and its assumed meaning (as signified). I find an ideal expression of the three relations in C.S. Pierce's division of the sign into *icon, index,* and *symbol.*[5] Pierce's *icon* is a sign connected to the signified by resemblance, similarity, or analogy between the relations of parts: it represents its object by virtue of its own character. Photographs, statues, and diagrams are simple examples of *icons.* An *index* has a real existential, dynamic, and physical connection with its signified: it represents its object by virtue of being really affected by it. The difference is clear from the examples:

> I see a man with a rolling gait. This is a probable indication that he is a sailor. I see a bowlegged man in corduroys, gaiters and a jacket. These are probable indications that he is a jockey or something of the sort ... A rap at the door is an index ... A low barometer with a moist air is an index of rain ... A weathercock is an index of the direction of the wind.[6]

A *symbol* is connected to its signified by a habitual mental association: it represents its object by virtue of a rule or convention. The link lies in a mental idea, not in resemblance or actual physical connection. So the Scales of Justice are a symbol, but the tilting of the grocer's scales is an index of weight.

The *Kidaris* as Index or *cucullus non facit monachum*

The simplest explanation might at first seem the most economical: he who wears a foreign hat is a foreigner.[7] Supporters of this hypothesis can point to a large number of Orientals in Late Archaic Attic painting. If we assume that these representations denote the presence of real foreigners in Late Archaic Athens, we may be further tempted to suppose that these Orientals appeared at Attic symposia and that Attic vase-painters recorded this international exchange. Scythian archers suddenly start to accompany Greek hoplites on Attic vases of the second half of the sixth century, sparking theories that the Peisistratids introduced a company of Scythian archers to Athens.[8] The continued popularity of this theme until ca. 500 can be explained by supposing that the archers stayed on after the fall of the tyranny; our *kidaris*-wearing symposiasts are the Scythian archers at ease in an Athenian *andron* and exemplify the openness of Late Archaic Attic society.[9]

The scenario is charming, but unlikely on several grounds. The argument for a Scythian military force in Athens of the sixth century rests on the iconography alone. There is no independent evidence in the Archaic period for Scythian police, a company of Scythian archers, or Scythian attendants for hoplites, all of which have been proposed. There are also internal weaknesses and inconsistencies in the iconographic evidence. It is difficult to square the persistent coupling of hoplite and archer with what is known of contemporary hoplite battle tactics.[10] Moreover, if Heracles occasionally dons a "Scythian archer" costume, he has mythological justification as the father of Skythes and *Stammvater* of the Scythians.[11] Pinney argues that the Scythians in art originated as attendants of Achilles and then evolved into generic heroic attendants; this may prove the most economical explanation for the Scythian archers.[12] Many figures defy neat categorization as "Scythian archers." Some carry bows but wear no hats or any other Oriental attribute;[13] some wear Oriental hats but carry no bows. Our symposiasts fit into the latter nebulous category. There is no clue that they are archers; only the *kidaris* can identify them as Scythians.

Our primary sources for Scythian costume in this period are Herodotus' description and Achaemenid imperial inscriptions and relief sculpture. Achaemenid inscriptions mention three groups of Sakai: *Saka haumavarga* (hauma-drinking Scythians); *Saka tigraxauda* (pointed-hat Scythians, from the Caspian and Aral seas); *Saka paradraya* (Scythians over the sea). The same three occur among the Throne-Bearers at Naqsh-i Rustam.[14] In the Besitun inscription, Shunkha is described as the chief of the Pointed-hat *Saka*; he is depicted with a very tall pointed hat and labeled by name.[15] We are thus able to identify with confidence the pointed-hat gift bearers of Delegation XI in the Persepolis Apadana reliefs.[16] After this point, we are in murky territory. The nationalities of Scythians on Persian reliefs are still problematic; although three names are recorded, the types of hat do not neatly fall into three mutually exclusive and distinguishable categories.[17] The very name "pointed-hat Saka" indicates that even for the Persians the hat served as an identifier; for the other two groups of Scythians we are left without clear iconographic indices. They both seem to have worn related forms of leather headgear.

Herodotus takes us no further. In his catalog of Xerxes' troops he outlines the costume of the Scythians. Here, too, the striking detail of the costume, which distinguished the Scythians from the other trousered Iranian peoples, was the hat. Herodotus describes it, using the word *kurbasia*, as "tapering to a point and standing stiffly erect" (7.64). By contrast, according to Herodotus, the Persians (and presumably the *Saka haumavarga* and the *Saka paradraya*) wore a soft felt hat called the *tiara* (7.61). This is apparently the hat described by Strabo (15.733) and it appears in both Iranian and Greek art.

In Attic vase-painting of the sixth century the same pointed hat decisively identifies many of the Scythian archers. Physiognomy and details of costume play a secondary or even tertiary role.[18] Thus, the lack of a single pointed hat among our symposiasts is a matter worthy of great concern. Raeck has already noted the absence and observed that some of the *kidaris*-designs, even early in the series, look like hats worn by figures believed to be Persians.[19] For example, with the *kidaris* of no. 3 (fig. 3) we should compare the cup by the Triptolemos Painter in Edinburgh, with the *kidaris* of no. 8 (fig. 14) the name vase of the Painter of the Oxford Brygos, and with no. 11 (fig. 22) the Thanatos Painter's white-ground lekythos in the Louvre.[20] At the same time, some symposiasts wear their hat "Scythian-style," with the end of the rear lappet tucked into a band around the hat (no. 5, fig. 7; no. 6, fig. 10).[21]

A similar fluidity occurs in the terms used by Greeks for Oriental hats.[22] The three words used by the Greeks (*kitaris* or *kidaris*, *tiara*, and *kurbasia*) generally seem to have served as synonyms; they all appear as the headgear for ordinary Orientals in Herodotus (1.132.1, 3.12.4, 5.49, 7.61.1, 7.90).

The upright *kitaris* (Plut. *Artax.* 26.4; Arrian 6.29.3), the upright *kurbasia* (Ar. *Av.* 487), and the upright *tiara* (Xen. *Anab.* 2.5.23; *Cyr.* 8.3.13) are all specified as the hat of the king. The precise meaning of *kitaris* is the most problematic precisely because it appears in more informative contexts. In the epitome of Ctesias it is equated with "crown" (*FGrH* 688 F 15.50) and has correspondingly been interpreted in two ways: as the cylindrical crown of the royal Achaemenid iconography and as the correct term for the "upright *tiara*."[23] The word may also occur in the text of Herodotus, where a meaningless *chitonas* in his description of Cypriot dress has been emended to *kitaris*, making it the normal term for Cypro-Persian headgear (7.90.4).[24] The definitions of all three words by ancient grammarians show that they, too, could not differentiate among hat names: Herodian (2.533, 25L) equates the *kidaris* with the *tiara*; Erotian (*Gloss. Hipp.* 55, 7Nach.) calls the *kurbasia* a *tiara*; and Galen's *Gloss. Hipp.* (116, 1K.) followed suit. Though there may have been, within the Iranian sphere, regional or hierarchical differences in headgear with corresponding differences of names, there can be no certainty that precise knowledge of such distinctions was acquired by any classical Greek.

The problems in distinguishing species of foreigners in Attic vase-painting exemplify the limitations of the material. We are hampered by the lack of independent evidence for the dress of most of the peoples represented. A further difficulty lies in differentiating between artistic convention and factual recording; developing internal artistic conventions clearly played a major role in the representation of all foreigners.[25] An appearance of order can be gained by a chronological approach in which Orientals are identified as Scythians before the Persian Wars and as Persians after the Persian Wars, but the capture of Sardis in the 540s had signaled the arrival of the Persians in the Greek sphere and should mark the start of an interest in Persians. In fact, the iconographic tradition shows no clear break at the fall of Sardis or the Persian Wars.[26]

Lack of interest on the part of the vase-painters may compound the difficulty. Some details from the group of *kidaris*-wearing symposiasts suggest that their ethnic ambiguity is unintentional, but ancient: the Triptolemos Painter cared so little about the design of an Oriental hat that he painted the two hats on the same cup with different shapes (no. 4, figs. 5–6). One *kidaris* (A) flops forward; the other (B) is rounded. Such unconcern about rendering the *kidaris* makes a striking contrast with the depiction of battling Greeks and Persians on a cup in Edinburgh attributed to the same painter and cited by Bovon as one of the more accurate representations of Persians.[27] A comparison of the *kidaris* on two works attributed to the

Brygos Painter suggests the same indifference: while no. 6 looks more Scythian, with its tied rear lappet (fig. 10), no. 7 looks more Persian (fig. 11). Again, of the two "Dourian" examples no. 8 looks Persian (fig. 14) and no. 9, with the side lappet's serrated lower edge, looks Scythian (figs. 17–18).[28] Though Bovon's researches have shown that painters of battle scenes gained some level of success in the accurate depiction of Persians and Persian regalia,[29] the painters apparently did not consider specific ethnicity important or even relevant for our *kidaris*-wearing symposiasts. A foreign hat was a foreign hat and various schemata of representation were equally acceptable.

In comparison we should note a small group of representations of banqueting Persians.[30] The two fragmentary cups of ca. 470 attributed to the Stieglitz Painter reveal a high level of precision in distinguishing the different ethnic types (figs. 26, 27).[31] Both clothing (long, patterned sleeves and *kandys*) and utensils (animal-head vessels and Achaemenid deep bowl) successfully characterize the banqueters as Persians.[32] The contrast with the group of symposiasts distinguished only by the *kidaris* could not be greater.

As a solution to the general problem of distinguishing Scythian from Persian in Attic iconography, Schauenburg placed reliance on the presence of a sparse (Scythian) or a full (Persian) beard.[33] Such an approach has the virtue of fitting into Achaemenid imperial iconography, where the king and his nobles always sport long flowing beards, and it works well for many of the *barbaroi* in Attic pottery of the late sixth and early fifth century. But when Schauenburg's yardstick is applied to our symposiasts, it is clear that they do not fit the schema. Of the twelve, four are bearded. Three have a full beard, but not the straggly ended Persian variety, and only one has a sparse pointed beard (no. 5, fig. 7; no. 8, fig. 14; no. 9, figs. 17–18; no. 12, fig. 24). The rest are clean-shaven and so by that measure are Greek. Even the earliest, whose long hair tends to suggest an indication of ethnicity, are clean-shaven (no. 1, fig. 1; no. 2, fig. 2). Only no. 5 can be convincingly argued as "foreign" in physiognomy (fig. 7).

Hats and beards aside, all the symposiasts have bare chests and some are totally nude. Both details are inconsistent with Greek stereotypes for Orientals: Herodotus reminds us that "among the Lydians, as indeed among nearly all the other *barbaroi*, even for a man to be seen naked brings him great shame" (1.10).[34] Of all figures in Attic painting identified as Oriental *barbaroi*, only the archers are nude. Vos explained that Hellenized Scythians in the hot climes of Attica decided to forego their national dress; the *kidaris*-wearing symposiasts are the same Scythian archers joining Athenians at a symposium.[35] Vos evidently never spent a summer in the Crimea. Why, if

"Hellenized," do these Scythians retain the most obtrusively barbarous element of their dress, clinging to their outlandish hats even forty years after dropping their pants?

The same range of problems afflicts any interpretation of the *kidaris*-wearing symposiasts as Persians or other contemporary Orientals. Peschel identifies the symposiast of the Berlin cup as a business traveler (no. 5, fig. 7).[36] Weber has proposed that the banquet of Attaginos recorded by Herodotus (9.16–17) appears on two cups (no. 8, fig. 14; no. 10, fig. 20).[37] Both these studies look at specific vases in isolation from the corpus. Moreover, Weber ignores the vases that in traditional ceramic chronology must antedate Xerxes' invasion. Her thesis, in any case, contradicts Herodotus on the main point of that banquet, that Greek and Persian dined side by side, sharing couches and confidences.

After some consideration of other possibilities, Jacobsthal decided that the *kidaris*-wearing symposiasts were metic artisans having a drink at the end of the working day.[38] He was finally swayed to this view by the reading of *acheti* on the London cup (no. 10, fig. 20), which he believed was "echtes oder fingiertes barbarisch"; a man uttering such a non-Greek word must be foreign, presumably one of the potters and painters of the Kerameikos who had such foreign-sounding names as Amasis and Lydos. Recent restudy of the inscription on the cup shows that it is probably incomplete, and that a lambda should be restored at the mouth of the speaker. The gibberish becomes an intelligible *kottabos* inscription, the dative of the name Laches used in response to the *toi* of the next man to the right, and the only positive argument for a foreign identification for the *kidaris*-wearing symposiasts is lost.[39]

The range of representations of men in Thracian garments in Attic red-figure provides a useful parallel to the "Scythians." Full Thracian dress (as described by Herodotus 7.75) is worn in vase-painting by men, some of whom appear in unequivocally mythological scenes. Other men, whose context is less specific, have a mixture of Greek, Scythian, and Thracian dress; some men wear only an *alopekis*.[40] Yet scholars reject "Thracians" as a parallel to the "Scythians" for precisely the reason they should have considered: some of the youthful Athenian horsemen on the Parthenon frieze wear articles of Thracian dress.[41] Accordingly, Schauenburg speaks of "eine Art Modetracht"—a fashion for Thracian garb among equestrian Athenians.[42] The realization that some Athenian youths definitely wore elements of Thracian dress leaves obvious the suggestion that just as *alopekis*-wearers may be Greek, so possibly may *kidaris*-wearers.[43]

In the cups of and near the Pithos Painter, a drinking horn in black often occupies the lower field of the tondo as if superimposed over the couch; it is not held by the symposiast but makes an effective pattern against the body and clothing (no. 1, fig. 1). The appearance of the drinking horn has seemed to provide an important iconographic clue for the identification of the symposiasts.[44] Fehr, for example, stated that of all depictions of Attic symposiasts after 530, the horn only appears on these repetitive cups. Though he hesitated to declare all the *kidaris*-wearing symposiasts Scythians, Fehr took the drinking horns as possible evidence that some are Scythians.[45] The drinking horn is known to have been the favored vessel of Scythians and northern barbarians;[46] in Greek art it is generally associated with Dionysos.[47] In the absence of Dionysiac imagery and any evidence to the contrary, it is reasonable to suppose that the vessel indicates the Scythian.

Or is it? A few other drinking horns do occur and they show that the categories "Dionysiac" and "Scythian" are neither comprehensive nor sharply delineated. Carpenter concluded that in Attic painting the drinking horn derives from the Corinthian komastic antecedents.[48] There is a small body of evidence for the use of drinking horns in East Greece, which may have been the result of East Greek sharing in the wider Anatolian *koine* (possibly sparked by contact with peoples further east and north); we may note the occurrence of ceramic drinking horns at Gordion.[49] In the East Greek sphere, drinking horns appear on the Larisa reliefs and a Samian black-figured amphora, and one ceramic version that is actually pierced to serve as a rhyton was excavated at Old Smyrna.[50] Closer to home, at Athens, we find that silver *kerata* were dedicated on the Acropolis; though it is usually assumed that these were Persian booty or other foreign imports, they attest to a readiness to give the vessel to Athena. The Pithos Painter's symposiasts may have been alone in their use of the drinking horn in the later sixth century, but at least some near-contemporary Attic komasts and a later symposiast wield one.[51]

The *Kidaris* as Symbol or "One Swallow Does Not Make a Spring"

Although a close study of the evidence makes the simple assumption that the *kidaris* indicates *barbaros* extremely difficult, there are other interpretive possibilities. Some have seen the *kidaris* as a symbol: it stands for the presence in the Greek symposium of some institution (*sumposiarchia*) or practice (Scythian drinking) that the Greeks associated with foreign culture. The first turns on the idea that to the Greeks of the Late Archaic and Early Classical period the Great King of Persia served as the archetype of all royalty. To allude to him was to allude to the institution of monarchy; the *kidaris,* as an Eastern hat, indirectly alludes to the king. Zahn suggested that an Athenian symposiast might humorously wear such a hat as the insignium of the office of *sumposiarchos,* or, in Plutarch's words, the *basileus tou sumposiou.*[52] Plutarch turns the phrase in the course of his discussion of the symposiarch's duties, when he uses the image of a symposiarch rewarding behavior like the legendary king of the Assyrians who offered a prize to the man who could invent a new pleasure (*Quaest. Conv.* 1.4, 622a-b). Elsewhere the topos of the king rewarding the inventor of pleasures is usually associated with the Persian king.[53] By Plutarch's time *basilikos* had even come to imply "symposiarchic,"[54] but there is no literary evidence of an equation between *basileus* and *sumposiarchos* in classical Greece. If anything, the office of *sumposiarchos* was originally (humorously?) modeled on the public institutions of the democratic or aristocratic state.

Further, the identification of *kidaris*-wearer as *basileus* on vases rests on the false assumption that the *kidaris* alone—not "upright" or marked in any special way—could signify "king."[55] The scepter denotes royal status in Attic art; the scepter, a royal attribute from Greek iconography, is inducted into representations of Oriental kings. Only later in the fifth century do clothing and context help to denote "king";[56] we might note the importation from the East of a fan bearer in some images in the second quarter of the century. The "upright tiara" comes later, evidently under the influence of drama and quite different in form. There is nothing of the king about our figures; the conceit of *basileus tou sumposiou* belongs to a later age.

Another interpretation focuses on the ancient tradition that Scythians drank their wine unmixed: the depiction of the *kidaris* is said to allude to the custom and, by extension, to uncontrolled drinking.[57] Traditions regarding the incontinence of other peoples on the Greek periphery were widespread.[58] A general belief that all *barbaroi* drink their wine unmixed would at least explain the lack of interest in ethnic specificity on the part of our vase-painters. Yet what precisely "Scythian drinking" connoted to an Athenian at the end of the sixth century is unclear. When Hartog collected ancient references to Scythian drinking habits, he found that as many described them as milk drinkers (i.e., uncouth) as drinkers of unmixed wine (i.e., uncouth); he decided that no pattern could be distinguished: "il est inutile à réduire ces traditions, qui, en fait, sont constitutives de l'aporie de leur personnage."[59] While it is indeed true that both milk drinking and unwatered wine drinking are marks of barbarian savagery according to a standard topos in later literature and thought, the nuances of the topos in the early tradition are less clear. The earliest references specify milk drinking rather than wine drinking. Even Anacreon, the earliest source for the unmixed-wine tradition, used Scythians as an example of loud, uncouth behavior rather than excessive drinking, making them a contrast with the code of behavior appropriate to the Greek symposium. Where Herodotus discusses Scythians seriously he describes them as milk drinkers (4.2); where he reports Laconian anti-Cleomenes propaganda, he mentions unmixed wine in an explanatory fashion, with reference to a peculiarly Laconian expression, "drinking *episkuthison*" (6.84). Strabo reasonably concluded that the Scythians had once been milk drinkers and only became wine drinkers after contact with Mediterranean civilizations (7.3.7). In the Archaic period "Scythian drinking" seems to refer primarily to uncouth behavior as evidenced by the use of unwatered wine (and doubtless other boorish customs) rather than excessive drinking per se.

Whereas some theories make the *kidaris* an index or attribute of the barbarian, the suggestion that *kidaris* equals "excessive drinking" or "drinking neat wine" transforms the object into a symbol: the Greek observer perceives a *conventional* link between *kidaris* and intemperate drink. But identifiable symbols are rare in Attic red-figure, as in Greek art generally, and where they occur, the bond between the signifier and its signified is a bond forged by broad cultural and religious conventions, not by purely iconographic conventions, as on Greek coinage or, for example, the New York "Brother and Sister Stele" where the pomegranate held by the youth may link the youth to the underworld.[60] The image does not appear only on a funerary stele; throughout Greek myth and cult the fruit has widely recognized chthonic associations. I know of no instance in Attic pottery of iconographic symbols that are not shared with the broader cultural milieu. If the *kidaris* is no exception, then the justification for reading it as a symbol here can only rest upon evidence that it served as a symbol in Late Archaic Greek culture generally. In the total absence of evidence of this kind, it seems recklessly complacent to accept a symbolic meaning for the hat on these Attic vases.

The vessels themselves fail to support any connection between the *kidaris* and disorderly drinking. Most of the *kidaris*-wearing symposiasts sedately engage in the same range of activities as their fellow drinkers; on the Leipzig cup all the drinkers abandon themselves equally (no. 4, figs. 5–6). The vase-painter had other means at his disposal to suggest advanced stages of drunkenness, which are familiar from other sympotic and komastic vases. The cup in Geneva exemplifies some of the available clues—an empty wineskin and an overturned amphora (no. 2, fig. 2).

Lissarrague has recently advanced an interpretation of the *kidaris*-wearing symposiasts as part of a broader discussion of the use of wine as an agent of liberation. Through wine one is freed from oneself to experiment with *altérité*. Occasionally images on drinking vessels render the "experimentation": in the series of vases known as the "Anacreontics" the wearing of women's clothing by men, and in the series of "Scythian symposiasts" the wearing of foreign headgear. The *kidaris* distinguishes the wearer from his bareheaded companions "comme un personnage à part, buveur hors de pair."[61] The distinctive appearance conferred by the *kidaris* is as undeniable as its Oriental nature, but objects from the Persian East in this period of Achaemenid imperial expansion should carry a heavy connotative burden. It is telling that a vase-painter would have placed so emphatically Oriental an object on an Athenian symposiast. Before drawing a conclusion about what an Athenian meant in distinguishing himself by wearing a *kidaris,* it is best to consider the cultural and historical context: the images appear on vessels produced for symposia of the wealthy in the second and third generations after the arrival of the Persians in Asia Minor.[62]

The *Kidaris*-Wearer as Icon: Sympotic Orientalizing

It seems to me that we need go no further than to read the symposiast with the hat as a symposiast with a hat, that is, as an *icon*. That the hat is of eastern origin is of course significant, but the significance is to be found in the phenomenon itself, and in its relation to the social context of Late Archaic Athenian society, not in the representation or its function within an artistic code.

There is a body of evidence, small, but sufficient to warrant serious attention, that suggests some Athenians deliberately adopted imported luxury goods, or local imitations, for use in the symposium. A series of Attic drinking vessels copies Oriental, most probably Achaemenid, metalware.[63] They begin to appear in the late sixth century, the same period as the *kidaris*-wearing symposiasts. Though a number have been found abroad, many appear in excavations at Athens, so that it cannot be argued that they were intended for an export market.[64] By a reasonable guess ceramic forms paralleled Attic imitations and adaptations in metalware, but there is no evidence yet to prove the case and ceramics must be our guide.

Attic ceramics of the late sixth and fifth centuries exhibit a wide range of adoptive types. They may be broadly categorized in three groups: direct imitation, adaptation to suit local needs, and adoption of superficial details to an otherwise Greek shape. The first two categories are particularly relevant to our discussion, and characterize the first two generations of adoption. A series of shallow bowls and *phialai* best exemplify direct imitation of shape. Though they are known from a number of sites, they have most secure contextual dates in the Athenian Agora excavations, where they seem to start at the end of the sixth century.[65] For the first half century their surface rendering is variable, indicative of attempts to capture the appearance of light shimmering on horizontally fluted metal. Experiments in black, added red, added white, and various combinations including tricolor effects are found.[66]

The adaptation of an Achaemenid form to suit Greek taste or custom is visible in a range of drinking vessels on which a handle and sometimes a resting surface is added to the Persian form. One such vessel is the somewhat rare straight-walled beaker with horizontal grooving whose earliest examples date to the second quarter of the fifth century.[67] Use of these vessels by symposiasts may even be attested iconographically: a straight-walled beaker is held by the right-hand symposiast on side B of the London cup (no. 10, fig. 21).

The most familiar example of Attic imitation of Achaemenid toreutics is the animal-head cup, which bears close similarity to Oriental animal-head rhyta, possibly through the intermediary of Athenian metalware versions.[68] The Greek artisan modified the vessel by adding a handle and even a foot; frequently the vessels are more profoundly Hellenized by the choice of animal.[69] The idea has long been mooted that Attic imitation of this vessel type was directly inspired by the capture of Achaemenid cups in the Persian spoils which, according to Herodotus, included *phialai* and *ekpomata* (9.80).[70] A straight animal-head cup was first imitated in the cups of the Brygan and Dourian Classes, which are usually dated ca. 480 and later, and so fit nicely into such a theory.[71] A bent animal-head vessel appears earlier, in the cups of the "Early Ram Class," which are now dated to the turn from sixth to fifth century.[72] In this case, a foot as well as a handle was added, ungainly but symptomatic of a ceramicist's concern for utility in the early days of imitation. Though the great popularity of animal-head cups came about after and possibly as a result of the Persian Wars, the Early Ram Class provides another instance of deliberate adoption of Oriental elements into the Attic symposium before the Persian Wars (for surely the symposium provided the locale for the use of the new animal-head cups).[73]

The "Old Oligarch" observed that unlike all other peoples, who used their own dress, the Athenians derived their attire from Greek and barbarian sources ([Xenophon] *Ath. Pol.* 2.8). In view of the evidence that some

Athenians affected luxurious Oriental toreutics in their symposia, we should reconsider the *kidaris*-wearing symposiasts. To describe the socioeconomic role of Greek imports in Iron Age Europe, Frankenstein and Rowlands created the term *prestige goods economy* ("the association of power with control over access to foreign goods which are assigned high status").[74] Late Archaic Athens did not have such a "prestige goods economy" but something akin. By the late sixth century, when the powerful Achaemenid Persian empire with its great material resources and rigidly aristocratic society was dominant in the East, the overall pattern of Attic material and social culture was well established, capable of reacting to new stimuli and absorbing new ideas without loss of integral character. No massive cultural "Orientalizing" like that of the late eighth and seventh centuries would recur. Something at once more superficial and more subtle could take place: the deliberate adoption of a select range of Oriental objects by wealthy Athenians as an effective statement of elitism.[75] Many have commented on the natural sympathy and parallel outlook probably shared by Greek and Persian aristocrats. Perhaps the wearing of a *kidaris* intimated to contemporaries the same range of political values as did the Laconizing of a later day.[76]

NOTES

I am grateful for the assistance of the members of the Ashmolean Library and Beazley Archive, Oxford, and of the Department of Greek and Roman Antiquities of the British Museum. I would like to thank the Social Sciences and Humanities Research Council of Canada and the Arts Research Board of McMaster University for defrayal of research expenses.

For gracious permission to include photographs of this small corpus of vases, I wish to thank Dr. D. v. Bothmer, Metropolitan Museum of Art, New York; M.J. Chamay, Musée d'art et d'histoire, Genève; Herr M. Ebnöther, Les Arcs; Mme. A. Giannikouri, Archaeological Institute of the Dodecanese, Rhodes; Dr. D.C. Kurtz, Beazley Archive, Ashmolean Museum, Oxford; Dr. F. Nicosia, Soprintendenza Archeologica della Toscana-Firenze; M. J.-P. Ottaviani, Musée Archéologique d'Aléria; Dr. G. Platz, Antikenmuseum Berlin; Prof. B. S. Ridgeway, Bryn Mawr College; Dr. H. Jung, Deutsches Archäologisches Institut, Rome; Mr. M. Vickers, Ashmolean Museum, Oxford; A. Kozloff, Cleveland Museum of Art.

1. The vessels under discussion are listed in rough chronological order in the Appendix and are referred to throughout by their numbering in that catalog. The following abbreviations are used:

Bovon (1963): A. Bovon, "La Représentation des guerriers perses et la notion de barbare dans la 1re Moitié du Ve siècle," *BCH* 87, 1963, 579–602.

Fehr (1971): B. Fehr, *Orientalische und griechische Gelage* (Bonn 1971).

Hoffmann (1989): "Rhyta and Kantharoi in Greek Ritual," *Greek Vases in the J. Paul Getty Museum* 4, 1989, 131–66.

Jacobsthal (1912): P. Jacobsthal, *Göttinger Vasen nebst einer Abhandlung Symposiaka, AbhGöttingen* NF XIV Nr. 1 (Berlin 1912).

Lissarrague (1987): F. Liassarrague, *Un flot d'images* (Paris 1987).

Raeck (1981): W. Raeck, *Zum Barbarenbild in der Kunst Athens im 6. und 5. Jahrhundert v. Chr.* (Bonn 1981).

Schauenburg (1974): K. Schauenburg, "Achilleus als Barbar; ein antikes Missverständniss," *AuA* 20, 1974, 88–96.

Schauenburg (1975): K. Schauenburg, "Eurymedon Eimi," *AthMitt* 90, 1975, 97–121.

Schoppa (1933): H. Schoppa, *Die Darstellung der Perser in der griechischen Kunst* (Coburg 1933).

Vos (1963): M.F. Vos, *Scythian Archers in Archaic Attic Vase-Painting* (Groningen 1963).

Weber (1984): M. Weber, "Ein Gastmahl in Theben?" *Gymnasium* 91, 1984, 485–95.

2. *Kidaris* is adopted here because to the modern reader it connotes "Oriental hat" without any further geographic or ethnic restriction.

3. See the comments of F. Frontisi-Ducroux and F. Lissarrague, "De l'ambiguité à l'ambivalence: un parcours dionysiaque," *AION* 5, 1983, 11–32, pp. 11–12.

4. M. Wegner, *Duris: Ein Künstler-monographischer Versuch* (Münster 1968), 188, in his brief discussion of the Florence cup (#8, fig. 14).

5. It is perhaps necessary to say that I am interested in Pierce's triad only insofar as it provides a useful description of fundamental interpretive differences in the literature: though it has been enormously influential in contemporary semiotic theory, the triad's ontological status is a matter of indifference for the present purpose.

6. C.S. Pierce, *Collected Papers,* II (Cambridge, MA 1932), 285.

7. Cf. Schoppa's programmatic statement in favor of relying on the *kidaris* to betoken a foreigner: (1933) 21.

8. See, e.g., Schoppa (1933), 9–10, with references, Vos (1963), *passim*, Raeck (1981), 10–21.

9. Vos (1963), 66–69, 89–90; Cat. #417–25.

10. K.-W. Welwei, *Unfreie im antiken Kriegsdienst* I (Wiesbaden 1974), 15–16; and G.F. Pinney, "Achilles Lord of Scythia," in W.G. Moon, ed., *Ancient Greek Art and Iconography* (Madison 1983), 127–46, pp. 130–31.

11. Schauenburg (1974), 91. Berlin-Charlottenburg F 2293: Brygos Painter, cup exterior, ca. 485 (*ARV*² 370.10); London E 65: Brygos Painter, cup exterior, ca. 490 (*ARV*² 370.13; *LIMC* III "Babakchos" #1, pl. 64); Athens 0.11: cup exterior (J.-J. Maffre, "Une gigantomachie de la première décennie du Vᵉ siècle," *RA* 1972, 221–32: 226–27).

12. G.F. Pinney, *op. cit.* (above n. 10).

13. These may well be Greek: J.D. Beazley, *CVA* Great Britain 3, Oxford 1, text to pl. I.5; Schauenburg (1975), 108–9; Raeck (1981), 22–25.

14. R.G. Kent, *Old Persian Grammar* (New Haven 1950), 137–38: DNa lines 25–26, 28–29. E.F. Schmidt, *Persepolis* III (Chicago 1970), 111–16, esp. 109, figs. 43–44, for the Scythian Throne-bearers at Nagsh-i Rustam.

15. L. King and R.C. Thompson, *The Sculptures and Inscriptions of Darius the Great on the Rock of Behistun in Persia* (London, BM 1907), 91, 157; pls. 13, 16.5. H. Luschey, "Studien zu dem Darius-Relief von Bisutun," *IranMitt* 1, 1968, 63–94: 79–80 (with his discussion of Schmidt's conclusions about Skunkha); pls. 31, 32, 38.6.

16. E.F. Schmidt, *Persepolis* I (Chicago 1953), pl. 37b.

17. Two of the three groups (Paradraya and Tigraxauda) have similarly pointed hats with rear lappets that curve upwards, though those of #24 (Paradraya) are slightly more domed than those of #15 (Tigraxauda) (*Persepolis* III, 116). By contrast, the third group (#14 Haumavarga) has a slight tip that projects forward and no rear lappet (Delegation XVII: *Persepolis* I, 43). Possibly the only ethnic breakdown is between Tigraxauda and Haumavarga, with the Paradraya as a purely geographic distinction.

18. Cf. Schauenburg (1975), 107–8; Vos (1963), 41–43.

19. Raeck (1981), 60–61, who ultimately accepted Vos' conclusions about the "Scythian" symposiasts in default of a better proposal. Jacobsthal (1912) in his first collection of the *kidaris*-wearing symposiasts hesitated on the question of the nationality of the hat, calling it variably Phrygian, Scythian, and barbarian.

20. Edinburgh 1887.213 (*ARV*[2] 364.46; Raeck [1981] P560; Bovon [1963] #4). Oxford 1911.615 (*ARV*[2] 399; Raeck [1981] P580; Bovon [1963] #2). Louvre CA 2980 (*ARV*[2] 1229.16; Raeck [1981] P583; Devambez, *AA* 1973, 711–19, figs. 1–4). Even Vos noted that the hat of #11 is Persian: (1961), 89.

21. Compare the rear lappets of the Scythians at Naqsh-i Rustam (E.F. Schmidt, *Persepolis* III, 111–16, figs. 43–44: #15, #24).

22. The terms are probably all loanwords to Greek. See the discussions of H.-W. Ritter, *Diadem und Königsherrschaft* (*Vestigia* 7: Munich 1965), 6–18 (esp. p. 8, n. 1, for a bibliography on the identity of the *kitaris* with the cylindrical crown); P.B. Sirch, "Tiara," *RE* Suppl. 14 (1974) 786–94, esp. 788; P. Calmeyer, "Stand der archäologischen Forschung zu den iranischen Kronen," *IranMitt* 10, 1977, 168–90, esp. 174–85.

23. *Cylindrical crown*: see previous note. *Upright tiara*; C.B.R. Pelling, *Plutarch. Life of Antony* (Cambridge 1988), 251.

24. Legrand made the emendation by comparison with Pollux 10.164. J.H. and S.H. Young, *Terracotta Figurines from Kourion in Cyprus* (Philadelphia 1955), 195–210, adduce archaeological evidence in support of the claim that Cypriot dress included a hat called a *kitaris*. See their comments p. 201.

25. See Raeck's comments (1981), 2–3. The problems are highlighted by the

disagreements about individual pieces, such as a cup in a Swiss private collection whose tondo depicts a figure called a Scythian by Vos (1963) #489 and Raeck (1981) S489, fig. 21, but a Persian by Schauenburg (1975), 105, pl. 38.2. On developing convention see J. Neils, "The Group of the Negro Alabastra: A Study in Motif Transferral," *AntK* 23, 1980, 15–20. Cf. the Persian-looking "Scythian archer" accompanying a hoplite on Berlin F 2295 (*ARV*² 364.45; R. Tölle-Kastenbein, *Pfeil und Bogen im Antiken Griechenland* [Bochum 1980]).

26. See K. Schauenburg (1975), 106–18, on the fluid boundaries between Scythian and Persian in Attic iconography, and esp. p. 113.

27. Edinburgh 1887.213; references above, note 20.

28. For the serrated lower edge of lappets, see E.F. Schmidt, *Persepolis* I, pl. 37b (Tigraxauda). Also Throne-bearer #24 of Tomb V (Paradraya): idem, *Persepolis* III, fig. 44, and Skunkha on the Besitun relief.

29. Bovon (1963). See, e.g., A.A. Barrett and M.J. Vickers, "The Oxford Brygos Cup Reconsidered," *JHS* 98, 1978, 17–24.

30. Raeck (1981) has already drawn the contrast between this group of Persian banqueters and the *kidaris*-wearing symposiasts: 61–62, 147–49. In addition to the two discussed here are a cup tondo in a Swiss private collection, dated ca. 500 (Schauenburg [1975], 113, pl. 35.1; Raeck [1981] S489, fig. 21) and a late column krater in Salerno, of ca. 400–375 (Schauenburg [1975] pl. 38.2; Raeck [1981] P592). Raeck draws attention to his P590, which may be another banqueting Persian: Rhodes (?), skyphos fr., C.S. Blinkenburg, *Lindos* I (Berlin 1931), pl. 129, #2714.

31. Oxford 1966.688 (*ARV*² 829.38. Bovon [1963] #8; Raeck [1981] P579). Bryn Mawr P-932, P-955 (*ARV*² 829.39. Raeck [1981] P559. *CVA* USA 13 Bryn Mawr 1, pl. 25. 1–2).

32. The Bryn Mawr fragment contains the earliest instance of the *kandys* in Greek art: E. Knauer, "Toward a History of the Sleeved Coat," *Expedition* 21:1, 1978, 23; eadem, "Ex Oriente Vestimenta," *ANRW* II *Principat* 12.3 *Künste* (Berlin 1985), 578–82, 607–23: p. 612. Hoffmann (1989), 140–41, aptly remarks that two details of the animal-head vessel on the Oxford fragment betray some level of Greek projection onto the Persian vessel: the presence of a foot (though unlike the stemmed foot of Greek productions and so probably a misunderstanding of use?) and the fact that it is a donkey head, which is not in the Persian toreutic "bestiary" for such vessels.

33. Schauenburg (1975), 107, 113.

34. Fehr (1971) observed that nudity for male symposiasts in Attica starts late in the sixth century: 76.

35. Vos (1963), 52–60.

36. I. Peschel, *Die Hetäre bei Symposiun und Komos in der attisch-rotfigurigen Vasenmalerei des 6.–4. Jahrh. v. Chr.* (Frankfurt 1987), 95.

37. Weber (1984). Compare E. Knauer's suggestion that the Bryn Mawr fragmentary cup is Attaginos' banquet (references above, note 32).

38. Jacobsthal (1912), 62, n. 2. In this he was followed by Schoppa (1933), who declared it "credible but unprovable" (75, n. 10). Schoppa was in any case more interested in the Scythian archers than the symposiasts.

39. E. Csapo and M.C. Miller, "The 'Kottabos-Toast' and an Inscribed Red-Figured Cup," *Hesperia* forthcoming.

40. Schauenburg (1974), 92–93, notes the difficulties of distinguishing nationality on the vases; see K. Zimmermann, "Thraker-Darstellungen auf griechischen Vasen," in R. Vulpe, ed., *Actes du II^c Congrès Internationale de Thracologie, I: Histoire et Archéologie* (Bucharest 1980), 429–46, on the range of "Thracians" from mythical to nonmythical to possible Athenians. A good example of the problem: D.M. Buitron, *Attic Vase-Painting in New England Collections* (Cambridge, Fogg Art Museum, 1972), 126–27, #70.

41. Summarized: F. Brommer, *Der Parthenonfries* (Mainz 1977), 231. See Schauenburg (1975), 109–10.

42. Schauenburg (1974), 92. Similarly, W. Techanu, "Eine Schale des Onesimos im Berliner Museum," *RömMitt* 46, 1931, 187–97, pl. 17–18, esp. 190, refers to the Scythian hat as a *modische Sportkleidung* for archers on the analogy of the Thracians. R. Tölle-Kastenbein, op. cit. (above note 25) 66. See H.A. Cahn, "Dokimasia," *RA* 1973, 3–22 and A.G. Geddes, "Rags and Riches: Costume of Athenian Men in the Fifth Century," *CQ* 37, 1987, 307–31, esp. 321. There is some slight evidence for a similar fashion among the Greeks of Klazomenai: R.M. Cook, "Old Smyrna: The Clazomenian Sarcophagi," *BSA* 69, 1974, 55–60: 58, #5 and fig. 5.

43. J. Beazley, "Al Mina, Sueidia," *JHS* 59, 1939, 1–44: 3–4 commented that he inclined to believe that the *kidaris*-wearers were "not all foreigners."

44. E.g., Raeck (1981), 61.

45. Fehr (1971), 101.

46. K. Tuchelt, *Tiergefässe in Kopf- und Protomengestalt* (Berlin 1962), 97–100, 114–17.

47. E.g., T.H. Carpenter, *Dionysian Imagery in Archaic Greek Art* (Oxford 1986), 117; H. Gericke, *Gefässdarstellungen auf griechischen Vasen* (Berlin 1970), 19–21, 177–86.

48. Carpenter, op. cit., (above note 47) 118. The same will have been true of its appearance in the hands of Laconian komasts, e.g., London, BM B3: C.M. Stibbe, *Lakonische Vasenmaler des 6. Jhs. v. Chr.* (Amsterdam 1972), 171, pl. 109, #308.

49. R.S. Young, *Three Great Early Tumuli* (Philadelphia 1981), 39, pl. 18H (Tumulus P, ca. 700 B.C., p. 10); cf. idem, "Gordion: Preliminary Report, 1953," *AJA* 59, 1955, 1–18: 3, pl. I.5.

50. *Larisa*: L. Kjellberg, *Larisa am Hermos, II: Die Architecktonischen Terrakotten* (Stockholm 1940), pls. 22–29: though Fehr (1971) argued that these show Greek and Scythian symposiasts drinking together, both use drinking horns: 107–8. Compare the Velletri terracotta relief, which, though Italian, has been argued by Akerström, detail by detail, to be East Greek in iconography: "Untersuchungen

über die figürlichen Terrakottafriese aus Etrurien und Latium," *OpRom* 1, 1954, 191–231, 204. *Samian amphora*: E. Walter-Karydi, *Samos VI.2: Samische Gefässe des 6. Jhs. v. Chr.* (Bonn 1975), cat. #109, pl. 13 = Fehr (1971), no. 42; J.-M. Denzter, *Le Motif du Banquet Couché* (= BEFAR 246: Paris 1982) p. 129 no. 7, fig. 118. *Smyrna Rhyton*: J.M. Cook, "Old Smyrna: Ionic Black Figure," *BSA* 60, 1965, 114–42, p. 135; E. Akurgal, *Alt-Smyrna, I: Wohnschichten und Athenatempel* (Ankara 1983), pl. M.

51. *Athenian Acropolis:* Tuchelt, op. cit. (above note 46) 114–17, gives references and discussion. *Komast*: Syracuse 2287, Gela Painter, white-ground lekythos (C.H.E. Haspels, *Attic Black-Figured Lekythoi* [Paris 1936], pl. 24a-b). *Symposiast*: Toronto ROM 959.17.95: Curtius Painter, cup (I), ca. 450 (*ARV²* 931.1). From the end of the fifth century a few fragmentary examples in Attic ceramic are known: H. Hoffmann, "The Persian Origin of Attic Rhyta," *AntK* 4, 1961, 21–24: 23, with references. The latter should be read with Hoffmann (1989); the ceramic drinking horns are presumably associable with Dionysiac cult.

52. Jacobsthal (1912), 62, n. 2 reports the suggestion. R. Zahn had not discussed the group in his dissertation, *Darstellung der Barbaren* (Heidelberg 1896).

53. The topos is of uncertain origin but was flourishing by the fourth century. F. Fuhrmann collected the parallels in *Plutarque: Oeuvres Morales Tome IX* (Paris 1972), 162: Theophrastos fr. 125 Wimmer = Athen. 4.144E; Clearchus fr. 50, 51A, 51D Wehrli = Athen. 12.539E, 12.514C, 12.529D; Aristoxenos fr. 50 Wehrli = Athen. 12.545ff. Plutarch elsewhere confuses Assyrians and Persians: *De Facie* 935B.

54. Sometimes *basilikos* means "symposiarchic" and relates to sympotic rules: e.g., Plut. *Mor.* 1095E and Athen. 1.3F; cited by W. Slater, "Aristophanes of Byzantium and Problem-Solving in the Museum," *CQ* 32, 1982, 336–49, p. 348, n. 63.

55. Jacobsthal draws attention to the existence of two *kidaris*-wearers on the Leipzig cup (#4, figs. 5–6).

56. Raeck (1981), 151–56.

57. Jacobsthal (1913), 62, n. 2 briefly considered the idea. Cf. Vos' use of the reputed Scythian fondness for wine in support of her identification of the *kidaris*-wearers as Scythians. F. Frontisi-Ducroux and F. Lissarrague, op. cit. (above note 3) 29, remark "Le seul bonnet scythe, *dont les connotations sont connues,* démarque ainsi le buveur. . ." Lissarrague (1987) 86–87, notes the Pithos Painter's addition of the drinking horn in support of this interpretation.

58. On the *aporia* of other *barbaroi*: F. Hartog, *Le miroir d'Hérodote* (Paris 1980), 170; Raeck (1981), 61, n. 230. Plato, *Laws* 367D-E.

59. Hartog discusses Scythian drinking: op. cit. 176–83, esp. 183–84.

Milk: Il. 13.5–6; Hes. fr. 150.15 M-W = Strabo 7.3.7; Hes. fr. 151 M-W = Strabo 7.3.9; Aesch. *TrGF* fr. 198 Radt = Strabo 7.3.7; Hdt. 4.2; Hippoc., *Aër.* 18; Ephorus *FGrH* 70 F 42 = Strabo 7.3.9; Antiphanes, *Bacchae* fr. 56 Kock = Athen. 10.441D; Diog. Laert. 1.104 (Cynic propaganda: the Life of Anacharsis).

Wine: Anacr., *PMG* fr. 356 = Athen. 10.427A-B; Hdt. 6.84; Plato, *Laws* 637E;

Arist. *Problemata* 3.7; Chamaileon fr. 10 Wehrli = Athen. 10.427B; Achaeus *TrGF* fr. 9 Snell = Athen. 10.427C (text uncertain); Hieronymus fr. 27 Wehrli = Athen. 11.499F.

60. New York, MMA 11.185. Illustrated: G.M.A. Richter, *Archaic Gravestones of Attica* (London 1961), fig. 109.

61. Lissarrague (1987), 16.

62. Hoffmann (1989) now views #6 and #7, like all such animal-head vessels, as products for funerary offerings "in substitution for precious metal originals" (164). As both are in the "early group" (Brygans and Dourians), whose iconography tends to relate to aristocratic pastimes like symposia (148), the question of the use of the actual vessels is not strictly relevant to our discussion of the iconography. They join a group largely composed of ordinary Attic drinking vessels.

63. H. Luschey, "Achämenidisch-persische Toreutik," *AA* 53, 1938, 760–72. G. Hafner, "Kretisch-Mykenisches in der späteren griechischen Kunst," *Festschrift für RGZM* III (1952) 85–86. H. Hoffmann, "The Persian Origin of Attic Rhyta," *AntK* 4, 1961, 21–24. B.B. Shefton, "Persian Gold and Attic Black Glaze: Achaemenid Influences on Attic Pottery of the 5th and 4th Centuries B.C.," *AArchSyr* 21, 1971, 109–11. Some of this material is discussed by D. Gill, though his interests are different: "Greek Fictile Imitations," *Pots & Pans: A Colloquium on Precious Metals and Ceramics: Oxford Studies in Islamic Art,* 3 (Oxford 1986), 9–30. The following is a partial and brief summary of material that I intend to discuss in greater detail elsewhere.

64. Contrast the black-figure "Cypro-jug" (*ABV* 441), for acquaintance with which I am indebted to J. Perreault.

65. The date concurs also with Luschey's findings about the time of introduction of the lobed Achaemenid *phiale* to the Greek world: H. Luschey, op. cit. (above note 63) 762.

66. *Phiale*: Agora P 9274, black, ca. 500 (B. Sparkes and L. Talcott, *Agora XII* #521, pl. 23, fig. 6). *Shallow bowl*: Agora P 11049, black with intentional red, ca. 500 (Agora XII #520, fig. 6). Agora P 23118, black, intentional red, ca. 520–480. Kassel T.550, black with white (Shefton, op. cit. [above note 63] 109, fig. 2; *CVA* Germany 35, Kassel 1, pl. 47.5). In the generation after the Persian Wars, Sotades experimented with tricolor effects: Boston 98.886, ca. 460 (*ARV²* 772d). London BM D8, similar, signed by Sotades (*ARV²* 772e). Shefton, op. cit. (above note 63) 109.

67. E.g., Agora P 25900 (*Agora XII* #199). Agora P 2779 (*Hesperia* 37 [1968] pl. 37a). Karlsruhe 329 (Shefton, op. cit. [above note 63] 109 and fig. 4; *CVA* Germany 7, Karlsruhe 1, pl. 34.11).

68. See the corpus of H. Hoffman, *Attic Red-Figured Rhyta* (Mainz 1962), where he discusses the classes in some detail; Hoffmann, op. cit. (above note 63) 22, on the details altered by potters. Hoffmann (1989), 162, stating that ceramic versions do not have good rims for drinking, argues that they are "dummy products" for funerary use in substitution for metalware vessels.

69. Hoffmann (1989), 164.

70. Luschey, op. cit. (above note 63) 763 (tentatively). Hafner, op. cit. (above note 63) 85–86. H. Hoffman, op. cit. (above note 63).

71. M. True, "New Vases by the Brygos Painter and His Circle in Malibu," *Greek Vases in the J. Paul Getty Museum* I, 1983, 72–84.

72. R. Guy, "A Ram's Head Rhyton Signed by Charinos," *Arts in Virginia* 21:2, 1981, 2–15, pp. 8–9, with references.

73. See H. Hoffmann's views (1989). See Guy's comments, op. cit. (above note 72), p. 8.

74. S. Frankenstein and M.J. Rowlands, "The Internal Structure and Regional Context of Early Iron Age Society in South-Western Germany," *Bull. Inst. Arch. London* 15, 1978, 73–112, pp. 75–76. See P. Wells, *Culture Contact and Culture Change* (Cambridge 1980).

75. K. De Vries has already briefly suggested that "local enthusiasts" might have liked to wear the *kidaris* at symposia: "East Meets West at Dinner," *Expedition* 15.4, 1973, 32–39, p. 39.

76. We might then regard the troubling features of #5 (and possibly the long hair of #2) as a dash of humor on the part of the painter.

APPENDIX: THE VESSELS

1. *The Pithos Painter:* Rhodes 13386, cup (I), ca. 510–500 (fig. 1).

Some fifty cups of and near the *Pithos Painter* share a uniform tondo decoration: a reclining youth who is viewed from the back but with profile face. He wears a *kidaris* and long hair. Below is often a black drinking horn. De Vries suggests that these cups, which are singularly sloppy, testify to a production for an Eastern export market, but more than half of the Pithos Painter's works have provenances outside of the borders of the Persian empire; a number come from Italy. The example here illustrated is one of the better-preserved cups, from Kameiros (*ARV²* 139.23). A, B: black.

Bibliography: ARV² 139–40. 23–63, lists forty-one symposium cups for the Pithos Painter (an incomplete list; see *Para.* 334, *Add.²*178. Vos [1963] #417–19). The same formula appears in two cups near the Pithos Painter (*ARV²* 141.2–3), and one of the related Group of Adria B 300 (*ARV²* 142.2). J.D. Beazley, "Al Mina, Sueidia," *JHS* 59, 1939, 1–44: 2–4. K. de Vries, "Attic Pottery in the Achaemenid Empire," *AJA* 81, 1977, 544–48, p. 548.

2. *Attic Unattributed:* Geneva, Collection Fondation Thétis, cup (I), ca. 510–500 (fig. 2).

A nude komast straddles an overturned amphora; the empty wineskin suspended beside him testifies to the late stage of his drinking. He wears red ribbons around his rounded *kidaris*, below which his long hair hangs over his shoulders. A, B: black.

Bibliography: J.-L. Zimmermann, *Collection de la Fondation Thétis: développements de l'art grec de la préhistoire à Rome* (Geneva 1987), #105, pp. 56–57, 165 (compared to the Pithos Painter).

3. *Colmar Painter:* New York, MMA 16.174.41, cup (A), ca. 500 (fig. 3).

One of six youthful symposiasts plays the double pipes. He wears a spotted *kidaris* that also has a brim; an interior curl suggests a floppy top. I: akontist.

Bibliography: ARV²355.35; Add.²221. Vos (1963) #420. G.M.A. Richter and L.F. Hall, *Red-Figured Athenian Vases in the MMA* (New Haven 1936), #36, pl. 35, 179.36, after which Raeck (1981) fig. 20; Lissarrague (1987) fig. 1.

4. *Triptolemos Painter:* formerly Leipzig, Museum des Kunsthandwerks 781.03.G, cup (A and B), ca. 500 (figs. 4–6).

Both exterior sides have two male symposiasts on cushions; one of each pair wears the *kidaris,* so that here exceptionally two men wear the *kidaris* on one vessel. These are particularly abandoned symposiasts. Both wear ribbons over their hats, like their bareheaded companions. I: komast.

Bibliography: ARV² 364.51. Vos (1963) #422. Jacobsthal (1912) 45, fig. 69 (A); 61 n. 2 F. Weege, *JdI* 31, 1916, 146, fig. 20 (after Jacobsthal). I would like to thank D.C. Kurtz for permission to use photographs after drawings in the Beazley Archive.

5. *Thorvaldsen Group:* West Berlin, Staatliches Antikenmuseum F 2270, cup (A and possibly B), ca. 500 (figs. 7–8).

This may have the same format as #4: on each exterior side recline a couple, though here they include one man and one woman. On A the man wears a *kidaris;* the head of the male on B is missing, though the downward curved line approaching the line of the pectorals may represent a dotted lappet (as such it would be unusually circular in contour). Of all the *kidaris*-wearing symposiasts, he of Side A is the only one depicted with distinctively foreign-looking physiognomy: like #1 and #2, his hair is long and worn loose under his hat. Most striking are his small pointed beard and thin curving moustache, both done slightly dilute as if to suggest blond hair. Both features occur on pointed-hat Scythians of sixth-century Attic painting, though they are not constant. The curl at the back of the symposiast's headgear appears to be a reminiscence of a tied-up neck lappet (see #6). I: satyr with drinking horn and large wineskin.

Bibliography: ARV² 455.3; *Paralipomena* 377Add.²243. Vos (1963) #421, pl. 19a. Greifenhagen, *CVA* Germany 21, Berlin 2, pl. 92.1–2. Jacobsthal (1912), 61. Pinney, op. cit. (above note 10) fig. 9.4, p. 129; cf. p. 127. See Raeck (1981), 37.

6. *Brygos Painter* (von Bothmer): Cleveland Museum of Art 88.8, bent ram-head cup (stemmed), ca. 480–70 (figs. 9–10).

On the neck three symposiasts recline. The two at right and center both have beards and wear himatia. He at the left plays the *diaulos* and similarly wears a himation. The rear lappet of his *kidaris* is raised as if tied, though no band is shown. A tied-up rear lappet is attested for Scythians on Achaemenid Persian reliefs.

Bibliography: R. Guy, op. cit. (above note 72) figs. 9–11; Recent Acquisitions, *The Bulletin of the Cleveland Museum of Art* 76.2 (Feb. 1989), p. 49. Cf. E.F. Schmidt, *Persepolis* III, fig. 44, Throne-bearers 15, 24. I am grateful to R. Guy for help with the cup.

7. *Brygos Painter:* Aléria, Musée Jerome Carcopino 2172, straight donkey-head cup (stemmed), ca. 480 (figs. 11–13).

The donkey's ears divide the decoration of the neck into three zones, each of which has a single komast wearing a himation; the booted central figure carries a *barbiton*. The komast between the left ear and the handle wears a high rounded *kidaris* with a curving interior line; he alone of the three is beardless.

Bibliography: Paralipomena 367. J. and L. Jehasse, *La nécropole préromaine d'Aléria, Gallia* Suppl. no. 25 (Paris 1973), #1902, pp. 49–50, 471–72; col. pl. V (reversed); pls. 33, 35b. H. Hoffmann, "Attic and Tarentine Rhyta: Addendum," in A. H. Cambitoglou, ed., *Studies in Honour of A.D. Trendall* (Sydney 1979), 93–95, 93.

8. *Douris:* Florence Museo Archeologico 3922, cup (A), ca. 480 (fig. 14).

One of seven reclining (3[A] + 3[B] + 1[I]), in a classic Dourian symposium arrangement. The *kidaris*-wearer is bearded like his companions (all male), and like them all, he wears a himation. They wear ribbons in their hair; he has his wrapped around his hat which is enhanced by an internal curl. He plays *kottabos* but in a noncanonical manner, wielding a stemmed cup by the foot.

*Bibliography: ARV*² 432.55*Add.*²237. Vos (1963) #423. Anna Magi, *CVA* Italy 30, Florence 3: pl. 90. Weber (1984), 491. Jacobsthal (1912), 57–58, figs. 79–80. Wegner, op. cit. (above note 4) 188.

9. *Manner of Douris* (Jucker): Collection Marcel Ebnöther, Les Arcs, woman's head kantharos (B), ca. 480 (figs. 15–18).

On the neck, six symposiasts recline, three women wearing chiton and himation and three bearded men in himation alone. They all hold some sort of drinking vessel. The *kidaris*-wearer, like his brother on Douris' cup in Florence, plays *kottabos* wielding his cup by the foot; the hetaira on the left of side A uses the more conventional hold. The *kidaris* is unusual in form on two counts: the "hat" part resembles a helmet; its cheek lappet has a scalloped lower edge, which must be a reminiscence, however incorrect, of the kind of neck lappets with lower serrated edges worn by the Scythians of Delegation XI at Persepolis.

Bibliography: Holger Termer, *Kunst der Antike* (Hamburg 1978), 17–21, #10. R. Guy, op. cit. (above note 71), 6–8, attributes the kantharos to Douris himself. I would like to thank D. Buitron-Oliver and K. Huber for their comments.

10. *Attic Unattributed:* London BM 95.10–27.2, stemless cup (A), 470–460 (figs. 19–21).

The *kidaris*-wearer is one of eight symposiasts (3 [A] + 3 [B] + 2 [I]). Though the work is careless, the figures are equipped with the usual, and even more than the usual number of accoutrements and inscriptions. The *kidaris* is a plain rounded form, but two thin lappets confirm its identity. Although the cup was originally declared an early example of Boeotian red-figue, Jacobsthal and others subsequently reidentified it as Attic; the employment of an Attic script supports an Attic identification.

Bibliography: Jacobsthal (1912), 59–62, fig. 82. P. Jacobsthal, review of G. Jacobi, *Scavi nella necropoli di Camiro 1928–1930,* in *GGA* (1931) 1–16: 10. R. Lullies, "Zur boiotisch rotfigurigen Vasenmalerei," *AthMitt* 65 (1940), 1–27: 6–7, pl. #3.1–2. B.A. Sparkes, "The Taste of a Boeotian Pig," *JHS* 87, 1967, 116–130, n. 56. Weber (1984) pl. 24. E. Csapo and M.C. Miller, op. cit. (above note 39).

11. *Leningrad Painter:* London E 351, pelike (A), ca. 470 (figs. 22–23).

In a komastic procession one youth leads another who wears a *kidaris* and carries a crooked stick; the procession continues on side B with a pipe player and youth carrying a wreathed krater. A thick garland is wrapped around the hat. Relief lines visible on the pelike indicate that the hat was originally drawn to have a curved upper profile; the "dimple" was a later change. S. Reinach interpreted the wrist-clasping gesture of the leader and the reluctant stance of the boy with his bowed head as a parody of a wedding; this does not account for the headdress.

Bibliography: ARV² 570.56Add.²261. Vos (1963) #425. S. Reinach, *Répertoire des Vases Peints* (Paris 1899) 343/1. Jacobsthal (1912) 61. F. Frontisi-Ducroux and F. Lissarrague, op. cit. (above note 3), 29, figs. 14.1–2. Lissarrague (1987) fig. 15. Cf. Engelmann, *AA* 8, 1893, 72.

12. *Nausikaa Painter:* Villa Giulia 3583, column krater (A), ca. 450 (figs. 24–25).

The latest of the series shows an abbreviation of a symposium: half of two reclining men. There seems to be a deliberate contrast between the two but it is perhaps to be read as one of age rather than ethnic. One is bearded and plays *kottabos;* it is he who wears the *kidaris.* Given their similar state of dress (himation), the full beard of the man at the right would be the most telling: it is not a shaggy Persian but a well-tended Greek beard. B: komos of three youths.

Bibliography: ARV² 1109.27. Vos (1963) #424. G.Q. Giglioli, *CVA* Italy 1, Villa Giulia I: III 1 C, pl. 10.1–2 (the detail in figure 2 shows the hat most clearly). For help in dating, I would like to thank T. Mannack, who is engaged in a study of the Later Mannerists.

War and the Symposium

Oswyn Murray

In this chapter I wish to consider a series of questions concerning the relationship between "la fonction guerrière" in ancient Greece and Greek drinking customs. In order to set these questions in context, however, I want to begin by discussing in general why it is that there can normally be found a close connection between the social use of alcohol and the creation of a warrior elite: indeed, Islam is perhaps the only major culture to have established a successful military caste without the use of alcohol. I therefore start by offering some theoretical observations, which are undoubtedly tainted with that somewhat unfashionable anthropological theory, functionalism, to explain what purposes alcohol serves in the military context.

The survival of a society depends on its ability to organize its social system on the basis of a surplus; in primitive societies this surplus is normally agricultural, and there is therefore often a direct link between the consumption of the surplus in ritualized feasting and its use as a vehicle for the creation of social values. Thus a society may either express its solidarity through religious or communal rituals of feasting, or seek to maintain an elite in a lifestyle higher than the rest of the community, for reasons of history or function.[1]

Since in a competitive world successful societies must also be military ones, it is a natural consequence that the grades of honor that can be created through the use of agricultural surplus are often apportioned in relation to military service: only priests eat better than warriors, and that is because there is no reason why they should stop eating. A fat priest is always a credit to the power of his god; but, while a well-fed warrior is a strong one, a fat warrior exhibits an element of the dysfunctional. So it is perfectly natural to find a close relationship between feasting and the organization of war. The Homeric feast is just one example of this primitive or "heroic" style of warfare:

Our nobles that rule in Lycia are great men, they eat fat sheep and drink the best honey-sweet wine. But they are powerful men, for they fight with the first of the Lycians. (*Il.* 12.318–21)

But I need not here go into the close relationship between the Homeric "feast of merit" and the military organization portrayed in the Homeric poems, which I have discussed elsewhere.[2]

Alcoholic beverages are a form of agricultural surplus, with the advantage of having a longer "shelf-life" than products such as meat or bread. It is often said that alcohol is easy to produce: "the process of fermentation occurs naturally even without human intervention."[3] But in a world before sugar, and with only the beginnings of selective fruit breeding, it is not as easy as all that to produce strong and pleasant fermentation: the grape in fact gives the Mediterranean area a distinct advantage over northern Europe, as is demonstrated for the ancient world by the constant influence of the luxury wine trade on less developed areas such as Etruria, Gaul, and Scythia. Wine was peculiarly suited to the role that it increasingly came to adopt in southern Europe from the eighth century B.C., as a vehicle of social differentiation and social change through a trade that was both economic and cultural.[4]

But alcohol in the military sphere also has other characteristics. Alcohol is quite different in its effects from the other so-called drugs in common supply, in being the only one with clear social uses: other drugs isolate the individual within himself, while alcohol creates fellowship. Whatever the problems that sometimes result from drinking, the act of drinking is usually viewed as a pleasant and sociable one. In many ethnographic reports, heavy emphasis is laid on the socially integrative functions of alcohol. Among American Indians on Skid Row, Brody found that "drinking unites Indians as Indians." As Heath says, "solitary drinking, often viewed as a crucial symptom of problem drinking, is virtually unknown in most societies":[5] it is in fact a characteristic often attributed to the stereotype of otherness, embodied in the uncivilized neighbors who do not know how to behave, as in the French phrase "boire en Suisses." In such fictional constructs it seems to hold the same position as the belief in the Greek world that barbarians drink unmixed wine. One may put the point in a more symbolic way: "through drinking together, people are able to identify with each other, to form symbolic blood covenants."[6] Personal experience, of course, suggests physiological reasons for this, in the release of individual defense mechanisms or inhibitions under the influence of alcohol, but expert opinion seems to regard the whole question as more complicated.

However, the fact of group bonding through shared drinking rituals is now widely recognized in anthropological circles.[7] The cultural historian of feasts and festivals finds much illumination in these comparative ethnographic studies, which concentrate on rituals rather than problems. In contrast, the huge sociological and medical literature seeks mainly to "problematize" in (Foucault's sense) the phenomenon: "it is a striking pattern that most non-anthropological writers who deal with alcohol tend to focus primarily on various problems that they consider derive from its use, whereas most anthropologists tend to focus more on the use." In fact "most societies that use alcohol are virtually free of alcohol-related troubles";[8] and this is of course especially true of ancient societies, whose use of alcohol was embedded in a social and ritual context, and whose experience of alcohol was confined to fermentation (among the Greeks diluted with water) rather than distillation. Alcoholism as a condition is effectively unknown to the ancient world.

Nevertheless, even in the sociological literature, the lines of relationship between social structure and alcohol are not entirely obscured, and modern studies can help in one particular area that is clearly relevant to warfare—the function of alcohol in stress-related activities. In the modern professional army, it is true, Dutch courage has been abandoned, on the grounds that it is incompatible with the skills necessary on the battlefield: pressing nuclear buttons or flying F-111s while drunk are not activities to be encouraged. Yet gin, rum, and brandy were the foundation of western supremacy on the battlefield: Nelson's sailors and Wellington's soldiers were not just drunk off duty. A ration of gin was the right of the soldiers at Waterloo, and Navy rum continued to be offered before going over the top in the First World War, until doctors discovered that alcohol made the blood run more freely;[9] the British navy did not abandon the daily ration of rum until a few years ago, well after the Second World War (though my grandfather was credited with trying to reduce it as Director of Victualling about 1907).[10]

Even when alcohol has been banished from the battlefield, the official response to it in military life remains deeply ambivalent. Though studies financed by the military authorities on alcohol use in the armed forces undoubtedly exist, they tend not to be published for obvious reasons of public confidence; but the impression remains that alcohol abuse and alcohol-related problems are relatively greater in military circles. Why then the ambivalence?

A comparative study recently carried out on the English police may explain some of the complexities involved.[11] London possesses two police forces, the uniformed Metropolitan Police and the C.I.D., the detectives. Both groups drink, naturally. But normally the Metropolitan Police do not drink on duty or during office hours; their sessions are reserved for the evening, and for those seasonal occasions of ritual release that every organization provides. The C.I.D. has, however, developed a whole series of rituals which permit its members to drink as often as possible, in groups of colleagues and usually during working hours at or near the workplace—birthdays, promotions, transfers, departures, the end of a case, the end of the week. All these occasions constitute an elaborate ritualized calendar related to the workplace. Those who have studied this phenomenon have come to the conclusion that these group drinking occasions serve to establish and to reinforce power relationships among individuals of different rank, through a specially constructed ritual space where equality and status are in conflict: drinking customs relate to power structures. They also have a psychological usefulness. The fundamental difference between the police and the C.I.D. lies in the structure of their working life. The uniformed policeman's lot, happy or not, is at least well organized; everything is subordinated to a fixed and regular regime; even the crises are normalized. By contrast, the C.I.D. does not possess such a clear ritual identity. It has no uniform, each job is different, and the structures necessary for it must be created or changed according to circumstance: the irregularity and insecurity of this life are compensated for by the creation of a ritual drinking structure.

Since it has been so kindly hidden from us by our lords and masters, let us seek to establish the theory of the role of alcohol in modern war for ourselves. A few years ago a young officer in the British Army of the Rhine created a scandal by resigning, and denouncing in the radical weekly *New Statesman* the abuse of alcohol among his fellow soldiers.[12] He seemed especially shocked and puzzled by the indifference of the military hierarchy to the drinking customs he described. Yet he should not have been; for even without the backing of sociological literature, a reading of such novels as Evelyn Waugh's trilogy *Men at Arms* or personal experience of "years in the Hampshire Militia" would reveal the basic importance of drinking rituals for the formation of the military virtues.

Modern military manuals in fact provide a justification for such activities.[13] In the contaminated postnuclear desert that will be the battlefield of the modern soldier, the day of the *Männerbund* will return: the elite army of today encourages the formation of small groups of male companions with a personal identity and personal loyalties. These loyalties that unite and preserve the group in moments of danger are created and maintained by the activities of the group at play: the drunken *komos* is an expression of the solidarity and the virility of its members, united in some potentially dangerous but ritually controlled act of confrontation with social norms. For in every situation drunkenness has its rules: drunkenness is a social state, not a physical condition, as long as a man has not reached the condition legally defined as "drunk *and* incapable." Earlier military training placed the emphasis on those qualities of leadership and discipline suited to armies deployed in mass formation; now it is mutual trust and equality that mark out the elite formations in western armies. No wonder the authorities turn a blind eye, or even encourage leisure activities that help toward this end.

A third general point about the military life may be attached to these last observations. It is the function of a warrior class to fight, but a warrior class which is always fighting tends to get killed off: preservation and use are in conflict. Or, to put it another way, armies are created and maintained in peace, and merely used in war. As a result every military caste suffers a necessary identity crisis most of the time: how is it to occupy itself off the battlefield? Since the days of the Homeric suitors on Ithaca, the consumption of the surplus Gross National Product has been an obvious answer; its ritualized consumption in the form of alcohol actually promotes the virtues required on the battlefield, without the dangers (or the expense) of realistic military maneuvers.

I

These observations are not of course my own. The whole debate was begun by Plato in the first two books of the *Laws*. The three old men, conversing in the shade as they journey across the parched countryside of a Cretan summer, begin to talk about the good uses of alcohol:

> In fact there is a great deal more that we ought to say on the whole subject of drunkenness: it is a science of no little importance, and needs a legislator of no little skill to understand it properly. I don't mean merely the question of drinking or not drinking wine, but the question of drunkenness itself, whether we should make use of it as the Scythians and the Persians do, and also the Carthaginians, the Celts, the Iberians and the Thracians—all of them warlike nations— or as you Spartans do. (*Laws* 1.637D)

Plato's discussion stands in fact at the head of that whole philosophical literature *peri methes,* which developed from Aristotle onward.

The analysis of Plato is however less an investigation of the effects of alcohol than a sociological analysis of those institutions where drunkenness is practiced. He makes a basic distinction: on the one side there are the military *syssitia* of Sparta and Crete, founded specifically to teach the military virtues and especially courage. On the other side there are the *symposia* of the Athenians, abandoned to pleasure and drunkenness: these *symposia* are "neither customary nor legal at Sparta and on Crete" (639D).

The opposition establishes two types of institution, the *syssition*, which produces the psychological state that we call courage, and the symposium, which has the effect of enfeebling the soul in its struggle against pleasure and disorder; and it allows Plato the possibility of creating paradoxical arguments in favor of the good uses of alcohol and of pleasure.[14] The *syssitia* of Sparta and Crete are criticized on grounds later elaborated by Aristotle, because they are directed solely towards the teaching of one single virtue, courage; but true courage, conscious of itself and its position among the other virtues, is different from and superior to Spartan courage—and even this true courage takes only fourth place in the hierarchy of virtues, after wisdom, temperance, and justice. Plato also criticizes the Spartan method of education for its concentration on the use of compulsion, and its failure to recognize the ambiguities of human nature, with the consequent importance of controlling man through pleasure rather than constraint. After this criticism, Plato offers a reasoned defense of the use of wine in a regulated and moderate manner, in a symposium reformed and controlled by the state. Wine offers all the benefits of companionship; it serves as a test of character and reveals the truth; it teaches the virtues of moderation and self-control through a controlled exposure to danger; it entices men to virtue through pleasure. For old men wine serves to moderate the natural severity of age. Wine therefore remains fundamental for the educational system proposed in the *Laws,* and for the social structure of Plato's ideal state, which rests on a fusion of the *syssition* with the symposium. It has been well pointed out by Glen Morrow in his excellent book, *Plato's Cretan City,* that this attempt at fusion causes one of the central problems in the interpretation of the *Laws,* for Plato never explains the institutional consequences of his initiative: "the unfinished character of this part of Plato's legislation has a deeper reason than the approach of death. It lies in the difficulty of reconciling two types of social organization, one essentially Dorian, and another which, as we have seen, is copied from his native Athens."[15]

There are three points I wish to emphasize about Plato's discussion. The first I leave as the background of this work: the majority of the arguments advanced by Plato can be paralleled in recent discussions among anthropologists and sociologists concerning the social uses of alcohol. The problems of the *syssition* and the symposium are not so different from the problems of their modern analogs.

The second point I wish to make is that we should nevertheless also read his arguments in their historical context. Morrow may have been right to talk of the difficulty of reconciling two types of social organization, but he was wrong to treat this as if it were solely a theoretical question, for it is here I think that we can find the ideology and the arguments that influenced the historical phenomenon of the development of the Athenian *ephebeia*. Vidal-Naquet in two classic articles of 1968 showed how the *ephebeia* was a traditional institution with its own myths and its origins in a distant past.[16] But he also accepted that it was precisely in the age of Plato's *Laws* that the *ephebeia* was remodeled. This apparently gradual process began before the mid-fourth century and was complete by the time that Aristotle wrote his *Constitution of Athens,* where a reformed and universalized *ephebeia* is described, apparently open to all Athenian citizens, and not just to those of hoplite census.[17] The details of the change escape us, but the ideology and the arguments used must have been those of Plato, who provides us with the theoretical principles of a fundamental revolution in Athenian social and political customs.

This development of the *ephebeia* towards the Spartan *agoge* belongs to a larger movement in social values that we call "laconism," which spread through the Athenian aristocracy and bourgeoisie of the fourth century. The movement certainly needed a Plato or a Lycurgus to reform it, for there was not always a correspondence between ideal and reality. The problems of turning the Athenian symposium into a Spartan *phidition* are well illustrated in the Demosthenic speech *Against Konon* (54). The young participants were all *epheboi* at Panakton, carrying out their year of garrison duties on the frontier. But the sons of Konon were poor soldiers:

> They used to spend the whole day after lunch drinking, and continued doing this the whole time we were on garrison duty. (54.4)

Ariston and his mess (*syssitoi*) complained to the generals about their drunken behavior, and from this a vendetta began. On their return to civilian life, Konon and his sons with a group of drinking companions waylaid Ariston, beat him up, and insulted him in a systematic and ritual manner. These are no lower-class hooligans: Ariston characterizes his aggressors as men who (34) "during the day put on sour looks and claim to laconise, and wear short tunics and single-soled shoes, but when they get together and are with each other leave no wickedness or foulness untried." It was not only Plato who had problems in reconciling the *syssition* and the symposium.

That brings me to my third observation, which is that the opposition that Plato sets up between *syssition* of courage and symposium of pleasure is a false one. Plato nowhere allows his Spartan interlocutor to describe the role of wine in the *syssition*. N.R.E. Fisher has pointed out that it is "drunkenness" (*methe*) rather than wine that is prohibited there;[18] and Plato does not intend to imply total abstinence, for at the end of the discussion the Athenian stranger contrasts Spartan and Cretan customs with Carthaginian laws that allegedly prohibit wine to soldiers on campaign, magistrates, and others (*Laws* 674). Plato therefore accepts that wine is permitted to Spartans; but he offers no discussion of its central importance and traditional use in Sparta, which are in fact not so different from his recommendations for a reformed symposium.

In fact we know certainly (as Plato also knew) that wine was not prohibited at Sparta—nor in Crete.[19] Wine was an important part of the compulsory contributions to the Spartan *phidition,* as is made clear by the large literature on Spartan customs of commensality, from Xenophon through the Hellenistic writers to Plutarch.[20] Plato's uncle himself, that Kritias who was one of the gentlemen with cauliflower ears of whom Plato talks elsewhere, in his elegy praising Spartan customs against those of Athens talks only of toasts (*proposeis*) as forbidden at Sparta; there they drink with moderation:

> This too is the established custom at Sparta, to drink from the same wine-bearing cup, and not to give toasts, calling them by name, nor to send the cup round from left hand to right. . . . The Spartan *koroi* drink only enough to lead the spirits of all to joyous hope and the tongue to friendliness and moderate mirth.

And again he says:

> The pledging of toasts beyond measure brings present pleasure but eternal pain; but the Spartan way of living is ordered equably, to eat and drink within measure, so they are able to think and to work; and no day is set aside to intoxicate the body with unmeasured drinking. (fr. 6 West)

It is moderation not abstinence that is the Spartan characteristic in all discussions outside Plato; and Plato's silence on the similarity between Spartan practice and his own proposals is disingenuous. Spartan rituals are indeed designed to display the proper use of alcohol and to relate its power to the distinction between citizen-equal and slave-unequal, as in the curious custom of humiliating helots by making them drunk on unmixed wine, and forcing them to perform comic and indecent songs and dances for the instruction (and entertainment) of their masters.[21]

In fact in the case of Sparta alone among ancient cities are we able to quantify the consumption of alcohol. Dicaearchus gives the monthly contribution of wine to the *syssition* as 11 or 12 Attic *choes*[22]—that is about 9 gallons, or over 100 gallons a year. Herodotus gives the usual dining ration for the kings as 2 *kotylai* (1 pint), which is double that for other Spartiates (6.57). These two sets of figures have caused a traditional problem, since ½ pint a day amounts to only 23 gallons a year, leaving more than 75 gallons to be accounted for. And if the higher figure is accepted, "at 12 *choes* a month, the Spartiate would be consuming wine at a rate approaching the highest levels attested for healthy adult males in military contexts."[23] However, we can I think lay greater reliance on another figure. Thucydides (4.16) records that the agreement between Sparta and Athens on the provisioning of the Spartans besieged on Sphakteria allowed them a daily ration of 2 *kotylai*: this is obviously the minimum requirement for the survival of a Spartan soldier. Modern medical opinion regards a maximum daily intake of three measures of alcohol (or 1½ pints of beer) as an appropriate limit; a society that expected all its members to consume as a minimum the equivalent of four pints of beer a day,[24] in a ritual setting that ensured that the process would take several hours, is not one oblivious to the pleasures of alcohol.

Plato's picture is of course developed from that of Kritias; he has exaggerated it in order to establish a fundamental opposition between Sparta and Athens, which did not in fact exist. He tries to establish a polarity, "Sparta–courage" against "Athens–pleasure." But pleasure was already part of the Spartan *phidition;* leaving aside homosexuality (which Plato disapproves of as unnatural—*Laws* 636C) and entertainment provided by helots, we can point to the institutional pleasantries and mockings that might not pass the door: there is a privilege of free speech within the *phidition* which demonstrates that the Spartan banquet too has its rules, and they do not exclude pleasure.[25] Plato has in fact had to revise the rules of the *phidition* in order to maintain his thesis, and at the same time he has forgotten that much more important contrast, between conviviality regulated by the state and private conviviality. But to consider this would lead us on to a wider question: why does Plato need an Athenian legislator for the construction of his ideal city, when that city is so close to the reality of Sparta?

II

Plato's attempt to establish an opposition between these two institutions of Sparta and Athens tends rather to lead to reflection on their similarities. Even if we were to accept a common Dorian origin for the commensality practiced in Sparta and Crete (and that is itself an open question, since both sets of practices belong within a wide spectrum of types of public commensality practiced in a variety of Greek cities, Dorian and non-Dorian), we must admit that the Spartan social system has been remodelled in an age when the hoplite army existed; and with this must go the acceptance that the *phidition* in its Archaic and Classical form is a development belonging to the age of the symposium.

Public *syssition* and hoplite reform seem in fact to be contemporary innovations. Many of the basic characteristics of the Spartan *phidition* are connected with those developments in commensality throughout Greece in the early Archaic period that we associate with the symposium. Whereas the Cretan *andreia* were seated at their meals (presumably the original custom),[26] it is certain that in the historical period the Spartan *phidition* was a meal taken in the reclining position.[27] The only concession to Spartan austerity was that Spartans reclined "on the wood": before the Hellenistic period (according to Phylarchus) no coverings or cushions were allowed on the couches.[28]

Moreover, at Sparta there was a clear distinction between the communal meal, or *aiklon,* and the subsequent session of drinking and eating various light foods, the *epaikla.*[29] The *aiklon* first appears in Alcman, both in the simple form and, significantly, in the derivative form *synaiklia* (fr. 95 Page); as Snell has shown, the prefix *syn-* is connected with a whole range of words especially related to the symposium in Alcaeus and other sympotic poets.[30] The *aiklon* may well preserve the oldest element of the Spartan communal meal: it is very simple, and centers around standard compulsory contributions and the famous and clearly disgusting black broth.[31]

But *epaikla* too are attested in the same period, and as part of a developed sympotic ritual. For it is the greedy Alcman, who loves not special food, but the common fare of the people (fr. 17), who also provides the first certain literary evidence for the arrangement of a reclining symposium:

Seven couches and as many tables crowned with poppy cakes and linseed and sesame, and among the flagons (?) honey cakes. (fr. 19)

Whether this does or does not refer to part of a normal *phidition* meal rather than to some special or festival occasion, the *epaikla* are clearly not a later development of the Classical period, but an element in the initial Archaic organization of the Spartan communal meal. The foods are the characteristic foods of the symposium, cakes and bread, wine, cheese, and figs, together with occasional products of the chase or the flock—the traditional austerity of the *aiklon* perhaps causing this departure from the normal Greek custom of eating meat only at the meal before the symposium.

The central importance of both parts of the Spartan system of commensality is shown by the fact that both *aiklon* and *epaikla* require compulsory contributions from the members of the *phidition;* in the first case these are standard, in the second graded according to wealth and prowess. In other words, we may say that the Spartan common meal in the Archaic period, though it may in part descend from some specifically Dorian practice of commensality, has been restructured in accordance with the normal Greek dyad of *deipnon* and symposium.

In Sparta, it is clear that hoplite reforms went hand in hand with the creation of a sympotic army, for the *syssition* was also a basic element in the military organization.[32] According to Herodotus it was Lycurgus who created the laws of Sparta "and after that their military institutions, the *enomotiai, triekades* and *syssitia*" (1.65). This enigmatic passage has never been completely explained, but it is immediately clear that the three groups have multiple connections with the world of the Greek symposium: "sworn bands," "groups of thirty," and "dining companions." These are the basic sympotic elements in the military structure of the Spartan state, which continued in some form or other at least until the battle of Leuctra.[33] The evidence for the size of the basic Spartan military unit is remarkably consistent. Still in 418 the *enomotiai* comprised thirty-two men (Thuc. 5.68.3), and in the mid-fourth century thirty-six men (Xen. *Hell.* 6.4.12); they would seem then to be effectively the same size as the *triekades;* on the basis of Plutarch *Lyc.* 12, the *syssitia* are usually held to comprise fifteen men, with two *syssitia* making one of the other units.[34] The Spartan technical vocabulary luxuriates in synonyms and variant names, and we cannot tell whether Herodotus' *enomotiai* and *triekades* are different groupings, the same groupings in different aspects, or different names for identical groupings. But the recurrent numbers fifteen and thirty (including officers?) are significant, for they imply a military organization based on the characteristic size for the Greek symposium; we must suppose a room for the *phidition* with space for seven couches, each holding two reclining men.[35] This is indeed the number of couches referred to by Alcman, and elsewhere in Greece the commonest sizes of *andron* are those with seven, eleven, or fifteen couches, that is with a wall length of two, three, or four couches.[36] In other words, the Spartan military system is not merely founded on and maintained by a primitive form of commensality; it is more specifically founded on the characteristic Greek development of that institution, the reclining drinking group or symposium.

This of course serves to date the establishment of the Spartan system of public commensality to the same period as its other military and social reforms, the seventh century. And it also enables us to establish a crucial link, between the Homeric military organization based on the common feasts of merit of the class of *basilees* in their great *megara,* and the adaptations of that organization in the hoplite age, based on the common feasts and common drinkings, the *syssitia* and symposia of the class of hoplites. Plato is in fact wrong to see these two institutions as separate; they are variant developments from the same type of institution. In most cities, the Homeric feasts that had supported a military caste were set on one side, as the *polis* developed its own military organization based on *phyle* and *phratria;* the symposium emerged as a development from the "feast of merit" toward the pleasure principle: it remained one of the dominant types of commensality, even retaining some political significance, but it existed outside (or rather parallel to) the new political and military institutions of the *polis*. The Spartan choice was, however, to build directly on this type of military feasting, by making all citizens compulsory members of the *syssitia,* thus renewing and reinforcing older customs of Doric commensality in the interests of creating a New Model Army: it is a perfect example of that "archaic form of rationality," the structuring of change through the transformation of existing institutions, which I have discussed elsewhere.[37] But in essence, as the conservative Athenian reformers of the fourth century saw, *syssition* and symposium are the same sort of institution; each represents a different development from the warrior feasts of the Homeric age.

III

One of the most striking features of the Archaic symposium is of course its function as a place of performance for poetry. The role of the poet in the transformation we have been discussing seems to me especially problematic. No one, I think, is in a position to say how the Homeric poems were originally performed. But what is significant is the *representation* of poetic performance given by Homer: the poet seems deliberately to describe himself as *aoidos* singing of the exploits of contemporary warriors in a banquet of warriors. There is only one exception to this general portrait, and that is the scene at *Od.* 8.256ff. where Demodocus sings the *epyllion* of the love of Ares and Aphrodite. That is specifically not a normal epic occasion, for it takes place in public before the people, and with the accompaniment of dance; the implication must be that the meter of the imagined song is not in fact epic, but lyric.[38] Otherwise the Homeric bard has a firmly fixed self-image, which may or may not correspond to the reality of poetic performance in late Dark Age Greece: he sings of the exploits of war before a group of warriors; through the art of memory he offers a substitute for war to the resting hero. His activity is therefore, as the ancient commentators saw, a form of *askesis* or preparation for the military life, as well as a moment of rest and reflection within it.

The advent of the reclining symposium in the mid-eighth century[39] had considerable effect on the self-representation of the poet, and it would be reasonable to connect this with the changing relationship between the poet and his audience. It may indeed be that our problem in envisaging a physical context for the performance of the Homeric poems relates to the fact that the Homeric descriptions are themselves attempts to accommodate the role of the poet to a changing environment: his picture of the *aoidos* may not so much reflect the traditional function of the bard as represent a claim to a new function. However that may be, we can detect a development of the poet's role in two directions.

One I mention briefly, because it does not directly relate to the military drinking group: a recurrent theme of early lyric poetry is the contrast between an old style of poetry and a new style suitable for the symposium: the content of this new style varies, but it is most often attached to the pleasures of the drinking group, to wine and especially to Aphrodite. Much of what is most characteristic of the themes of monodic lyric belongs to this self-conscious development away from the conceptual world of the Homeric *aoidos,* in the social context of a symposium which saw itself in conflict with the Homeric model.[40]

The same polarity as we observed between Spartan military *syssition* and Athenian symposium of pleasure emerges here; for alongside a new poetry of pleasure there developed a military poetry that is also, I believe, new. It seems that here too the model of the poet offered by Homer was refused.

It is true that some have wished to see signs of experimentation with forms of poetry based on Homeric themes, but specifically designed for performance in the symposium, in the art of Stesichorus;[41] others have pointed to the evidence for historical epic themes transformed into elegiac meter in the works of Mimnermus, Panyassis, and Ion of Chios, whether these represent a lost tradition of "elegiac epic" for symposia, or a new development of elegy from the symposium to the public festival.[42]

But these hypotheses will only add nuances to a picture whose main lines seem clear. Elegy, whether or not it existed earlier, became in the seventh century one of the dominant forms of sympotic poetry, and one of its main themes (perhaps its earliest theme) was war. Elegiacs were not perhaps the only meter in which military poetry could be composed, but they seem from the start to have been the chief meter. Ewen Bowie has argued persuasively that this genre originated in the military drinking group:[43] my article so far may indeed be taken as an attempt to explore the social setting in which such poetry was performed. It was not of course a tradition confined to Sparta: Archilochus, Callinus, Mimnermus, and Solon demonstrate how widespread such military sympotic poetry was. If Sparta came to be especially associated with this type of poetry, that is a consequence of the formal establishment of the *syssition*.

The warrior symposium has then a genre of poetry related especially to it. In some ways it performs a function analogous to that envisaged above for Homeric epic, as leisure activity and training for a warrior elite. But such a characterization raises two problems that need discussion.

The first is this: leaving aside the possibility of historical narrative elegy, war elegy exhibits a quite different tone from heroic epic. Epic instructs through memory and indirect example: the *klea andron* may be thought to inspire the present warrior, as still on occasion with Mimnermus and even Tyrtaeus, but direct exhortation is avoided. Elegy, however, works primarily through such direct exhortation. Its tone is set by the earliest known example, Callinus fr. 1:

> How long will you stay reclining? When will you recall your strong spirits, you young men? Are you not ashamed to neglect so much the borderlands? You seem to rest in peace, but war possesses all the land.

This is an appeal to the warrior youth of the country, reclining on their sympotic *klinai,* to remember their duty; it is surely sung at the symposium.[44] But why the change in tone? Memory, when it is used, is not a simple recall of times past, but either part of an explicit statement to remember and emulate the heroes of old, or a promise of a similar future *kleos* for the contemporary warrior. And explicitly for the first time a group is addressed: corresponding to the *ego* of the lyric of pleasure is the *vos* of military elegy, "you young men": here the singer fades into the background, and the audience is the center of attention.

My second problem begins from these "young men." Who are they? At least in Sparta they are organized in small groups, *enomotiai*, sworn bands, *syssitia*, with all the psychological bonding that this implies. In the elegiac and lyric poetry devoted to political and social themes, such bonding is reflected in a whole vocabulary belonging to the psychology of the group: the range of words with the prefix *syn-* that were mentioned earlier, the appeals to companionship, the importance of oath and *pistis,* all these reflect the world of the *hetaireia*, the group apart, united in action whether for or against the rest of the community. The Theognidean corpus shows that this mode of thought was endemic in such a social organization. But military elegy at least in Sparta (and as far as we can see elsewhere) makes no appeal to the individual group. Those addressed are an undifferentiated *o neoi;* occasionally they may be contrasted with the older man or the *gymnetes*, they may be exhorted to stand by their fellow soldiers, or groups of traditional form (*choris Pamphyloi kai Hylleis ede Dumanes*, Tyrtaeus fr. 19, 1.8); but there is no appeal to group loyalty within the *syssition* or *enomotia*, no recall of the ties of sympotic companionship such as exists in elegy elsewhere (and indeed in epic itself). Instead they must remember past exploits, family and fatherland, and be mindful of future glory. My second problem, then, is why does military elegy not exploit the themes and vocabulary that exist elsewhere—why does it ignore the value of group loyalty as expounded by Plato and by modern military thinking?

I have no conclusive answer to these two questions, but let me attempt an explanation by combining them. Homeric epic operated in a world of relatively certain and unchanged values, envisaging an audience whose hereditary status as warriors was reflected in their pleasure in recalling a heroic past, with whose aspirations and values they could identify; in a traditional society a wider audience at a festival performance might still accept such aristocratic values. But the coming of hoplite tactics brought with it a need to widen the warrior elite, to create for the first time a warrior class that might eventually comprise as much as a third of the community, and that indeed at Sparta became identified with the citizen body itself.

Military elegy was developed from the necessity to create a new form of bonding directly related to the military experience. The aim of elegy remained that of education and preparation for the world outside, beyond the place of performance; but the greater insistence of elegy, the technique of direct address rather than oblique recall—these reflect the need to adapt the old warrior values to a different group. The urgency in this changing consciousness, and the official public aim behind it, perhaps precluded the slow and natural development of forms of military poetry adapted to the interests of the small group. Military elegy became the first *public* poetry, the first that was directed to a class as a whole rather than to its constituent groupings; in contrast political poetry long continued to exhibit to the full the range of metaphors and the vocabulary to be expected in any political culture based on the *hetaireia* or the club.

Of course one should not exaggerate this distinction: Alcaeus talks as a warrior about politics, and his great hall gleams with arms described in loving detail (fr. 357): "these we must not forget since first we undertook this task." But this confusion of war and companionship belongs rather to the ideology of *stasis,* which is perhaps a different thing; Plato is surely being ironical when he seeks to demonstrate that the ideal of Theognis is more valuable than that of Tyrtaeus (*Laws* 630A).

The absence of this type of language in military poetry thus appears as less strange than it might seem at first sight. It is the public status of the warrior class as a whole that is reflected in Greek elegy, rather than the interests of those groups of which it is composed. For these groups are not (as perhaps they were in early Rome) still private groups in the service of the community, but groups controlled and organized by the *polis.* Their poetry is a public poetry, emphasizing loyalty to the community rather than to the group; their rewards and penalties are in terms of public honor. The poetry is not concerned with questions of the creation and maintenance of group loyalties but with relating these loyalties to a larger whole, the class of the hoplites: the mythology and the psychology are public. Only in the event of *stasis* can a tension begin to exist between the group of warriors and the city.

IV

The relationship between *symposium* and war is not of course exhausted by these remarks; at least two other Greek societies require investigation from the same angle—Crete and the Thebes of Pelopidas. The question of rites of initiation and acceptance into the drinking group needs discussion. I have also deliberately omitted one of the most important types of evidence— the enormous repertoire of images of the heroic warrior on sympotic pottery and of the heroic warrior imagined as hoplite. One may very well ask what these images conveyed to the symposiasts who used them—why, when in literature little trace exists of a connection between symposium and the world of epic, is so much attention paid to epic warfare in sympotic art? More specifically, I would especially like to understand better those representations of the group of warriors as reflections of the warrior mentality.[45]

Let me end by attempting a diachronic sketch of the development of the military symposium. I see the origins of the warrior group in Homeric institutions, where a military elite was formed and defined by virtue of certain practices of commensality. These activities were accepted and even encouraged by the community, because they created a group of warriors at the service of the community in times of war. In this society relations of loyalty and companionage were clearly recognized. But with the arrival of the hoplite army there was a break. Loyalty to the community took on more importance, and the elegiac poetry of the first generations reflected this change of mentality so clearly because it was itself a part of the mechanism of change. The same age saw the development of the orientalizing-style symposium of pleasure in Greece, which transformed traditional rituals of commensality. Two ways of development opened up. Either the symposium became an agent in the withdrawal of a traditional elite from its public functions into a private world of pleasure, or it had to accept the control of the *polis* as it rearranged and employed traditional forms of commensality. Spartan society in particular succeeded in creating out of Homeric and Dorian customs a hoplite army at the service of the state, by the deliberate extension of these aristocratic and military rites of commensality to the entirety of the hoplite and citizen class.

This remodeling of traditional institutions of commensality never lost its appeal to the Greek cities; it functioned in the classical period as the myth of the peasant soldier functioned in late Republican Rome, as a focus of attention for successive reformers. We know little of those cities where the class of hoplites maintained itself in power. But the example of Athens in the fourth century reveals the consequences of the return of the hoplite, in the attempts by the state to control and universalize the social institutions of hoplite warfare. The tendencies to laconism are signs of this reversal of values, and Plato's myth in the *Laws* evokes this debate by its playful inversion of the traditional but false polarity between Spartan *syssition* and Attic symposium.[46]

NOTES

1. See in general my introductory essay, "Sympotic History," in O. Murray, ed., *Sympotica* (Oxford 1990), 3–13.

2. "The Symposion as Social Organisation," in R. Hägg and N. Marinatos, eds., *The Greek Renaissance of the Eighth Century* B.C.: *Tradition and Innovation* (Stockholm 1983), 195–99.

3. D.B. Heath, "A Decade of Development in the Anthropological Study of Alcohol Use, 1970–1980," in M. Douglas, ed., *Constructive Drinking: Perspectives on Drink from Anthropology* (Cambridge 1987), 16–69, p. 20.

4. See the survey of B. Cunliffe, *Greeks, Romans and Barbarians: Spheres of Interaction* (London 1988).

5. Heath, op. cit. (above note 3), 31 and 49.

6. E.M. Jellinek, "The Symbolism of Drinking: A Cultural-Historical Approach," *Journal of Studies on Alcohol* 38, 1977, 849–66, p. 864.

7. As the collection of essays edited by Mary Douglas (above note 3) shows; see also the standard bibliography on the subject, D.B. Heath and A.M. Cooper, *Alcohol Use and World Cultures: A Comprehensive Bibliography of Anthropological Sources* (Addiction Research Foundation, Toronto 1981).

8. Heath, op. cit. (above note 3), 36.

9. J. Keegan, *The Face of Battle* (London 1976), 181ff., 241.

10. Falsely, for although a virtual teetotaller, "he knew that for the sailor a warming drink that requires any preparation is frequently impossible, and he was as particular about the rum ration as he was about every other supply for the Fleet" (Lady [Oswyn] Murray, *The Making of a Civil Servant* [London 1940], 69).

11. I owe this information to Peter Manning of Michigan State University, coauthor of the study.

12. M. Yardley, "What Shall We Do With the Drunken Soldier?" *New Statesman*, 2 Oct. 1981, 15–16.

13. I refrain from documenting the following remarks, having been required many years ago to sign the Official Secrets Act.

14. For the development of Plato's thought here, see the fundamental study of M. Tecusan, "*Logos Sympotikos*: Patterns of the Irrational in Philosophical Drinking: Plato Outside the *Symposium*," in Murray, op. cit. (above note 1), 238–60. There are also interesting comments in E. Belfiore, "Wine and *Catharsis* of the Emotions in Plato's *Laws*," CO 36, 1986, 421–37, although I cannot accept her view that Plato's discussion of the benefits of drunkenness is confined throughout to its effects on those over forty.

15. G.R. Morrow, *Plato's Cretan City: A Historical Interpretation of the Laws* (Princeton 1960), 398.

16. "La Tradition de l'hoplite athénien" and "Le chasseur noir et l'origine de l'éphébie athénienne," reprinted in *Le Chasseur noir*² (Paris 1983), 125–74.

17. Arist. *Ath. Pol.* 42; Lycurg. *In Leocr.* 76; see the detailed commentary by P.J. Rhodes, *A Commentary on the Aristotelian Athenaion Politeia* (Oxford 1981), 502–10. It is true that few scholars have been able to accept the assertions of our two sources that the *ephebeia* was universal, but I agree with the conclusions of M.H. Hansen, *Democracy and Demography: The Number of Athenian Citizens in the Fourth Century* B.C. (Herning 1986), 48–50.

18. N.R.E. Fisher, "Drink, *Hybris* and the Promotion of Harmony in Sparta," in A. Powell, ed., *Classical Sparta: Techniques behind Her Success* (London 1989), 26–50; see esp. 27–29 on this point.

19. At Cretan *andreia* two cups of (heavily diluted) wine were provided, according to Dosiadas, *FGrH* 458 F 2 = Athen. *Deipnos.* 4.143 C-D.

20. A representative selection of these is given in Athenaeus' discussion of Spartan dining in the *Deipnosophistae* 4. 138ff. The best account of the whole subject remains the thesis of A. Bielschowsky, *De Spartanorum Syssitiis* (Diss. Breslau 1869); H. Michell, *Sparta* (Cambridge 1964) is unreliable, often misreporting both ancient evidence and the views of earlier scholars.

21. Plut. *Lyc.* 28; on the ritual degradation of helots see J. Ducat, "Le Mépris des hilotes," *Annales ESC* 29, 1974, 1451–64. The possibility of similar entertainment elsewhere is discussed by B. Fehr, "Entertainers at the *Symposion:* The *Akletoi* in the Archaic Period," in Murray, op. cit. (above note 1), 185–95.

22. Fr. 72 Wehrli; Plutarch (*Lyc.* 12) says 8 (presumably Spartan) *choes.* H. Michell, *Sparta* (Cambridge 1964), 287ff. gets these two testimonia the wrong way round; see rather Bielschowsky, op. cit. (above note 20), 23–27.

23. T. J. Figueira, "Mess Contributions and Subsistence at Sparta," *TAPA* 114, 1984, 87–109, p. 94. Figueira assumes the presence of many guests and nonmembers, which I doubt, given the general tradition of Spartan exclusiveness.

24. Measurements of consumption in terms of modern wine are misleading. Greek wine was a natural fermentation and yet remained sweet: since it failed to eliminate all the sugar, we may assume that it reached close to the upper limit for natural fermentation, of 16–17 percent alcohol by volume; diluted 1 part of wine to 2 or 3 of water, this is roughly equivalent in terms of both liquid intake and alcoholic strength to the range of modern beers. I therefore prefer to use these for comparative purposes.

25. E. David, "Laughter in Spartan Society," in Powell, op. cit. (above note 18), 1–25.

26. For Crete see Pyrgion *FGrH* 467 F 1 ap. Athen. *Deipnos.* 4.143E.

27. Only Varro seems to couple Crete and Sparta in his *De Gente Populi Romani,* as sources for the old Roman habit of sitting at meals (see Servius on *Aen.* 7.176); but it has long been recognized that this refers to a hypothetical original Spartan custom, later abandoned; for the Romans traditionally contrasted Crete and Sparta in this respect, as in Cic. *Mur.* 74.

28. There are many passing references to reclining Spartans; for reclining on the wood, see Phylarchus *FGrH* 81 F 44 ap. Athen. 4.142A; cf. Athen. 12.518E; Cic. *Mur.* 74; Suda s.v. *phiditia* and *Lykourgos;* and in general Bielschowsky, op. cit. (above note 20), 20ff.

29. On these two Spartan institutions see esp. Athen. 4.138–42; Bielschowsky, op. cit. (above note 20), 18–20.

30. B. Snell, *Dichtung und Gesellschaft* (Hamburg 1965), 71 n. 22; cf. W. Rösler, *Dichter und Gruppe* (Munich 1980), 33–40.

31. A recipe for *haimatia* or *zomos melas* is given in Bielschowsky, op. cit. (above

note 20), 19: blood, the stock from the boiled pork, salt and vinegar—a sort of liquid black pudding, which those who had not bathed in the Eurotas found totally unpalatable: Plut. *Lyc.* 12.

32. Already in the nineteenth century the connection between *syssition* and military organization was the subject of controversy between the followers of C.F. Hermann and C.O. Müller: see the section "Quae ratio inter syssitia et rem militarem intercesserit, ostenditur," in Bielschowsky, op. cit. (above note 20), 32–44. Since then the vast literature on Spartan military organization seems rather to have lost sight of its basis: the most illuminating remarks are those of A.J. Toynbee on "The Social Effects of the 'Lycurgan' Reform," in *Some Problems of Greek History* (Oxford 1969), 322–25, who compares the Spartan *syssitia* with the mess groups of ten men of the Ottoman Janissaries: "the psychological value of the comradeship fostered by the *syssitia* explains why this form of corporate life was maintained so zealously by the Spartan military authorities, as well as by the members of the *syssitia* themselves" (p. 323).

33. At this battle, Polyaenus (*Strat.* 2.3.11) still gives the Spartan divisions as *lochoi, morai, enomotiai,* and *syssitia.*

34. The figure of ten given in the scholia to Plato *Laws* 633A is I think rightly disregarded.

35. Two men to a couch is of course normal and is vouched for in the Spartan context by a number of anecdotes, e.g., Athen. 4.142D.

36. The description of the *Karneia* refers to groups of nine, and is called a mirror of their military *agoge* (Demetrius of Skepsis ap. Athen. 4.142E-F); but this is an artificial grouping for festival purposes, in which each group of nine is composed of members of three separate *phratries*—that is, normal groups are deliberately mixed together. As Walter Burkert pointed out in discussion, the festival *Karneia* seeks to recall an original pre-*polis* organization of the Spartan community.

37. See "Cities of Reason," *Archives Européennes de sociologie* 28, 1987, 325–46, esp. 333–66.

38. Cf. B. Gentili, *Poetry and Its Public in Ancient Greece* (Eng. trans., Baltimore 1988), 14ff.

39. A date that I intend to justify elsewhere.

40. This too is a theme I hope to develop elsewhere.

41. L.E. Rossi, "Feste religiose e letteratura: Stesicoro o dell'epica alternativa," *Orpheus* 4, 1983, 5–31.

42. E.L. Bowie, "Early Greek Elegy, Symposium, and Public Festival," *JHS* 106, 1986, 13–35; cf. W. Rösler, "*Mnemosyne* in the *Symposion*," in Murray, op. cit. (above note 1), 230–37.

43. "*Miles Ludens?* The Problem of Martial Exhortation in Early Greek Elegy," in Murray, op. cit. (above note 1), 221–29.

44. For this interpretation see R. Reitzenstein, *Epigramm und Skolion* (Giessen 1893) 50; G. Tedeschi, "L'elegia parenetica-guerriera e il simposio: a proposito del fr. 1 W. di Callino," *Riv. stud. class.* 26, 1978, 203–9.

45. Cf. F. Lissarrague, "Dionysos s'en va-t-en guerre," C. Bérard, ed., *Images et société en Grèce ancienne* (Lausanne 1987), 111–20, and the remarks of B. D'Agostino on warriors in Etruscan funerary art, "Military Organization and Social Structure in Archaic Etruria," O. Murray and S. Price, eds., *The Greek City* (Oxford 1990), 59–82.

46. Earlier versions of this chapter have been read to audiences in Leicester, Paris, Naples, and Venice, as well as to our symposium in Hamilton; I am grateful to these for many helpful comments. I should especially like to thank Henry Blyth, Walter Burkert, Malcolm Chapman, Godfrey Fowler, and Peter Manning for assistance in many different fields, from anthropology to medicine and military discipline, and for instructing me in the habits of drinking groups as diverse as Breton fishermen and the British police.

The Age for Reclining and Its Attendant Perils

Alan Booth

Never smell of wine, lest the philosopher's words be said of you: "This is not a kiss but a wine sip". . . . If even without wine I am all aglow, if I feel the fire of youth and am inflamed by hot blood, if I am of a strong and lusty habit of body, then I will readily forgo the wine cup, in which I may well suspect that poison lurks. The Greeks have a pretty proverb which perhaps in our language loses some of its force: "A fat paunch never breeds fine thoughts." Impose upon yourself such fasting as you are able to bear. . . . [1]

This admonition, addressed by Jerome to a young ascete, serves to recall one point on which Christian and pagan moralists agreed: eating, drinking, and sexual indulgence constitute an intimate and unholy trinity. It is recorded, for example, both of Pythagoras and of Socrates that they advocated, by their example and teachings, restraint in these pursuits.[2] Again, it was by offering the combined pleasures of food, wine, and flesh, that perfidious Capua, if Livy be believed (23.18.12), demoralized and set on the slope to defeat that otherwise vigorous arch-enemy of Rome, Hannibal's army. Censorious Romans would typically dub such indulgence neither Etruscan nor Sabellian nor Punic, but, by a tradition established already in Plautus, Greek.[3] Philo (*De Vita Contempl.* 48–56), however, reverses the charge, alleging that imitation of Italian extravagance in dining, wining, and lovemaking is tainting Hellene and barbarian. Such luxury had indeed come to be regarded as an integral aspiration and perquisite of the same Roman civilization that naturalized the study of rhetoric, Greek in provenance, as the crown of its liberal culture.[4] Thus cultivation of oratory and the elegant banquet, along with the use of the promenade and the toga, are the enticements to Romanization, to vice and servitude too, adds Tacitus (*Ag.* 21), promoted by Agricola to enervate the British. And Dio (62.6.4) has Boudicca signal in even sterner terms the insidious practices and effects of Roman refinement:

I supplicate and pray the goddess Andraste for victory, preservation of life, and liberty against men insolent, unjust, insatiable, impious— if, indeed, we ought to term those people men who bathe in warm water, eat artificial dainties, drink unmixed wine, anoint themselves with myrrh, sleep on soft couches with boys for bedfellows—boys past their prime at that—and are slaves to a lyre-player and a poor one too.

As the case of the Greco-Roman Nebuchadnezzar, Lucius, so piquantly reminds us, the ability to imbibe while reclining distinguished man from brute.[5] It was also a right that set gentleman apart from slave.[6] This dignified position was never attained by Martial's Maximus Syriscus, who, flitting between tavern stools, ate his way through the fortune left him by his former owner: "Oh, what stupendous gluttony, to gorge ten millions! And still more stupendous, not even to recline at table!" (*Epigram. 5.70*). In grief over the defeat at Pharsalus, Plutarch claims (*Cat. 56*), the Younger Cato, who would thereafter recline only to sleep, sat to dine, a gesture no doubt intended to mourn the imminent passing of his world. So, while Greek symposium and Roman convivium were recognized to share and foster a degree of decadence associated not only with the pleasures of the palate but also of the pillow, they were considered at the same time to be an irrevocable development in a secure and sophisticated society. This point is pithily put by Juvenal, who has supping and sipping alone in pristine purity disappear with the reign of Saturn (13.33–46). In Plato (*Laws* 1.637A) the Spartan speaker specifies the absence of symposia as an essential factor in the modesty and order of his unusual civilization:

For our law banished entirely from the land that institution which gives the most occasion for men to fall into excessive pleasures and riotings and follies of every description; neither in the country nor in the cities controlled by Spartiates is a drinking-club to be seen nor any of the practices which belong to such and foster to the utmost all kinds of pleasure.

Not unexpectedly, it was from the convivial path to perdition that Christian asceticism also sought to woo souls. Thus, Jerome (*Epist. 22* [7]) recalls how, in his desert retreat, he struggled to repress fantasies about dancing girls by shunning his customary fare and subsisting on water and raw food; this dietary deprivation was to him even more severe than the rejection of his family (ibid. 30). The future saint, who had been liberally educated at

Rome, designates the offending tastes as "Roman delights" and regards exposure thereto as an unexceptional part of growing up. In short, throughout antiquity concerns are voiced about the effect of the joys of reclining upon the character of the young well-born male.

Juvenal's satire on the vanity of human wishes concludes by identifying as one worthy object of prayer "a stout heart . . . that can endure any kind of toil; that knows neither wrath nor desire, and thinks that the woes and hard labours of Hercules are better than the loves and the banquets and the downy cushions of Sardanapalus" (11.357–62). Cicero might well have prayed that his student-son Marcus, taken by the high life at Athens, should mature along such lines; tradition made Marcus a perpetual wastrel.[7] On the other hand, Polemo, the future paragon of scholarly toil, was salvaged from the impetuous thirsts of youth, which had led him to conceal money throughout the city so that he might purchase instantaneous gratification of his desires (Diog. Laert. 4.16):

And one day, by agreement with his young friends, he burst into the school of Xenocrates quite drunk, with a garland on his head. Xenocrates, however, without being at all disturbed, went on with his discourse as before, the subject being temperance. The *meirakion*, as he listened, by degrees was taken in the toils.

Polemo had been straying along the road shown the youthful Hercules by Prodicus' Vice, where choice in food and drink, sound and scent, bedding and bed partners constitutes life's challenge (Xen. *Mem.* 2.1.21–33).

Since, therefore, society's convivial institutions were acknowledged as both a desirable part of life and a persistent danger for the young, we should expect to find conventions concerning the age at which license freely to participate in the symposium and convivium, license to accept invitations there to recline, was to be granted. Now the ages approved by the Rome of the late Republic and early Empire and by classical Athens can be determined with some precision. An awareness of these ages may in turn enhance our appreciation of certain passages in ancient literature. To Rome first.

That the right to recline was enjoyed by Roman males in their later teens emerges from Polybius' eulogy of the young Scipio Aemilianus. When the latter was not yet eighteen years old, he attached himself to the historian who memorializes the youth's aim to obtain, above all else, a reputation for moderation. His success in this pursuit, we are informed, was the more praiseworthy since some of his coevals "had abandoned themselves to cat-

amites, others to the society of courtesans, and many to musical entertainments and banquets, and the extravagance they involve" (31.25.4). Two
centuries later the Younger Seneca likewise identifies the luxurious banquet
and infatuation with pretty *servuli* as symptoms and causes of decadence
in the young; he laments that the schools of philosophers and rhetors are
shunned by adolescents enraptured by the cuisine of their spendthrift
friends, and he finds himself too outraged to mention

> the troops of luckless slave boys who put up with other shameful
> treatment after the banquet is over . . . the troops of catamites, rated
> according to nation and colour, who must all have the same smooth
> skin, the same amount of youthful down upon their cheeks, and the
> same way of dressing their hair, so that no boy with straight locks
> may get among the curly-heads. (*Ep.* 95.24)

Evidently the revellers present in the moralist's mind are teenagers who
might be expected to attend classes on a regular basis, from puberty up
to the age of eighteen or so.[8] These wayward youths, one would then
assume, upon arrival at a crucial fork in life's path, have shied from virtue's
rocky road to coast instead along the paved highway of pleasure.

This interpretation finds eloquent confirmation in an autobiographic
reflection of Persius, who remembers the potential freedom to experiment
sexually that was granted him by the *toga virilis* (5.34–44):

> At the age when the path of life is doubtful, and wanderings, ignorant
> of life, parted my trembling soul into the branching cross-ways, I
> placed myself in your hands, Cornutus; you took up my tender years
> in your Socratic bosom . . . With you, I remember, did I pass long
> days, with you pluck for feasting the early hours of night. We two
> were one in our work; we were one in our hours of rest, and unbent
> together over the modest board.

Assumption of the *toga virilis*, then, was on the one hand recognized to
bestow freedom to recline, and on the other to render desirable some
restraint and guidance. This conclusion is borne out by Apuleius' account
of the corruption of his stepson, Sicinius Pudens.[9] According to the orator's
vituperations, the boy, who had been attending school and showing promise
of eventually matching the eloquence of his deceased brother, was seduced
into the clutches of his uncle, Aemilianus. Hitherto a *praetextatus*, Sicinius
received at once the toga of manhood and exercised uncontrolled freedom

to indulge his appetites: in the company of the most dissolute adolescents he turned his life into one prolonged feast of whoring and drinking. It was Sicinius himself, avers Apuleius, who ruled his uncle's household and assumed the role of "master of the feast." The charge is clear: this youth did not benefit from the proper *tirocinium convivii* deemed necessary to mold the use of the freedom bestowed by the toga of manhood.

In his *Quaestiones Romanae* (33), Plutarch asks why, in days of yore, Roman fathers never dined out without taking along those of their sons who were still in boyhood.[10] This question provides confirmation, as do reports of usage at the imperial court, that *praetextati* were not normally invited out to *convivia*. Suetonius (*Aug.* 64.3) records that Augustus never dined with his grandsons, his adopted sons Gaius and Lucius, unless they sat at the foot of his couch. Since this information is attached to remarks about Augustus' care of the princes' rudimentary education, one may assume the occasions in question to have been meals during official boyhood; once Gaius and Lucius had assumed the *toga virilis* in 5 B.C. and 2 B.C. respectively, they enjoyed the right of attending senatorial banquets, where they no doubt reclined in Augustus' presence (Dio 55.9.4, 55.10). Now the same Suetonius remarks that Claudius would always invite to formal *convivia* his own children, along with the sons and daughters of distinguished men, and he would have them sit at the foot of the couches as they ate, after old-fashioned custom (*Claud.* 32). The children of Claudius here in question should be Octavia, Britannicus, and Nero between his adoption and his assuming the *toga virilis*.

According to Suetonius (*Claud.* 43), Claudius sealed his fate at Agrippina's hand in the autumn of 54, when he expressed the intention of giving Britannicus the *toga virilis* and designating him successor. In his *Nero* (33), the biographer informs us that this emperor had the fatal draught administered to Britannicus while the latter was dining with him. Suetonius in *Titus* (2) tells us that Titus, who was believed to have tasted the poison too, was reclining beside Britannicus. Perhaps Suetonius imagined that Britannicus had assumed the toga of manhood before his murder; otherwise, as Tacitus' account reveals, Suetonius has missed a point of etiquette, just the sort of point, moreover, that he relishes remarking upon. Towards the end of his *Annals* (12.65), Tacitus has the freedman Narcissus pray, in the last days of Claudius, that Britannicus may reach maturity and be designated to succeed Claudius. Then the historian has Agrippina, faced with her waning power as the emperor Nero eludes her influence, affirm that Britannicus is now adult and the rightful successor. So Nero, the narrative continues, murdered Britannicus, whose fourteenth birthday was approaching. But Tacitus, who evidently believes that the *toga virilis* has not yet been donned, sets the victim apart from the reclining Nero (*Ann.* 13.16.1): "It was the regular custom that the children of the emperors should take their meals in sight of their relatives, seated with other nobles of their age at a more frugal table of their own. There Britannicus was dining."

So, in proper imperial practice, before assumption of the *toga virilis*, princes did not recline but sat, and they did not participate fully in the *convivium*. This practice reflects a general convention whereby the right to recline came with the grant of the garb of manhood. Let us look further now at the dangers that could beset the new adult at this stage in his social development.

Seeking to explain the popular custom of granting the *toga virilis* at the festival of *Liber Pater,* Ovid suggests that parents may wish to commend their emancipated sons to the keeping of a heavenly father (*Fasti* 3.775–76). It seems fair to see here, besides a play on the god's title, an allusion to a widespread concern about the potential behavior of youths who could now recline and drink; some paternal protection from the god of intoxication would not go amiss. Octavian's avoidance of drunkenness and its concomitant follies at this juncture is treated with some insistence by Nicolaus of Damascus.[11] The latter has Octavian assume the *toga virilis* about the age of fourteen; he then describes how Ateia continued to monitor the youth's conduct; this supervision combined with his innate sense protected him from the advances of conniving women (8–12). After the African War, Nicolaus notes, Caesar and Octavian kept company "in the theatres and at drinking parties" (18), and a passage that would explain Caesar's decision to adopt his nephew mentions (28): "* * * of silver according to the customs of his country, nor to be in attendance with the young men as they get drunk, nor to remain at drinking parties past evening, nor to have dinner before the tenth hour other than at the house of Caesar, Philippus and Marcellus." The youth, moreover, "abstained from sex just at the time when young men are particularly sexually active" (36). Clearly, Octavian exercised the right to recline in the years following his assumption of the *toga virilis*, but, at this stage, he is made to respond to such direction as would consolidate his morality and place his adolescent reputation beyond a slur.

In Octavian's case the "conniving women" were no doubt power-hungry, but they evoke too the sex-hungry sort typified by the Clodia of Cicero's *Pro Caelio,* the Clodia who fished impressionable lovers from among the Tiber's youthful bathers (36). The pose of an indulgent parent pardons Caelius' involvement here. But Cicero responds also to allegations about homosexual submission on his client's part. Such muckraking, affirms the orator, is generally launched against those who have enjoyed a handsome, attractive appearance in adolescence (6), but in Caelius' case this recourse is futile (9):

> So far as the age of Marcus Caelius might have given room for such suspicion, it was protected, first by his own conscience, and in the second place by his father's own carefulness and severe training. As soon as his father had given him the gown of manhood . . . he was brought to me at once by his father. No one ever saw this young Marcus Caelius, while he was in that early youth, in the company of anyone but his father or myself, or in the irreproachable household of Marcus Crassus, while he was being trained in the most honourable pursuits.

At the crucial formative period—that is, during the year following assumption of the *toga virilis* (11)—Caelius, so Cicero's words may be taken to imply, not only associated generally but also dined either with his father, Cicero, or Crassus, thus completing impeccably his *tirocinium convivii* and preserving the chastity of his person.

Allegations about the young Julius Caesar's pathic conduct at the court of King Nicomedes stained his reputation indelibly, so Suetonius reports (*Caes.* 49.2): "Gaius Memmius makes the direct charge that he acted as cup-bearer to Nicomedes with the rest of his wantons at a large dinner-party, and that among the guests were some merchants from Rome, whose names Memmius gives." It may be presumed that such invective, in its full-dress form, began as does Cicero's "Fall of Antony" (*Phil.* 2.44–45): "You assumed a man's gown, and at once turned it into a harlot's. . . No boy ever bought for libidinous purposes was ever so much in the power of his master as you were in Curio's." Then the invective will have proceeded along lines similar to the sketch of the formation of Catiline's followers (*In Cat.* 2.23): "All the activity of their lives and all the efforts of their waking hours are devoted to banquets that last till dawn. . . These boys, so dainty and effeminate, have learned not only to love and be loved, not only to dance and sing, but also to brandish daggers and sow poison." Indeed Antony himself will have included such material in an attack on Pompey "right from his taking the pure white toga" (Cic. *Ad Att.* 7.8). Was there a real threat that the recent recipient of the *toga virilis* would be homosexually seduced during his *tirocinium convivii*?

Cicero notes that, on donning the toga of manhood, the youth might apprentice himself forthwith to the rigors of military life (*Cael.* 11). Sallust contrasts such traditional training with contemporary decadence (*Bell. Cat.* 7.4): "To begin with, as soon as the young men could endure the hardships of war, they were taught a soldier's duties in camp under a vigorous discipline, and they took more pleasure in handsome arms and war horses than in harlots and banquets." Predictably, Sallust has Catiline supervise such a *tirocinium* as would produce for him suitably depraved followers (14.5–7):

> But most of all Catiline sought the intimacy of the young; their minds, still pliable as they were and easily moulded, were without difficulty ensnared by his wiles. For carefully noting the passion which burned in each, according to his time of life, he found harlots for some or bought dogs and horses for others; in fine, he spared neither expense nor his own decency, provided he could make them loyal to himself. I am aware that some have believed that the young men who frequented Catiline's house set but little store by their own chastity; but that report became current rather for other reasons than because anyone had evidence of its truth.[12]

Sallust's testimony might reasonably beget the notion that mentions of homosexual use of freeborn youths owe more to rhetoric than to reality. Polybius castigates the extravagance of Roman youth in the matter both of mistresses and slave catamites. Likewise Seneca's party-crowd is rebuked because of its appetite for pretty slaves. Did homosexual submission bear such a servile stigma that freeborn boys would only be tempted most exceptionally?

The clearest answer to this question is afforded by remarks of the level-headed Quintilian. Where he discusses whether instruction at home is preferable to schooling, he recognizes the concern that morals may be corrupted in school. But he adds (1.2.4): "The teacher employed at home may be of bad character, and there is just as much danger in associating with bad slaves as there is with immodest companions of good birth." He proceeds to lament the influences to which the child is exposed in the normal household (1.2.6–8):

> We rejoice if children say something over-free, and words which we should not tolerate from the lips even of an Alexandrian page are greeted with laughter and a kiss. We have no right to be surprised. We taught them: they hear us use such words, they see our mistresses and our male concubines; every dinner party is loud with foul songs,

and things are presented to their eyes of which we should blush to speak. Hence springs habit, and habit in time becomes second nature. The poor children learn these things before they know them to be wrong. They become luxurious and effeminate, and far from acquiring such vices at schools, introduce them themselves.

Quintilian's point is clear: because of his home environment, the child acts provocatively like a catamite to attract attention and so develops a pathic nature.[13] Again, Quintilian stresses that the teacher of rhetoric must control the urges of his pupils who are arriving at manhood and advises (2.2. 14–15):

I do not approve of boys sitting mixed with young men. For even if the teacher be such a one as we would desire to see in charge of the morals and studies of the young, and can keep his youthful pupils under proper control, it is none the less desirable to keep the weaker members separate from the more mature, and to avoid not only the charge of corruption but the merest suspicion of it.

It is here assumed that adolescents will have both passive and active homosexual tendencies. These tendencies will have been fostered by their childhood exposure to behavior at banquets. Quintilian no doubt envisages a danger that an ill-supervised class may gain the reputation of being a venue where assignations are made and invitations to seductive dinners pressed.

Quintilian describes the customs of the whole segment of society that would enjoy a liberal education. Thus, his testimony tends to weaken any notion that homosexual liaisons among the freeborn were limited to a Hellenizing minority among the upper classes. In the late Republic and early Empire, once youths had assumed the *toga virilis* at about the age of fifteen, they were liable to be homosexually courted by invitations to a *convivium* where they now had freedom to recline. So, in the twenty-first poem, whose subject may well be Iuventius, Catullus evokes a realistic situation wherein the beloved has been dined, wined, and seduced; Aurelius, "father of all starvations," does not have the resources to operate with flair in one of the common courtship rituals of his society. Again, the situation evoked in the pseudo-Ciceronian *In Sallustium* is not merely rhetorical (21): "But you, the parasite of all tables, the harlot of all chambers in your youth and in later years their adulterer, are the disgrace of our whole order."

Let us move now from Rome into the Greek world. As the Younger Pliny (*Ep.* 10.161) reminds us, donning the ephebic cloak was regarded as equivalent to the assumption of the *toga virilis*. That the new Greek adult would be exposed to homosexual advances as he reclined is revealed by the tale of the Pergamene ephebe in the *Satyricon* (85—87), where Eumolpus operates in the opposite fashion to Persius' Cornutus. The initial seduction took place in a dining room where "moral guardian" and ephebe happened to be reclining, too relaxed to retire to their bedrooms after making merry on a holiday. Similar opportunity for seduction was sought and offered in classical Athens.

First, some reflections of Isocrates.

> If possible avoid drinking-parties altogether, but if ever occasion arises when you must be present, rise and take your leave before you become intoxicated; for when the mind is impaired by wine it is like chariots which have lost their drivers; for just as these plunge along in wild disorder when they miss the hands which should guide them, so the soul stumbles again and again when the intellect is impaired.

This advice, offered to Demonicus in the address that bears the latter's name (32), warns against the type of decadence that is said in the *Antidosis* (286) to be menacing Athens' young men: drinking bouts, parties, soft living, childish folly, neglect of all efforts to improve themselves. Isocrates has Nicocles identify passions for boys and women as indulgences to which even the morally best succumb; Nicocles prides himself on having shown self-control here "at an age in which we find that the great majority of men most frequently go morally astray" (*Nicocles* 39, 45). Now an Athenian youth might be led morally astray by his male lover.

At Athens homosexual liaisons between males of the citizen class were so accepted that, in his prosecution of Timarchus (135–40), Aeschines admits to having chased several potential *eromenoi,* to having made a pest of himself in gymnasia, to having written love poems, and to having been involved in scuffles with rivals. He defends this conduct as honorable and his courtship practices as legitimate; for, he reasons, since the law forbids a slave to love a freeborn boy or follow him, the law's intention is to encourage the freeborn man to act in this way. But, continues the orator, the legislator intends the *erastes* to postpone talk of love until the boy has intelligence sufficiently mature to assess the sincerity of the lover's intentions. It is not difficult to identify this age of consent. For, in this speech, Aeschines examines the legal concern for the conduct and protection of the potential and actual citizen, first as a *pais,* next as a *meirakion,* then throughout the rest of his adult life (7–8). The transition from *pais* to *meirakion* occurs when the young Athenian is registered as a demesman at the age of eighteen

(18–22; [Aristotle] *Ath. Pol.* 42.1–2). The *meirakion,* unlike the *pais,* is responsible under the law for his own actions. So, as Aeschines charges Timarchus with deliberately prostituting himself, he stresses thus his accusatory moderation (39): "For I remit all the sins that as *pais* he committed against his own body . . . But what he is guilty of having done after he reached years of discretion, when he was already a *meirakion,* and knew the laws of state, that will I make the object of my accusation." Evidently, then, Aeschines regards the age of civic majority as the recognized age of consent. There are clear indications that attendance at the symposium was not acceptable before this same age.

In Plato's *Symposium,* Alcibiades describes his attempts to seduce Socrates, whose genuine goodwill he had ascertained: he arranged to meet with Socrates alone, but the latter made no overtures. Alcibiades invited Socrates to train with him in the gymnasium where they wrestled together without others present. But again Socrates made no sexual advances. "Then, as I made no progress that way, I resolved to charge full tilt at the man . . . Accordingly I invited him to dine with me, for all the world like a lover scheming to ensnare his favourite" (217C). Alcibiades was reversing the behavior typical of *erastes* and *eromenos* first here, and then by detaining Socrates in conversation after their second dinner, by proposing that he stay the night because of the lateness of the hour and by joining Socrates, once the slaves had withdrawn, on the dining couch where Socrates intended to sleep. This account then reveals that, by a standard rite of courtship, an *erastes* might organize a dinner and symposium to provide opportunity for social contact with an *eromenos,* in the hope that the latter might linger after the other guests had left. If such potential access was considered improper before the beloved had reached majority, then the age of eighteen should have been considered the youngest acceptable age for reclining.

Ready confirmation for this conjecture is provided by a fragment of Antidotus (fr. 2 Kock): "Before I was registered in my deme and received the ephebic cloak, whenever the conversation happened to fall on how to be a parasite, I always drank in the art eagerly and proved that I had a precocious understanding in grasping it." The craft learned in boyhood would evidently be exploited on reaching majority. Again, Xenophon's idealizing description of Persian education (*Cyr.* 1.2.8) contains the observation that Persian boys receive beneficial instruction by taking food and drink with their teachers instead of their mothers—which was presumably Greek and, more specifically, Athenian practice. Then Xenophon, drawing his inspiration from Greek reality, immediately specifies that Persian boyhood extends until transition to the ephebic class. In this Persian system such passage occurs at the age of sixteen or seventeen. But it is a justifiable inference that, at Athens, boys regularly ate with their mothers up to the age of eighteen. We should believe, moreover, that Plato and Aristotle allude to Athenian convention, when, in the *Laws* (2.666A), the former would not allow consumption of wine before the age of eighteen, and when, in the *Politics* (7.15.7, 9), the latter associates political maturity with the right to recline and drink. The Athenian reader was expected already to subscribe to the notion that the right to participate in the symposium should come first with attainment of ephebic status.

Plato's *Laches* introduces the fathers Lysimachus and Melesias, who are concerned about the upbringing of their sons. They have resolved "to give them most constant care, and not—as most fathers do when their sons begin to be *meirakia*—let them run loose as fancy leads them, but begin forthwith by taking every possible care of them" (179A). The immediately mentioned aspect of this unwonted supervision is that the *meirakia* dine with their fathers. The stage in question I take to be the sons' attainment of majority, *meirakion* here possessing the technical force met in Aeschines. In the normal run of things, new adults, those now past the age of eighteen, might recline where they chose. These *meirakia*, exceptionally, keep company with their fathers, and such training would, ideally, have produced paragons at the opposite end of the scale from the dissolute Alcibiades of the vituperative tradition. In Isocrates' sixteenth speech (29), the younger Alcibiades relates how his father, having attained adult status and impatient for glory, served in the Potidaean expedition and received crown and panoply for his valor. But, according to a fragment of Antiphon (Athen. 12.525B), at this stage in his life—to wit, just when he had attained his majority—Alcibiades went to learn female ways from the licentious women of Abydus, with the aim of promoting his career by skillful sexual receptivity. The symposium, we may be sure, was an understood occasion for such sexual politics.

Those still at the age of boyhood might attend the symposium under certain conditions, which Lysias, marking the younger Alcibiades as perverse from his earliest years, has the latter flaunt (14.25):

When the man was a *pais*, he was seen by a number of people in the house of Archedemus the Blear-eyed . . . drinking as he lay at length under the same cloak; he carried on his revels till daylight, keeping a mistress while he was still *anebos*, and imitating his ancestors, in the belief that he would not achieve distinction in his later years unless he could show himself an utter rascal in his youth.

Such activities, the context confirms, constitute the most outrageous conduct imaginable in one under the age of majority. With it may be contrasted the propriety that we see exercised in Xenophon's *Symposium* (1.1–8). There Autolycus, who has been victorious in the boys' *pancration* at the *Panathenaia,* is entertained by his suitor Critias, along with other guests including the beloved's father. The boy does not recline but sits. Callias is praised by Socrates for having included the father in such meetings. "For," says Socrates (8.11), "the virtuous lover does not make any of these matters a secret from the father of his beloved." If Callias proceeds properly, he will not meet privately with Autolycus until the latter is major; by that time he will have demonstrated his genuine goodwill by his restraint. Such is the ideal social behavior for which Aeschines finds a legal basis (*Timarchus* 139–40): "But, I think, so long as the boy is not his own master and is as yet unable to discern who is a genuine friend, and who is not, the law teaches the lover self-control, and makes him defer the words of love till the other is older and has reached years of discretion." The *eromenos,* once he has gained his majority, will behave with modesty, receiving advances as he reclines in the company of his lover but not initiating them, as would a wanton Alcibiades.

So at Athens, the new adult, aged eighteen, usually acquired the right to accept invitations to recline. At this stage he was considered sufficiently mature to cope with sexual advances. This situation, provided that it occurred within certain conventions, was apparently viewed more favorably at Athens than at Rome. But a similar rite of seduction did exist at Rome, to which were exposed Roman "ephebes," recipients of the *toga virilis,* some three years earlier. At Athens, as at Rome, there was a general concern about the indulgences of young adults at this convivial stage. Xenophon directs further advice to his Athenian reader on this topic in the *Constitution of the Lacedaemonians* (3.1–5). There he describes the controls imposed when Spartiates pass from the stage of boys to that of *meirakia,* imposed, that is, at the precise moment when other Greeks, he says, would free their sons from *paedagogi* and teachers and all supervision. Xenophon thinks here of the conduct of eighteen-year-old Athenians who contrast with their Spartiate counterparts: "When the latter have taken their place at a public meal, you must be content if you can get an answer to a question." Once the Attic *ephebeia* was tightened into the form described by the Aristotelian *Constitution of Athens* (42.3), attention was likewise given to decorum in dining. We may fairly detect there an institutionalized *tirocinium symposii,* a formalized *contubernium.*

Hercules at the crossroads—this scene does then indeed represent a dilemma that recurs throughout antiquity. The exact point in his development, which has set him thus at life's crucial fork, is clearly signalled (Xen. *Mem.* 2.1.21): "When Hercules was passing from boyhood to *hebe.*" He has reached the ephebic age, he has freedom of choice, and he must select between the joys of eating, drinking, and lovemaking on the one hand, and edifying toil on the other. This parable eloquently arrays concerns met elsewhere about the social formation of the new adult, he who could henceforth recline. According to the Epicurus of Diogenes Laertius (10.132), "it is not an unbroken succession of drinking-bouts and of revelry, not sexual love, not the enjoyment of fish and other delicacies of a luxurious table, which produce a pleasant life." But to such indulgences the philosopher will surely have been abandoned in the hostile tract "On Epicurus' Ephebic Service" (ibid. 10.4). His early adulthood no doubt matched Isaeus' (Philostr. *Vit. Soph.* 20): "As a *meirakion,* this sophist had devoted his time to pleasure, for he was the slave of eating and drinking, dressed himself in elegant stuffs, was often in love, and openly joined in drunken revels . . . But when he attained to full manhood he so transformed himself as to be thought to have become another person . . . He reduced his table, and left off his amours as though he had lost the eyes he had before." In the fourth century after Christ, when Athenian students were probably recognized to have attained adulthood by their middle teens after the Roman model, extravagance on the part of novice recliners was still a noted danger. Libanius confesses that one of the several attractions held out to him by Athens' riotous student life was the prospect of dissipating his resources and incurring debts through hosting dinner after dinner.[14] In Rome of the second century B.C. Sulpicius Gallus was subjected to this abuse from Scipio Aemilianus (A. Gellius, *Noct. Att.* 6.12.5):

> For one who daily perfumes himself and dresses before a mirror, whose eyebrows are trimmed, who walks abroad with beard plucked out and thighs made smooth, who at banquets as an *adulescentulus* has reclined in a long-sleeved tunic on the inner side of the couch with a lover, who is fond not only of wine but of men—does anyone doubt that he does what wantons commonly do?

Persius kept his reputation at the *convivium* pure through the protection of Cornutus' "Socratic" bosom; the allusion of course is to the reported purity of Socrates' relationship with Alcibiades. In fourth-century Rome the conduct of the young at banquets was still calling forth concern, for an enactment of A.D. 370 seeks to restrain students, who have travelled to the ancient capital for their education, from base associations and frequent attendance at unseasonable *convivia*: "We furthermore grant to you as prefect the authority that, if any student in the City should fail to conduct himself as the dignity of a liberal education demands, he shall be publicly flogged, immediately put on board a boat, expelled from the City and returned home."[15]

NOTES

1. *Ep.* 52.11–12. Unless specified otherwise, translations are from the editions of the Loeb Classical Library, with some adjustments.

2. See Diog. Laert. 8.19; Xen. *Mem.* 2.1.1.

3. The Greeks might claim that corruption came to them from the East, and in turn the Romans too could trace the origins of their decadence to points further east than mainland Greece; cf. Sall. *Bell. Cat.* 11.4–7. The passages listing Roman objections to Greek symposia are assembled by W. Kroll, *Studien zum Verständnis der röm. Lit.* (Stuttgart 1924), 2.

4. Sallust's Marius opposes the study of Greek-based oratory to the pursuit of Roman manliness (*Bell. Jugu.* 85.31–37). The notion of Greek depravity will also underlie the Elder Seneca's depiction of contemporary students of rhetoric as effeminate (*Controv.* 1 *Praef.* 8–10).

5. [Lucian] *Asinus* 48; Apul. *Met.* 10.17 in the text of D.S. Robertson (Paris 1965).

6. Columella *de Agricult.* 11.1.19; Petr. *Sat.* 64 at end; 68.4; cf. Xen. *Mem.* 2.1.15–16.

7. Cf. Sen. *Suas.* 7.13; Plin. *H.N.* 14.147; Dio 46.18.5.

8. Quint. *Inst. Or.* 2.2.3; Plin. *Ep.* 5.5.8.

9. P. Valette (ed. and trans.), *Apulée: Apologie*[2] (Paris 1960), 98.

10. Plutarch continues: "Did Lycurgus introduce this custom also, and bring boys to common meals that they might become accustomed to conduct themselves toward their pleasures, not in a brutish or disorderly way, but with discretion, since they had their elders as supervisors and spectators, as it were? No less important is the fact that the fathers themselves would also be more decorous and prudent in the presence of their sons; for 'where the old are shameless,' as Plato remarks, 'there the young must also needs be lost to all sense of shame'." Direct reflection appears here on the need for some kind of *tirocinium convivii*.

11. In the edition of J. Bellemore (ed. and trans.), *Nicolaus of Damascus: Life of Augustus* (Bristol 1984).

12. Sallust has already traced the moral corruption of Rome to tastes imported by Sulla's army from Asia (13.3): "Nay more, the passion which arose for lewdness, gluttony, and the other attendants of luxury was equally strong; men played the woman, women offered their chastity for sale." Does this give ground to suspect that Sallust's apparent fairness aims to damn?

13. Writing of the marriage feast of Livia and Augustus, Dio sheds this light upon the potential for corruption of behavior (48.44.3): "One of the prattling boys, such as women keep about them for their amusement, naked as a rule. . . . "

14. A.F. Norman (ed. and trans.), *Libanius' Autobiography* [Oration I] (Oxford 1965), 19. Sexual misconduct is not mentioned here. But when Libanius began his teaching career at Constantinople, he was accused of improper involvement with students (Eun. *Vit. Soph.* 495).

15. C. Pharr (trans.), *The Theodosian Code* (Princeton 1952), 14.9.1. Sexual misconduct is implied but not specified here.

Triclinium and Stibadium

Katherine M.D. Dunbabin

We are better informed about the physical environment of dining in classical antiquity than about almost any other activity. Written descriptions of dinners and symposia can be compared with illustrations, often detailed, in all the major media;[1] these in turn can be used to complement the archaeological record. In the ancient house, as well as in some public buildings, the dining room is one of the few whose function is often clearly indicated: by the layout of the room, by its decoration, or by its fittings. Naturally this is not always so; of course one could dine elsewhere than in a regularly appointed dining room. But any discussion must be based upon the numerous securely identifiable examples, where clear evidence exists that they were intended for dining.

The first contribution of archaeology is to illuminate the differences between Greek and Roman practice. In a luxurious Greek house, the *andron* complex is clearly marked off by its plan, and, in the most lavish examples, by the decoration of the floor. A good example is the House of the Mosaics at Eretria, dated to the early to mid-fourth century B.C. (fig. 1).[2] Here there are two clearly identifiable *andrones* (nos. 7 and 8–9) on the far side of the peristyle, firmly separated from the more private section of the house to the east. The more elaborate of the two (nos. 8–9) has a vestibule, with a pebble mosaic of sphinxes and panthers, followed by a room 4.68 m square, with a platform or trottoir around the edge, 0.95 m wide and raised 3 cm above the central area. Such a room, it has been calculated, could hold seven *klinai*, 1.85 m long, on the trottoir, starting from the off-center door.[3] A pebble mosaic in the vestibule and a panel at the entrance greet the guests as they enter. The central area is also decorated with a pebble mosaic with a frieze of griffins and Arimaspians and of fighting beasts, designed so as to offer a figured scene on each side to be enjoyed by the guests on the couches nearest to it. The larger room (no. 7) is 6.70 m square, with a similar trottoir around the edge, offering space for eleven *klinai*; the floor here is plainer, a simple pebble mosaic covering both trottoir and center, while the walls were decorated with painted stuccos.

The plan is that characteristic for Greek *andrones*, in both private and public architecture; it recurs in other houses at Eretria, with almost exactly identical dimensions.[4] At Olynthus, a standard-sized *andron* for seven couches with an anteroom, situated in the corner of the house next to the entrance, seems to have been a feature of the original layout of the houses in the new quarter of the town (fig. 2).[5] A similar plan is found on a larger scale in palaces of the late Classical and early Hellenistic periods as at Vergina or in the aristocratic houses of Pella.[6] It also characterizes many public dining rooms, from the fifth century B.C. onwards, such as those in the South Stoa of the Agora or the Pompeion at Athens (fig. 3); and it is found at sanctuaries with dining facilities such as the Asklepieion at Corinth or Troizen, or the sanctuary of Artemis at Brauron.[7] In several of these public rooms traces are preserved of more permanent fittings: cuttings for the couches in the raised trottoir, or actual stone couches, and solid stone tables in front of each couch. These permit reconstruction of the characteristic form of a dining room as having an uneven number of couches, usually seven, nine, eleven, or sometimes more, arranged anticlockwise around the wall, and averaging between 1.70 m and 1.90 m in length; a separate table for each couch; and an open space in the center of the room. Illustrations show normally one or two guests reclining per couch.[8]

In the Hellenistic period, the place of dining in private houses undergoes a change. At Delos, there is no sign of this type of nearly square *andron* separated from the main living rooms of the house. Instead, nearly all the houses of Delos, large or small, have one broad oblong room, larger than the rest, opening off one side of the court or peristyle; this room often gives access to two smaller rooms, either at the sides or back.[9] In the wealthiest houses, such as the House of the Trident or House of the Masks, these broad rooms are lavishly decorated, and their mosaic pavements are laid out with an ornamented central "carpet" and a plain band around the edge, corresponding to the trottoir in earlier *andro" (fig. 4).[10] Such rooms, therefore, clearly did serve as dining rooms, but they must have had other functions as well, since the doors opening onto the side or back rooms would have been blocked by the couches when they were laid out for dining. Moreover, they are not differentiated architecturally from similar rooms in smaller houses, which often form the only available living quarters. The change reflects a decline in the notion of the symposium as an activity requiring its own special setting, separate from the main living quarters of the house. In the richer houses at least, the tendency is now for the reception and entertainment of guests to dominate the layout of the house as a whole.[11]

With the Greek pattern may be contrasted the Roman fashion of the *triclinium*: three couches, each holding up to three diners in comfort, fitted closely together around a single central table, which may be round or rectangular (fig. 5). Numerous writers of the late Republic and early Empire attest to the standardization of the type and to the strict social rules that governed the order of seating at formal parties.[12] The many identifiable *triclinia* at Pompeii and Herculaneum confirm their picture. Although the movable couches, often of precious material, that were most commonly used, especially in the more luxurious settings, have seldom survived, cuttings in the walls occasionally attest to their location.[13] More informative are the rooms with permanent masonry couches, found fairly frequently at Pompeii; they are characteristic of public and semipublic settings but are found also in private houses. An example of the latter may be seen in the summer *triclinium* of the Casa del Moralista (III.4.2–3): the three flat couches run continuously around the walls; a single rectangular table stands between them, with a semicircular recess, presumably for the wine krater, in its fourth side. The room, with its black walls, is elegant but crowded, with very little space available for the servants.[14] A row of well-preserved *triclinia*, presumably serving a semipublic function, runs along two sides of a peristyle in the Portico dei Triclini in the *Pagus Maritimus*: they have masonry couches revetted at sides and front with white marble, a single round table in the center, and niches beneath the sides of the couches where objects could be stored. Like some of the garden *triclinia* to be considered shortly, they are equipped with pipes to permit jets of water to play in the center of the tables and to run along ledges at the front of the couches.[15] Less elegant is the arrangement in the Casa del Criptoportico (I.6.2–4).[16] Three sloping couches of masonry covered with red plaster run in a horseshoe around the walls, with higher *fulcra* at the two ends; the central couch is 4.41 m long, the other two 4.68 m. Along the front runs a ledge where cups could be put down, leaving only a small space free for access at the end of the *lectus imus*. Low benches run along the ends of the couches and the walls in front, where children or other inferior persons could sit. There is a single small round table between the couches, and a stand against the wall to the right, where the service for the wine could be set (figs. 6, 7).

In the absence of permanent couches of masonry, *triclinia* are frequently identifiable by their layout. Both wall-paintings and pavement design often distinguish clearly between the forepart of the room, for reception of the guests, service, and entertainment, and the inner part for the couches; and the pavement of this inner part may be divided into a more highly decorated center and a plainer surround.[17] Such clearly identifiable dining rooms at

Pompeii and the other Campanian towns are normally fairly small, about 6 m × 4 m maximum; they have room only for the one standard set of couches suitable for nine guests. Larger rooms exist but do not necessarily offer any more space for the *triclinium* itself. Thus two houses at Pompeii, the Casa del Labirinto (VI.11.9/10) and the Casa di Meleagro (VI.9.2), have rooms resembling the Corinthian *oeci* described by Vitruvius, with rows of columns along three sides separating the central area from a surrounding gallery; but the area between the columns available for the couches is no larger.[18] Other rooms are simply larger rectangles, without internal colonnades; the largest, in the Casa del Menandro (I.10.4), measures 11.50 m × 7.60 m, almost twice the usual size.[19] No indication is given here, however, of the layout of the couches, and the room may have served other functions beside dining. In general, it is seldom clear how the couches were laid out in these big rooms. Vitruvius speaks of Cyzicene *oeci* which could hold two *triclinia* facing each other, and of larger square *oeci* which could, in some unspecified way, hold four; in both cases he is speaking of a Greek custom.[20] We hear occasionally of banquets of twelve guests, like the notorious *cena dodekatheos* of Octavian, and there were fourteen, plus two latecomers, at Trimalchio's; but it seems that in the late Republic and early Empire it was not considered good form to entertain large numbers at a single *triclinium*.[21] Richer houses frequently have more than one dining room, scattered through appropriate locations in the house, suitable for different seasons (as Vitruvius recommends), for different occasions (more public or more private), or simply to provide variety: there is no one typical location.[22]

A common feature at Pompeii are the garden *triclinia*, for outdoor or semioutdoor dining in summer (fig. 8). An article published in 1950 listed about forty, to which subsequent research, and especially the excavations of W. Jashemski in gardens and vineyards, have added many more.[23] The majority are masonry couches, with fittings similar to those indoors, though traces survive also of wooden ones. They are set up on a terrace next to the house, in the peristyle, or in garden or vineyard under a pergola (fig. 9). Most are very simple, but a few are lavishly appointed and decorated.[24] Often there are special water effects, where the diners reclined with fountains splashing around them, or jets of water in the middle of the table.[25] Among the better preserved or more elegant examples may be cited that in the Casa dell'Efebo (I.7.10–12), with a nymphaeum fountain at the back and water running between the couches (figs. 10–12);[26] the *biclinium*, on the terrace of the so-called house of Loreius Tiburtinus (House of Octavius Quartio, II.2.2), where the guests must have taken their food from dishes floating in the basin in front;[27] and the *triclinium* grotto in the *praedia* of Julia Felix (II.4), with a waterfall down the back wall.[28]

The garden *triclinia* are not found only in private houses; many were apparently available for hire for public or semipublic festivities. Some are found in inns and taverns, where their provision for formal dining (that is, for reclining) contrasts with the simpler form of eating and drinking shop where one sat at table.[29] Others form settings for cult meals attached to temples, best exemplified at Pompeii by the double *triclinia* in front of the Temple of Dionysus.[30] *Triclinia* (and *biclinia*) are also found attached to tombs for memorial banquets, as in the tomb of Cn. Vibrius Saturninus at Pompeii, and frequently at Ostia.[31] In addition to such permanent *triclinia* it must always have been more common to set up movable equipment wherever one chose; but they serve as a reminder of the range of locations available for the celebration of banquets outside the house.

In the later centuries of the Empire, the basic *triclinium* layout continues to be clearly exemplified in both domestic and more public rooms for dining. At Ostia, for example, a row of masonry *triclinia* opens off the central courtyard of the Caseggiato dei Triclinii (I.12.1), identified as the headquarters of a *collegium*;[32] while in the Schola del Traiano (IV.5.15), of similar purpose, the main room on the central axis is marked out as a *triclinium* by the plan of its early third-century black-and-white mosaic.[33] But there is one important difference here from the Pompeiian dining rooms (at least from those whose function is indicated unmistakably by fittings or layout), and that is the scale. Although these rooms are still laid out for three continuous couches, they are no longer intended to have space for a maximum of nine guests, with a central table within the reach of all. The room in the Schola del Traiano measures 9.50 m × 8.50 m; the strip of mosaic for the couches is 1.50 m wide, but each side is ca. 5–6 m long, two or three times the length of a normal couch in Pompeii. I would guess that at least six diners, perhaps more, could be accommodated on each side; the notion that the ideal *convivium* is composed of no more than nine guests has clearly been abandoned. In this particular case, the semipublic nature of the building may be partly responsible for the change, since a *collegium* required more space for its members; but it is reflected in domestic architecture at this period too.

Masonry couches are rare in the houses of the High Empire;[34] it is most often the layout of the mosaic pavement that permits the identification of a room as a *triclinium*. Two typical forms may be distinguished. One is a U-shape: a central rectangular panel is surrounded on three sides by a rectilinear area for the couches. The second type is a T + U: as well as the U-shape for the couches, the entrance to the room is marked by the addition of a horizontal bar to the central panel, to provide more space here for service or entertainment. Minor variations can include marking off an area at the back of the couches, for service and access; and substituting two panels for the ends of the bar of the T, over which the couches can be extended if extra space is required without spoiling the design of the mosaic as a whole. These characteristic plans can be found in houses in almost every region of the Roman Empire except the northern provinces. They are freely adopted in the East, as numerous houses of the second and third centuries A.D. in Antioch demonstrate.[35] Among the clearest examples may be quoted the T + U design of the Atrium House and the House of the Triumph of Dionysus, with separate panels of figured decoration in the crossbar of the T and the upright shaft (fig. 13);[36] and the simpler U-shape, with a single central panel between the couches, in the House of Narcissus and the House of the Drinking Contest (fig. 14).[37] There is no trace at Antioch of the older Greek *andron* plan, nor of the Hellenistic broad room; the Atrium House, with its T + U mosaics, is generally regarded as one of the earliest houses at Antioch, possibly before the earthquake of A.D. 115.[38] By this date, therefore, it seems that Roman fashions of dining had been adopted in the Greek world, at least as far as the layout of the room was concerned.

The mosaics at Antioch are generally decorated with small figured panels, offering a single viewpoint. This raised certain problems for the designer, given the layout of the couches. Solutions vary: if there is a separate bar to the T, it usually faces the guests at their entrance. Other panels may be turned towards the principal guests on the central couch, as with the two panels at the end of the shaft in the Atrium House (fig. 13), or a single scene might be set to be best appreciated by the guests of honor. Many of the guests must have been confronted for much of the time, after the tables were removed, by the sight of a finely worked panel upside down or sideways; it does not seem that this was a matter of major concern, though there are a few experiments with scenes or figures oriented to give all the guests something to look at.[39] The subjects of the panels, on the other hand, are often chosen to be appropriate for the occasion: Dionysus is common, and so are scenes illustrating banquets or symposia, mythological and allegorical.

The North African provinces contain a large number of houses where *triclinia* are clearly and unmistakably indicated, frequently by their mosaics.[40] In a prosperous but remote town such as Volubilis, most of the rich houses in the newer section of the town have a large dominant room opening onto the peristyle, usually on its main axis. These often have a triple-bayed entrance, and a fountain or a special decoration is frequently placed beyond the portico of the peristyle. In several the floors are clearly marked with mosaics in the T + U layout. Two good examples are the House of Dionysus and the Seasons, and that of the Ephebe (figs. 15, 16).[41] In both houses the two ends of the bar of the T are marked off as separate panels, exactly corresponding to the breadth of the U-portion; if desired, the couches could be extended over these to give extra space for guests, without destroying the effect of the mosaic as a whole. The central part of the floor is composed of individual small compartments in which the figures are placed at different angles (a common method of composition in African mosaics); this makes it easier to distribute them so that all the diners have something to look at, though this rule is by no means always followed.

Another town where many of the houses have clearly identifiable *triclinia* is Thysdrus [El Djem]. In the House of the Months is a room with a T + U mosaic marking out the position of the couches; its irregular layout suggests that it was designed with a specific set of furnishings in mind (fig. 17).[42] The T-portion has a pattern whose compartments contain images of various forms of food: fish and fruit, game, birds, a lobster, vegetables, all carefully displayed before the eyes of the guests to whom similar delicacies are presumably to be served. Along the base of the couches runs a narrow strip, decorated with the debris of a meal: fish-bones, lobster claws, seashells, etc., just as they would be dropped on the floor by the diners during the meal. It is a late descendant of the tradition of the *asarotos oikos* mosaic, whose original was the famous work of Sosus of Pergamon described by Pliny; its use here is appropriate to its setting.[43] The room seems to have formed part of a complex that also contained a very much larger dining room, considerably earlier in date. This was a huge room, 16.50 m square, probably dominating a peristyle in front of it. A colonnade ran around three sides, resembling the Corinthian *oeci* described by Vitruvius.[44] The central area within the columns was marked out by a regular T + U mosaic to form a *triclinium* 13.20 m long and 10.30 m wide.[45] The fashion now is clearly for rooms as large as the resources of the patron would permit, marked out for one single set of couches, capable of holding up to three or four times the conventional number of nine guests recommended by earlier writers. Such numbers would have required a change in the method of serving, since the central space is much too wide for a single table; either the servants must have brought small individual tables to each guest, or a ledge must have run along the front of the couches, corresponding to the border on the mosaic here. The gallery behind the colonnade will have enabled guests to get to and from their places more easily, and perhaps provided space where slaves in attendance on the diners could stand, but many *triclinia* nearly as large as this have no gallery.[46]

A further African example of this type comes from the House of Neptune at Acholla, where two rooms are identifiable as *triclinia* (fig. 18).[47] On the main axis of the peristyle is a colonnaded *oecus-triclinium,* 11.20 m by 9.50 m, the area within the columns marked out with a T + U mosaic. It opens through three bays onto the peristyle, with fountains on the far side of the portico. On the south side of the peristyle is a much smaller *triclinium,* with a U-shaped pavement whose central area contains baskets of fruit and other *xenia*-motifs. Very clear here is the way in which the requirements of dining dominate the decoration of the house: the rooms are designed and laid out expressly for this purpose, and the subject matter of the mosaics frequently alludes to it. There can be little doubt that the owners of these houses see this as their most important social activity. There is a steady tendency in the later examples to expand the width of the bar of the T, presumably in order to provide more space for entertainment and service.[48] The attention paid to providing vistas onto the peristyle, with its fountains, and the wide-open doorways suggest that this area too may have been used for entertainment.

The plans I have been examining are characteristic of the second and third centuries A.D., but they do not disappear totally after that date. An example from Complutum [Alcalà de Henares] in Spain shows a similar *triclinium* plan in a house of the late fourth or early fifth century A.D., the Casa de Baco (figs. 19, 20).[49] The corridor leading to the *triclinium* has a mosaic showing a row of servants offering cups of wine to the guests; at the entrance to the *triclinium* is a panel with busts of the Seasons. The *triclinium* itself has a broad U-shaped design, with an asymmetrical space for the couches, longer on the right than the left. A central rectangle shows Dionysiac scenes: a drunken Dionysus, and satyrs treading the grapes, all, surprisingly, facing away from the guests on the couches, though they would greet them on entry. Opposite is a small apse: not, apparently, a fountain, but perhaps intended to hold the krater for the wine.

In general, however, literary sources and figured representations alike attest to a different fashion for dining in late antiquity: the semicircular *sigma*-couch or *stibadium.*[50] Rooms designed for dining in this fashion can also frequently be identified by the layout of the mosaics. In the villa at Dargoleja in Spain, for instance, a rectangular room had the mosaic divided into two portions; the front half is richly decorated, the back marked out with a broad semicircle and a smaller semicircle at its center: space for the couch and the table (fig. 21).[51] Proof of the use for dining of rooms marked out in this way comes from the house called the Villa of the Falconer in Argos, where the design marks not only the semicircle but also the seven individual wedge-shaped segments into which the couch was divided (fig. 22).[52] Immediately in front of the space for the couch was a panel with a Dionysiac *thiasos,* turned towards the diners for their entertainment. Also marked on the mosaic is the semicircular table, with a plate bearing fish on it. This helps to clarify the much-discussed question of the function of the numerous tables of this shape that have been found in both Christian and secular contexts from the fourth century onward, including several recently found *in situ* in the early Byzantine houses of Apamea.[53] They are still sometimes taken to be invariably a sign of Christian activity, used as altar tables or tables for the *agape.* Thus, one found in the Omega House in Athens has been used to argue that it indicates Christian activity in a house that previously belonged to a philosopher.[54] But the Argos mosaic and the Apamea finds prove conclusively that such tables could serve as normal secular dining tables with a *sigma*-couch.

Rooms might also be designed with an apse to hold the *sigma*-couch, leaving a conveniently large space in front for the servants and entertainers. Here too there is a problem with the definite identification of such rooms, since apses can serve so many functions in later Roman architecture. There has been a tendency to identify many such rooms as Christian chapels; for example, a building in Histria with such a room was considered by many to be the bishop's palace, with the apse serving as a *synthronon* for the seats for the clergy.[55] But Noel Duval has shown conclusively that it should be seen as the raised support for a *stibadium* couch in an ordinary domestic house, and he has argued the same for many similar rooms previously misinterpreted.[56] The mosaics again are often helpful in identifying apses used for dining, marking out the space for the couch and showing appropriate themes in the space left free. An example can be seen in another building whose function has been disputed, the Edifice des Saisons at Sufetula [Sbeitla] in Tunisia: off the peristyle, in the traditional position for a *triclinium,* opens a big apsidal room flanked by a pair of nymphaea on either side. The apse (a later addition) was slightly raised, and the greater part marked out with a semicircle in a repetitive pattern leaving a smaller semicircle at its center for the table; across the chord of the apse runs a figured band that includes the Seasons with their gifts. The room in front of the apse is nearly nine meters square.[57]

The *sigma*-couch could not hold as many guests as some of the huge *triclinia* looked at above. The couch in the Villa of the Falconer at Argos is marked into seven segments, presumably one per guest (fig. 22);[58] some of the other rooms identifiable as designed for *stibadia* offer slightly more space but nothing comparable to the largest of the *triclinia*.[59] Those who wished to give larger parties than a single *sigma* would hold might, however, construct for themselves a room with three apses, a triconch;[60] a good example is in the so-called Palace of Theodoric at Ravenna, where an inscription on the mosaic in the central square invites the guests to take the fruits of the Seasons.[61] For a small party, one presumably set up the *sigma* in one apse alone; for a larger one all three could be used. The ultimate luxury must be the rare multiconch rooms, best seen in the Maison de Bacchus at Cuicul [Djemila] in Numidia (fig. 23).[62] This house already possessed a large colonnaded *oecus-triclinium;* at a later stage, a room with seven apses was added alongside it. This room is nearly 27 m long, with a vestibule in front; the apses are over 4 m in diameter, with a larger one at the back. Evidence of its use for dining is given by the little basins for water at the entrance and flanking the rear apse, and by the provision of drains to allow the floor to be flushed down after the meal; in these drains, according to evidence unfortunately never reported in detail, the excavators found large quantities of broken glass.[63] A room of this size would hold banquets for about fifty guests, magnificent occasions indeed: the mosaic in the central space, which shows hunting and amphitheater scenes, suggests a link with the celebration of official spectacles in the city.

By the fourth and fifth century, there is no doubt that, despite the occasional persistence of the *triclinium* layout, the fashion for the curving *sigma*-couch had prevailed.[64] A few rooms manifestly designed for its use can be dated earlier. Best known is the House of the Buffet Supper in Antioch (figs. 24, 25).[65] This is paved with a mosaic, dated by Levi to the Severan period, which follows the curving shape of the couch. Within the outer strip is a horseshoe-shaped area, set with the various provisions for the meal. A display of food in silver dishes, interspersed with garlands, loaves of bread, and drinking vessels, is spread out in front of the guests in the order in which it would be served: appetizers of eggs, artichokes, and pigs' trotters, a fish, a ham, at least two types of fowl, and a cylindrical cake. In the center is a circle that marks the position of the table, with a scene of Ganymede serving drink to the eagle; when the guests progressed to drinking, the table would be removed and the mosaic with its appropriate theme revealed. Beyond the semicircle is a panel containing the krater for the wine, among peacocks, *putti* with birds, and other allusions to luxury. The actual use of the room is slightly problematic: originally apsidal, following the curve of the mosaic, it was later altered through the addition of an extra rectangular section at the back. This might imply that a new owner wished to use it with rectangular couches rather than a *sigma*, or that extra space was required for some purpose behind the couch.

Another early example is the mosaic of an apsidal room from Sainte-Colombe, Vienne (figs. 26, 27).[66] The large rectangular part of the room is decorated with a continuous vine scroll, in the center of which Lycurgus is fighting with the vine. The scroll continues around the curve of the apse, within which is a group of Dionysiac figures reclining on cushions, drinking and making music. They surely echo the actual layout of the room: real drinkers must have reclined above them, similarly looking out into the activities in the main part of the room. The report of the excavation mentions the remains of a plinth surrounding the mosaic, which might suggest the base of a platform for the couch, though the information is not precise enough to be certain. Lancha suggests a late second-century date for the mosaic on the basis of style, though this criterion is difficult to apply to a unique work such as this; she believes also that the houses of this quarter of Vienne were destroyed by a flood ca. A.D. 220, and that the activity of the Vienne mosaic workshops came to an end fairly soon afterwards, which would give it a more definite *terminus ante quem*.[67]

This raises the question of the date at which the fashion for the curving *sigma* couch was introduced. Although sometimes taken as characteristic of late antiquity—even as if it were specifically Christian—it is undoubtedly much older: Martial twice refers to it unmistakably[68] while the Younger Pliny describes at length the *stibadium* in his Tuscan villa.[69] Its introduction is often associated with the fashion for the round tables of expensive citron wood that came in at the end of the Republic, and the older handbooks write as if, by the time of Martial or soon after, it had driven out the traditional fashion for rectilinear *triclinia*.[70] The archaeological evidence studied above shows this conclusion to be demonstrably not true: rectilinear *triclinia* continued to be the predominant form, both in Italy and the provinces, well into the third century A.D. A round table in any case could be—and often was—used with a regular *triclinium*. On the other hand, the *Historia Augusta*'s life of Elagabalus (not a very reliable source), claims that Elagabalus was the first to lay out a *sigma* on the ground, not on couches;[71] and this seems at variance with the literary evidence for the earlier existence of the *sigma*. If it deserves any credence at all, it may mean nothing more than that he had the actual cushions placed on the ground, since it occurs in the context of his amusing habit of releasing the air from inflated cushions while his guests were reclining on them.

Despite the literary evidence for the use of the *sigma* in the first century A.D., to the best of my knowledge no rooms are marked out specifically for a *sigma* couch before the late second or beginning of the third century.[72] In the face of the large quantity of evidence for regular *triclinia* all through this period, I conclude that the fashion for *sigma*s was not strong enough before this date to justify the permanent decoration of a dining room in this way. It is possible that we should see a contrast here between the fashions adopted by Martial and his smart set at Rome, and normal middle-class habits in the provinces; but there may also be another explanation for the discrepancy. Clear earlier evidence does indeed exist for semicircular arrangements for dining in the open air. The Younger Pliny describes the marble *stibadium* in his Tuscan villa: it was outdoors, under a vine pergola, with water gushing around it, and the food in little dishes floating on the basin in front or balanced on the rim.[73] The watery part of this corresponds to some of the fountain *triclinia* in Pompeii discussed above, but the majority of these were rectilinear. However, the shape also has at least one parallel there: among the outdoor garden *triclinia,* one is known with a semicircular couch of masonry, in House VIII.3.15 (fig. 8).[74] A few decades after Pliny, the form was used for one of the grandest of all open-air *stibadia* in the Serapeum of Hadrian's Villa at Tivoli; the support for the couch circles the curve of the apse, with water splashing all round and a basin in front. For larger occasions, as Ricotti has shown, a second *stibadium* could be set on the ground within the curve of the masonry couch, again with a small basin in front.[75]

The suggestion that the *stibadium*-form may be primarily intended for outdoor banquets fits in fact with much of the figured evidence. On numerous works, banqueters are seen reclining out of doors on a semicircular cushion, often with an awning hanging from trees. They may be hunters, as on the mosaic of the Small Hunt at Piazza Armerina,[76] or the silver plate from Cesena;[77] a similar setting is used for the rustic feast, for instance on a Coptic textile in the Brooklyn Museum (fig. 28).[78] In the Ilias Ambrosiana, Greek and Trojan warriors recline on *stibadia* on the ground, outside their tents or in a bare landscape.[79] The theme is used in funerary painting for the funerary banquet or the banquet in paradise: in a tomb-painting from Rome the diners recline at a *sigma*-couch under a vine pergola,[80] while one of the paintings in the Hypogaeum of Vibia shows the Banquet of the Blessed reclining on a cushion set among bushes and flowers (fig. 29).[81] It is also fairly frequent on sarcophagus lids, where it occurs in several contexts. On sarcophagi with the myth of Meleager from about A.D. 150 onwards, it is used for the meal after the Calydonian hunt; from here it passes to the nonmythological hunting sarcophagi, while others use it for bucolic scenes of rustic feasts (fig. 30).[82] The earlier versions leave no doubt that the scene takes place in the open air, with the diners sometimes reclining directly on the rocky ground; later a more regular *sigma*-cushion appears, but there are still often allusions to a natural setting, such as outcrops of rock or a *parapetasma* hanging from trees. The Christians in turn adopt the theme of the *stibadium* banquet in both catacomb painting and sarcophagi, sometimes with clear indications of an outdoor setting.[83]

But not all the scenes from late antiquity that show diners on *sigma* couches take place in the open air. Some are doubtless intended to take place indoors, in the rooms specially designed for this use. For instance, a mosaic from Ephesus shows four revellers reclining on cushions spread on a built-up couch, with no allusion to the open air. In front is a huge silver krater and a hot-water container, and a couple of tiny animals nibble at the remains of the food. The mosaic decorates an apsidal space set into one wing of an older peristyle; this is surely designed for dining.[84] Later, illustrations of luxurious banquets in fifth- and sixth-century manuscripts show the guests reclining on a *sigma*-couch in an architectural setting: Dido and Aeneas, in the *Vergilius Romanus,* or Pharaoh and his guests in the Vienna *Genesis.*[85]

By the late Empire, therefore, illustrations show the *sigma*-form in use both for outdoor meals, sophisticated or simple, and for regular indoor dining in a room specially appointed. But paintings from Pompeii and the early Empire suggest that there may still have been a clear distinction in the fashions there. Some paintings show, more or less clearly, banquets with rectilinear couches, which take place apparently in regular *triclinia.* Three paintings in the Casa del Triclinio (V.2.4) actually decorated a *triclinium.*[86] On one, a drunken guest leans over and vomits, while another sits to have his shoes removed. The background here is certainly an indoor scene; the guests recline on three straight-sided couches, though the painter has trouble with the perspective (fig. 31). The second, where the drinking party is accompanied by extracts from the guests' conversation, takes place under hangings, but since there is no other indication of exterior setting, these are likely to be indoor tapestries, rather than awnings against the sun. The couches are even less clearly rendered here, but a sharp edge beneath the elbow of the right-hand guest, over which the drapery hangs in folds, suggests that here too separate straight-sided couches are intended. There are also several examples of paintings from Pompeii where the diners recline in a semicircle, and I believe these all to be outdoor scenes. One is known only from an engraving, and the details may not be entirely reliable.

It shows a regular *sigma*-couch and a table; the setting is uncertain, but the light structure around the diners suggests a pergola outdoors, rather than indoor architecture.[87] More often we see an obvious outdoor picnic, with the figures on a cushion on the ground and an awning hanging from trees. Erotes and Psyches appear as the actors in several such scenes from the House of M. Lucretius (IX.3.5), with statues of Dionysus or of Psyche herself behind them (fig. 32).[88] Slightly more formal is the banquet painted in the Tomb of Vestorius Priscus: the guests recline on a regular *sigma*-couch with a table in front of them, but the scene is set in the open air, with a *velum* above, peacocks on pedestals at the sides, and flowers and grass in front.[89] This type of picnic occurs most often as a feature of rural scenes and friezes, especially of those with Egyptianizing elements; the actors are often pygmies (fig. 33).[90] In a frieze that decorated the real outdoor *triclinium* of the Casa dell'Efebo (I.7.10–12), there are two groups in the midst of a landscape with Nilotic elements: in one eight guests (?pygmy Ethiopians) recline on a couch with a fountain basin replacing the table; in the other there are five guests on a cushion under a pergola, again with a fountain in front of them (fig. 34).[91] From Rome come two paintings that appear to be the earliest of the genre, probably from early in the reign of Augustus. In the Columbarium of the Villa Pamphili a group of figures lies on the ground in a semicircle in the open air;[92] in the yellow frieze in the Casa di Livia groups reclining in an approximate semicircle under a *velum* can just be made out in two places.[93]

These last examples suggest an association of the *stibadium* in its early form with popular festivals, but the fashion was not confined to such occasions. Among all the descriptions of luxurious dining from the late Republic, there is one that may offer an early example of the use of the *stibadium* in a permanent architectural form: Varro's aviary at Casinum.[94] The guests dined in the *tholos,* between the colonnades of the aviary; within it was a little lake, with a revolving table for the food set on a column on a little island at its center. The guests must have reclined in a semicircle around the edge of the lake, where the table was within their reach.

The *stibadium* may therefore be taken as originally a fashion for outdoor banquets, derived at first from the numerous religious festivals in the Roman, and earlier in the Greek world, which called for outdoor feasting. This is indeed a natural conclusion from its derivation from the Greek *stibades,* whose literal meaning is the leaves or foliage on which the participants at such feasts reclined, originally just strewn over the ground or stuffed into a mattress or cushions.[95] The original form of such feasts would have involved a simple, apparently impromptu setting, but growing luxury already in the Hellenistic period required an ever-more complex provision of furnishings and of special places to dine. Varro's description, undoubtedly under Hellenistic influence, shows how thoroughly such picnics in the late Republic, their original religious content vanished or changed, had become an opportunity for the display of wealth and luxury, while still retaining some of the associations of the simple outdoor meal on cushions set on the ground.[96] Such feasts were particularly associated with Dionysus, although not confined to his worship; and the traditional imagery of the primitive celebration is retained for scenes of the Dionysiac feast on sarcophagus lids as late as the second and early third century A.D. The revellers recline spread out in a row on the rocky ground, sometimes with only an animal skin beneath them (fig. 35).[97] In some of the early paintings of outdoor symposia, the cushions are spread rather irregularly over the ground rather than forming the single continuous mattress standard in later representations; but the tendency for the guests, if there were more than two or three, to arrange themselves in a semicircle would have been natural. It is not clear when the curved couch first came to be used indoors, although perhaps the *cenatio rotunda* of the Domus Aurea is relevant here.[98] Martial's references do not point explicitly to indoor celebrations rather than to outdoor parties, though the *sigma* inlaid with tortoiseshell of 14.87 would be more appropriate for indoor use. There still remains a gap, however, between these references and the definite testimony to the indoor use of the *sigma* provided by the representations in art and by the rooms specially designed for it: as I have shown, there is no unambiguous testimony for this use before the beginning of the third century.

It is, however, possible to conjecture why the *sigma* came to be preferred for indoor architecture. One reason is likely to have been that it left a wide space open in the room in front, which could be used for the entertainment. In the traditional *triclinium,* despite the steady tendencies to expand the bar of the T in front of the couches and to widen the distance in the center between them, the space must always have been somewhat cramped. The wide semicircle of the *sigma,* especially when it was placed in an apse, left the main area of the room free in front; in the triconches too, all three couches alike looked out onto the central square. Another reason for the adoption of the *sigma* may have been that the conventions for such feasts were originally more relaxed than those for the formal Roman dinner party with its traditional *triclinium* and strict order of precedence in seating, and the *sigma* therefore recommended itself for less formal occasions. But the *sigma* subsequently developed its own order of precedence: at first the middle position may have been the more honorable, while by the late Empire the guest of honor reclined *in cornu dextro;*[99] either position would have offered a better view of the entertainment than the traditional *triclinium.* There is no trace left in these later *stibadia* of the informality associated with the outdoor feast; the *sigma* has become the setting for formal and grandiose banquets, a symbol of traditional luxury.

But customs in the late Empire were beginning to change. A late fourth-century mosaic from Carthage illustrates a banquet where the participants, instead of reclining, sit upright on high-backed benches before long rectangular tables (fig. 36).[100] Sitting at table had long been the normal practice for those of inferior social position, and in taverns;[101] but the mosaic shows a rich and formal dinner. Parts of seven benches are preserved; there may originally have been eight, with three guests at each. Numerous well-dressed servants bring food and drink; musicians and dancers entertain the guests. It may well represent an *epulum* given by the patron to a *collegium* or similar group.[102] It is clear therefore that there is no hint of social inferiority implied here by the seated position of the diners; the thousand-year-old custom of reclining, to which many aristocrats in their luxurious villas would continue to cling for many years yet,[103] was ceasing to be regarded as a necessity for an occasion such as this.[104]

NOTES

The following abbreviations are used:

Colloque Apamée 1980: J. Balty, ed., *Actes du Colloque Apamée de Syrie. Aspects de l'architecture domestique d'Apamée, Brussels 1980* (Brussels 1984).

Levi (1947): D. Levi, *Antioch Mosaic Pavements* (Princeton 1947).

Marquardt-Mau (1886): J. Marquardt, *Das Privatleben der Römer* (4th ed. rev. A. Mau, Leipzig 1886).

Reinach *RPGR* (1922): S. Reinach, *Répertoire des Peintures Grecques et Romaines* (Paris 1922).

Salza Prina Ricotti (1987): E. Salza Prina Ricotti, "The Importance of Water in Roman Garden *triclinia,*" in E.B. MacDougall, ed., *Ancient Roman Villa Gardens,* Dumbarton Oaks Colloquia on the History of Landscape Architecture 10 (Washington, D.C. 1987), 137–84.

Soprano (1950): P. Soprano, "I triclini all'aperto di Pompei," in *Pompeiana* (Naples 1950), 288–310.

Spinazzola (1953): V. Spinazzola, *Pompei alla luce degli scavi nuovi di via dell'Abbondanza* (Rome 1953).

1. E.g., B. Fehr, *Orientalische und griechische Gelage* (Bonn 1971); J.-M. Dentzer, *Le Motif du banquet couché dans le Proche-Orient et le monde grec du VIIe au IVe siècle avant J.-C.* (Rome 1982); R. Hurschmann, *Symposienszenen auf unteritalischen Vasen* (Würzburg 1985); S. De Marinis, *La Tipologia del banchetto*

nell'arte etrusca arcaica (Rome 1961). No comparable study exists of the iconography of banqueting scenes in Roman art.

2. P. Ducrey and I. Metzger, "La Maison aux mosaiques à Erétrie," *AntK* 22, 1979, 1, 3–21, pls. 1–7; K. Reber, "Zur architektonischen Gestaltung der *Androñes* in den Häusern von Eretria," *AntK* 32, 1989, 1, 3–7.

3. Cf. Ducrey, op. cit. (above note 2), 6, for these and the following measurements.

4. Ducrey, op. cit. (above note 2), 6; P. Auberson and K. Schefold, *Führer durch Eretria* (Bern 1972), 84–96.

5. D.M. Robinson and J.W. Graham, *Excavations at Olynthus 8, The Hellenic House* (Baltimore 1938), 171–85, listing twenty-nine identifiable examples at Olynthus as well as references to examples elsewhere in the Greek world; W. Hoepfner and E.-L. Schwandner, *Haus und Stadt im klassischen Griechenland,* Wohnen in der klassischen Polis I (Munich 1986), 43–74, distinguishing the original plans from later developments in the fourth century. Cf. also ibid., 108–12, 178–79, 202, on *andrones* at Kassope, Priene, and Abdera.

6. Vergina: M. Andronikos, *Vergina. The Prehistoric Necropolis and the Hellenistic Palace,* SIMA 13 (Lund 1964), 6–7, fig. 10. Pella: Ch. Makaronas, *ArchDelt* 16 A, 1960, 72–83; H. Lauter, "Les éléments de la *regia* hellénistique," in E. Lévy, ed., *Le Système palatial en Orient, en Grèce et à Rome,* Actes du Colloque de Strasbourg, 1985 (Leiden 1987), 345–55.

7. Ch. Börker, *Festbankett und griechische Architektur,* Xenia 4 (Konstanz 1983), with further refs.; esp. 12–13 with notes for details of dimensions and remains of fittings. Recent bibliography on *hestiatoria* in R. Etienne and J.-P. Braun, *Ténos I. Le Sanctuaire de Poseidon et d'Amphitrite* (Paris 1986), 165–70.

8. Cf. Plato *Symp.* 175C, and 213A-B, where Alcibiades squeezes onto the couch between Agathon and Socrates. Hoepfner and Schwandner, op. cit. (above note 5), 178–79, identify the standard *andron* in Priene as having space for only three *klinai,* slightly above the usual size. Cf. also E. McCartney, "The Couch as a Unit of Measurement," *CPh* 29, 1934, 30–35, with refs.

9. Cf. J. Chamonard, *Délos VIII. Le Quartier du Théâtre* (Paris 1922), 1, 169–74; C. Krause, "Grundformen des griechischen Pastashauses," *AA* 1977, 173–79. In the modern literature these broad rooms are usually referred to as *oeci,* a term I have avoided, except where there is written testimony to its use, because of its potential for confusion.

10. Chamonard, op. cit. (above note 9), 171, pl. XIII; id., *Délos XIV. Les Mosaiques de la Maison des Masques* (Paris 1933). The Maison des Masques, with its two "broad rooms" on either side of the peristyle as well as the large one on the central axis, is very untypical in plan, and is perhaps not to be seen as an ordinary private house.

11. Krause, op. cit. (above note 9), 173; Hoepfner and Schwandner, op. cit. (above note 5), 244–45. Unlike Krause, who believes that in smaller houses the

whole family must have used these rooms as living quarters, Hoepfner and Schwandner argue that they form specifically the men's quarters (reflecting a growing eastern
influence), while the women must have used the upper stories and the courtyards.

12. Cf. Marquardt-Mau (1886) I, 302–6; A. Mau, s.v. *Convivium, RE* IV
(1901), 1201–8; A. Hug, *RE* 7A (1948), 92–101, s.v. *Triclinium*.

13. E.g., couch from *triclinium* in House IV.2.18: J. Overbeck and A. Mau,
Pompeji in seinen Gebäuden, Alterthümern und Kunstwerken[4] (Leipzig 1884), 426–
28, fig. 228; A. Mau, *Pompeji in Leben und Kunst*[2] (Leipzig 1908), 389–90, fig.
206. Cuttings for couches in the walls of a room in the Casa dei Dioscuri (IV.9.6/
7): L. Richardson, *Pompeii: The Casa dei Dioscuri and Its Painters* (*MAAR* 23,
1955), 46–48. Cuttings and fragments of the feet of couches in the Casa dell'Efebo
(I.7.10–12): A. Maiuri, *NSc* 1927, 45–49, 79–80. Others: H. Thédenat, *Pompéi*
(Paris 1910), 80.

14. Spinazzola (1953), II, 750–56, figs. 731–32.

15. O. Elia, "Il portico dei Triclini del Pagus Maritimus di Pompei," *BdA* 46,
1961, 200–11; K. Schauenburg, "Zur 'Portikus der Triklinien' am Pagus maritimus
bei Pompeji," *Gymnasium* 69, 1962, 521–29. They can be dated to shortly before
A.D. 79.

16. Soprano (1950), 294–95, no. 4; Spinazzola (1953), I, 121–22, 442–45, figs.
149, 499.

17. Cf. A. Barbet, *La Peinture murale romaine: les styles décoratifs pompéiens*
(Paris 1985), 66–70: a normal division in Second Style *triclinia* of one-third for the
forepart of the room and two-thirds for the dining area; ibid., 130–35: more uniform
decoration in the Third Style, but with a system of bipartition into zones persisting,
and predominating in the Fourth Style. The design of the floor may have a small
panel or *emblema* at the center of the couch area: cf. Thédenat, op. cit. (above
note 13), 80. Few examples are found of the type of T-shape decor common on
later *triclinium* mosaics (below, 125–26), but there is one in *signinum* in the Casa
di Cerere (I,9,13): Barbet, op. cit., 114, fig. 70. In the *triclinium* of the Casa
dell'Efebo (I.7.10–12), a T-shaped pavement of *opus sectile* has an *emblema* of
much finer workmanship in the center of the bar of the T, between the couches:
Maiuri, *NSc* 1927, 45–46, fig. 20; this combines the two systems of floor design
(fig. 10).

18. Vitr. 6.3.8; A. Maiuri, "Gli *oeci* vitruviani in Palladio e nella casa pompeiana
ed ercolanese," *Palladio* 2, 1952, 1–8. Tetrastyle *oecus* in Casa delle Nozze d'Argento
(V.2.1), with vaulted ceiling over central portion of dining area: ibid., 2–3. The
overall measurements are: Casa del Laberinto, 6.70 m × 6.80 m; Casa del Meleagro,
6.57 m × 5.82 m; Casa delle Nozze d'Argento, 10.75 m × 5.28 m; but in all
three rooms the area between the columns allows little more than ca. 4 m × 3.5
m for the couches.

19. A. Maiuri, *La Casa del Menandro e il suo tesoro di argenteria* (Rome 1933),
168–75. B. Tamm, *Auditorium and Palatium* (Lund 1963), 144, points to the
similarity of the room to a basilica, and believes it to have been used for meetings.

20. Vitr. 6.3.10; 6.7.3. Richardson, op. cit. (above note 13), 63–65 identifies as

a Cyzicene *oecus* almost exactly corresponding to Vitruvius' description the big room (9 m × 7.5 m) at the east end of the great peristyle in the Casa dei Dioscuri; this could have held two *triclinia* facing one another, but looks as if it were intended for one, facing out onto the portico of the peristyle. See A. Wallace-Hadrill, "The Social Structure of the Roman House," *BSR* 56, 1988, 59–64, 67–68, on the difficulties of pinning down the uses of such rooms, and their semipublic nature.

21. Suet. *Aug.* 70.1; Petr. *Sat.* 31 with Friedländer's note ad loc. Cf. Cic. *In Pis.* 67 (five and more packed on a couch, as a sign of Piso's lack of taste), and *Ad Att.* 13.52.2 (Caesar's entourage entertained at three separate *triclinia:* but we are not told how many there were). Mau, *BdI* 1883, 80, reports a room at Pompeii with space for twelve guests but does not give measurements.

22. Vitr. 6.4.2; also Var. *De L.L.* 5.162. Cf. Wallace-Hadrill, op. cit. (above note 20), 90–94; and 93, n. 147, his arguments against the theory of L. Richardson, *Pompeii. An Architectural History* (Baltimore-London 1988), 157–58, who identifies as "ladies' dining-rooms" a series of rooms with alcoves alongside the regular *triclinia*. Wallace-Hadrill, much more plausibly, sees these rooms as *cubicula*.

23. Soprano (1950), 288–310; W. Jashemski, *The Gardens of Pompeii* (New Rochelle 1979), 89–97, 215–16, 230–31, 243–44, 247, 253, and 346 n. 1, listing those discovered since Soprano, to a total of fifty-six. Cf. also P. Zanker, "Die Villa als Vorbild des späteren pompejanischen Wohngeschmacks," *JdI* 94, 1979, 498–502.

24. Extra fittings include a step for ascending the couch, a seat for children or inferiors, bases for wine jugs and so forth, a ledge along the front, and niches for storage; a base in the Casa dell'Efebo is assumed to have held the statue of an ephebe with candelabra for dining after dark, which was found elsewhere in the house: references all in Soprano (1950).

25. Salza Prina Ricotti (1987), 169–72. L. Richardson, "Water *Triclinia* and *Biclinia* in Pompeii," in R. Curtis, ed., *Studia Pompeiana et Classica in Honor of Wilhelmina Jashemski* I (New Rochelle 1988), 305–12, includes an unconvincing attempt to query whether some of these, notably the *triclinium* of the Casa dell'Efebo and the *biclinium* in the "House of Loreius Tiburtinus," were actually used for dining; his similar earlier query (*Pompeii,* op. cit., above note 22, 295) about the *triclinium*-grotto in the *Praedia* of Julia Felix, appears now to have been withdrawn. It is indeed likely that many of these *triclinia* served principally for drinking rather than eating, but to claim that they cannot have been used for dining underrates the resourcefulness of the slaves in serving food and the Romans' evident propensity for dining damply. The suggestion that they may have been seen primarily as a "new and interesting form of fountain" is very implausible.

26. Maiuri, *NSc* 1927, 52–61; Soprano (1950), 295–96, no. 5, fig. 31; Jashemski, op. cit. (above note 23), 92–93; Zanker, op. cit. (above note 23), 500–2.

27. Soprano (1950), 305–6, no. 25; Spinazzola (1953), I, 404, figs. 458–59; E. Salza Prina Ricotti, "Forme speciali di triclini," *Cronache Pompeiane* 5, 1979, 104–30; ead. (1987), 169–72, quoting parallels with Pliny's description of his Tuscan *stibadium* (below notes 69, 73); Zanker, op. cit. (above note 23), 471–80.

28. F. Rakob, "Ein Grottentriklinium in Pompeji," *RömMitt* 71, 1964, 182–94;

Salza Prina Ricotti (1987), 172–73. A very similar water *triclinium* has been discovered in the House of the Wedding of Alexander (Pompeii VI, Ins. Occid. 39–41): W. Jashemski, in E.B. MacDougall, ed., *Ancient Roman Villa Gardens* (Washington, D.C. 1987), 74–75, fig. 46.

29. E.g., J. Packer, "Inns at Pompeii," *Cronache Pompeiane* 4, 1978, 12–24, figs. 5, 8; Jashemski, op. cit. (above note 23), 167–80. At least part of the dining facilities in the *Praedia* of Julia Felix was available for the public (above note 28); the *triclinium* in the Casa del Criptoportico appears to have been designed for public use in the last phase of the house: Spinazzola (1953), I, 121–22. For sitting in taverns, cf. T. Kleberg, *Hôtels, restaurants et cabarets dans l'antiquité romaine* (Uppsala 1957), 114–15; Packer, op. cit. 49, with refs.

30. O. Elia and G.P. Carratelli, "Il santuario dionisiaco di Pompei," *PP* 188–89, 1979, 442–81.

31. Soprano (1950), 304, no. 21; V. Kockel, *Die Grabbauten vor dem Herkulaner Tor in Pompeji* (Mainz am Rhein 1983), 40, 109–11, pl. 31. Ostia: G. Calza, *La necropoli del porto di Roma nell'Isola Sacra* (Rome 1940), 56, fig. 16; 69, fig. 21; M. Floriani Squarciapino, *Scavi di Ostia III.1, Le necropoli* (Rome 1958), 96, 117–27.

32. G. Becatti, in G. Calza, ed., *Scavi di Ostia I, Topografia generale* (Rome 1953), 132: seat of the *fabri tignuari,* built ca. A.D. 119–20; G. Hermansen, *Ostia. Aspects of Roman City Life* (Edmonton 1981), 62–63, fig. 12.

33. G. Becatti, *Scavi di Ostia IV, Mosaici e Pavimenti marmorei* (Rome 1961), 199–201, no. 379, pl. LXXXVIII; Hermansen, op. cit. (above note 32), 71–74, suggesting that it may have been the seat of the *navicularii.*

34. Buildings with permanent masonry *triclinia* seem to be characteristic of meeting houses for dining clubs and similar groups. In addition to the Caseggiato dei Triclinii in Ostia (above note 32), compare a building in Hadrumetum [Sousse] in Tunisia, with a row of three *triclinia* down each side and a big one in the center, all paved with mosaics typical of the early second century A.D.: A. Ennabli, "Maison aux banquettes ou à banquets à Sousse," *La Mosaique Gréco-Romaine* II, Colloque Vienne 1971 (Paris 1975), 103–18, pls. XXXVII–XLII.

35. R. Stillwell, "Houses of Antioch," *DOP* 15, 1961, 47–57; J. Lassus, "Sur les maisons d'Antioche," *Colloque Apamée 1980,* 361–72. Stillwell includes a number of examples where the floor is divided into two rectangular panels of unequal size, without space for the normal arrangement of three couches: these should probably not be classified as *triclinia.* Several seem rather to be *cubicula,* while others may be designed for the semicircular *sigma*-couch (below, note 50).

36. Levi (1947), 15–25, figs. 1–2, pls. I–II; 91–100, figs. 36–38; F. Baratte, *Catalogue des mosaiques romaines et paléochrétiennes du musée du Louvre* (Paris 1978), 87–92, no. 43, figs. 83–85. For the date of the Atrium House, see below, note 38; the House of the Triumph of Dionysus is placed by Levi in the Hadrianic/Antonine period.

37. Levi (1947), 60–66, fig. 23; 156–59, pl. XXX; ascribed by Levi respectively to the Hadrianic/Antonine period and the Severan.

38. Levi (1947), 16; Baratte, op. cit. (above note 36), 92, places it between A.D. 115 and the mid-second century.

39. Most successful perhaps in the House of the Calendar (Levi [1947], 36–39, fig. 12, pl. V), where the broad shaft of the T contains the figures of the months radiating in a circle. For some other solutions, see Stillwell, op. cit. (above note 35).

40. Cf. R. Rebuffat, "Maisons à péristyle d'Afrique du Nord. Répertoire de plans publiés," I *MEFR* 81, 1969, 659–724; id., II, *MEFRA* 86, 1974, 445–99; R. Rebuffat and G. Hallier, *Thamusida* II (Paris 1970), 290–301, 317–27 and tables 334–35. Rebuffat classifies as *triclinia* not only rooms marked out as such by mosaics, but also those recognizable by other traits: "accès direct ou quasi direct au péristyle, grande taille relative, tripartition de l'entrée" (*MEFR* 81, 1969, 661). I have concentrated on those where the design of the mosaics makes the identification certain, although I accept that rooms identical in plan were doubtless also so in function. Cf. also Y. Thébert, "Private Life and Domestic Architecture in Roman Africa," in P. Veyne, ed., *A History of Private Life I. From Pagan Rome to Byzantium* (Cambridge, MA 1987), 364–78.

41. Maison de Dionysos et des Quatre Saisons: R. Etienne, *Le Quartier Nord-Est de Volubilis* (Paris 1960), 39–41, pl. VI; Rebuffat, *MEFR* 81, 1969, 667, no. 5; Etienne, "Dionysos et les quatre saisons sur une mosaique de Volubilis (Maroc)," *MEFR* 73, 1951, 93–117; id., *Publications du Service des Antiquités du Maroc* 10, 1954, 58–89. Maison à l'Ephèbe: R. Thouvenot, *Publications du Service des Antiquités du Maroc* 7, 1945, 114–31; Rebuffat, *MEFR* 81, 1969, 671, no. 25; L. Chatelain, *Publications du Service des Antiquités du Maroc* 1, 1935, 8–10. Both probably date from the end of the second or beginning of the third century A.D. (Etienne, *Quartier Nord-Est*, 147–49).

42. Maison des Mois: L. Foucher, "Une mosaique de triclinium trouvée à Thysdrus," *Latomus* 20, 1961, 291–97, pls. XI–XVIII; id., *Découvertes archéologiques à Thysdrus en 1961* (Notes et Documents n.s. 5, Institut d'Archéologie, Tunis, n.d.), 50–51, pl. XXXV. The arms of the U differ not only in length (between 2.90 m and 3.17 m), which is not uncommon, but also in width, between 1.77 m and 2.01 m; and the border at the base of the *lectus imus* on the left is set obliquely. The date is probably early third century A.D.

43. Plin. *H.N.* 36.184; cf. H. Meyer, "Zu neueren Deutungen von Asarotos Oikos und kapitolinischem Taubenmosaik," *AA* 1977, 104–10, with earlier refs.; G. Hagenow, "Der nichtausgekehrte Speisesaal," *RhM* 121, 1978, 260–75. The *asarotos*-motifs form a frieze also in front of the couches on the mosaics of the Lateran Collection and of Aquileia. For the *xenia*-motifs on the Thysdrus mosaic, see S. Gozlan, in Y. Duval, ed., *Mosaique romaine tardive* (Paris n.d. [?1981]), 73–87.

44. Vitr. 6.3.9. Following Rebuffat, *MEFR* 81, 1969, 662, I have in general avoided using the word *oecus* except for rooms of this type, although it is often loosely used for any large reception hall.

45. Foucher, *Découvertes archéologiques à Thysdrus en 1961* (op. cit. above note 42), 27, pl. XXXVI; the black-and-white mosaic is typical of the first half of the second century A.D.

46. For example, the *triclinium* in the House of the Dionysiac Procession at Thysdrus, which measures 8.40 m × 6.90 m: Foucher, *La Maison de la Procession Dionysiaque à El Jem* (Paris 1963), 29, 48–62.

47. S. Gozlan, "La Maison de Neptune à Acholla-Botria (Tunisie)," *Karthago* 16, 1971–72, 41–99; ead., "Les pavements en mosaïque de la Maison de Neptune à Acholla-Botria (Tunisie)," *MonPiot* 59, 1974, 71–135; S. Gozlan and A. Bourgeois, "Nouvelles recherches à la Maison de Neptune (Acholla-Botria)," *BAC* n.s. 17B, 1981 (1984), 75–88: the construction of the house is placed in the third quarter of the second century A.D. The pavement of the big *oecus-triclinium,* whose central portion shows a Triumph of Neptune, is damaged, but the bar of the T probably contained two separate panels, as in the Houses of Dionysus and the Seasons and of the Ephebe at Volubilis (above note 41).

48. E.g., Foucher, *Découvertes archéologiques à Thysdrus en 1961* (op. cit. above note 42), 14, 27 n. 76. For entertainment at dinner, see C.P. Jones, below, 185–97.

49. D. Fernandez-Galiano, *Complutum I. Excavaciones* (Madrid 1984), 129–36, 158–60; *II. Mosaicos,* 134–86 (with a list of *triclinium*-mosaics in T + U, 157).

50. Marquardt-Mau (1886) I, 307–9; G. Rodenwaldt, *RE* 2A (1923), s.v. *sigma,* 2323–24; for representations in art, see below, notes 77–85. Cf. also the article of J. Rossiter, below, 199–214.

51. J. M. Blazquez, *Mosaicos romanos de Sevilla, Granada, Cadiz y Murcia,* Corpus de Mosaicos de España IV (Madrid 1982), 43, no. 34, fig. 9: fourth-fifth century A.D.; J.-G. Gorges, *Les Villas hispano-romaines* (Paris 1979), 262, pl. XXVIII, 2.

52. G. Åkerström-Hougen, *The Calendar and Hunting Mosaics of the Villa of the Falconer in Argos* (Stockholm 1974), 34–36, 101–17, pls. 7, VII–VIII; probably early sixth century A.D.

53. C. Donnay-Rocmans and G. Donnay, "La Maison du Cerf," *Colloque Apamée 1980,* 155–70, with discussion 179–80; N. Duval, "Les maisons d'Apamée et l'architecture 'palatiale' de l'Antiquité Tardive," ibid., 464; J.Ch. Balty, "Notes sur l'habitat romain, byzantin et arabe d'Apamée: rapport de synthèse," ibid., 478, 495–96. The two in the Maison du Cerf were found, one in a large rectangular room (A), the other in a small apsidal room (F); both, therefore, were presumably used for dining. The final state of the house appears to belong to the sixth century A.D. For other examples of such tables, and the problem of their use, cf. O. Nussbaum, "Zum Problem der runden und *sigma*förmigen Altarplatten," *JAC* 4, 1961,

18–43; G. Roux, "Tables chrétiennes en marbre découvertes à Salamine," *Salamine de Chypre IV* (Paris 1973), 133–96.

54. E.g., J. Camp, *The Athenian Agora. Excavations in the Heart of Classical Athens* (London-New York 1986), 210–11, fig. 185.

55. E. Condurachi, "Quelques maisons byzantines des villes pontiques," in G. Robertson and G. Henderson, eds., *Studies in Memory of D. Talbot Rice* (Edinburgh 1975), 174–77; id., *Dacia* n.s. 1, 1957, 259: "nous considérons ce palais soit comme un tribunal, avec salle d'audience terminée en abside, soit comme un édifice religieux comportant une chapelle intérieure."

56. N. Duval, *RA* 1980, 328; id., *Colloque Apamée 1980*, 459–60.

57. N. Duval and F. Baratte, *Les ruines de Sufetula: Sbeitla* (Tunis 1973), 65–68; D. Parrish, "The Mosaic of Xenophon and the Seasons from Sbeitla (Tunisia)," in *Mosaique. Recueil d'hommages à Henri Stern* (Paris 1983), 297–306, with earlier refs.

58. Above note 52.

59. The smaller of the two *sigma*-tables found in the Maison du Cerf at Apamea had space for seven guests: Donnay, op. cit. (above note 53), 179. Literary sources appear to indicate between five and eight as preferred numbers at a *stibadium*, and up to twelve as possible occasionally: Marquardt-Mau (1886) I, 307 (not all the passages cited here refer explicitly to *stibadia*).

60. I. Lavin, "The House of the Lord: Aspects of the Role of Palace triclinia in the Architecture of Late Antiquity and the Early Middle Ages," *Art Bulletin* 44, 1962, 1–27; Duval, *Colloque Apamée 1980*, 457, 460–61. See also the examples quoted by Rossiter, below, 203.

61. G. Ghiradini, "Gli scavi del Palazzo di Teodorico a Ravenna," *MonAnt* 24, 1916 (1918), 782–94; F. Berti, *Mosaici antichi in Italia*, Reg. 8a, *Ravenna I* (Rome 1976), 77–81, nos. 58–60, pls. XLVII–LI. The association with Theodoric is not proved.

62. J. Lassus, "La salle à sept absides de Djemila-Cuicul," *AntAfr* 5, 1971, 193–207; M. Blanchard-Lemée, "Nouvelles recherches sur les mosaiques de Djemila," in R. Farioli Campanati, ed., *III Colloquio internazionale sul Mosaico Antico, Ravenna 1980* (Ravenna 1983), 277–86; ead., "La 'Maison de Bacchus' à Djemila," *BAC* n.s. 17B, 1981 (1984), 131–43. Blanchard proposes a date in the mid-fifth century A.D. for the multiapsed room, while Duval in the following discussion suggests that it may belong to the Byzantine period.

63. Quoted by Lassus, op. cit. (above note 62) 199, from the excavator, Y. Allais.

64. Among the rich houses at Apamea, for instance, there is only a single example of a traditional *triclinium* with a T + U mosaic, in the Maison aux Colonnes bilobées, where it dates from the second half of the third century A.D.; all the other houses have a large room ending in apse or alcove, and presumably used with a *sigma*, as the numerous remains of *sigma*-tables attest: Balty, *Colloque Apamée 1980*, 476–78, 495–96, and cf. id., *Guide d'Apamée* (Brussels 1981), 63, fig. 56.

65. Levi (1947), 127–36, pls. XXIII–XXIV, CLII–CLIII; 625 (date).

66. J. Lancha, *Recueil général des mosaïques de la Gaule III. Narbonnaise 2. Vienne.* X^e supplément à *Gallia* (Paris 1981), 157–63, no. 331, pls. LXXVII–LXXXI; H. Lavagne, "Rome et les associations dionysiaques en Gaule," in *L'Association dionysiaque dans les sociétés anciennes, CEFR* 89 (Rome 1986), 145–47.

67. Lancha, op. cit. (above note 66) 163; for the general chronology cf. ead., *Mosaïques géométriques. Les ateliers de Vienne-Isère* (Rome 1977), 195–98.

68. 10.48; 14.87: describing *sigmas* that hold respectively seven and eight guests.

69. *Ep.* 5.6.36; see below, note 73.

70. E.g., Marquardt-Mau (1886) I, 307; Rodenwaldt, *RE* 2A (1923), s.v. *sigma*, 2323: "Während im 1. Jhdt., wie Beispiele aus Pompeii zeigen, die griechische Form des Trikliniums sich noch neben dem Sigma hielt, scheint in den folgenden Jahrhunderten die halbrunde Form die übliche geworden zu sein. . . . "

71. *SHA: Elagabal.* 25: *primus denique invenit sigma in terra sternere, non in lectulis.* Duval, *Colloque Apamée 1980,* 459, announces an article, "Sigma et stibadium dans l'*Histoire Auguste*," in the *Historia Augusta Colloquium 1980*; this, to my knowledge, has not yet appeared.

72. Apses are found earlier in rooms probably or certainly used for dining, but without evidence that they were intended for a *stibadium:* for example, the apse in the "Auditorium of Maecenas" is completely occupied by a nymphaeum, while a regular rectangular *triclinium* appears to have been laid out in the main area of the building: S. Rizzo, in *L'archeologia in Roma capitale tra sterro e scavo* (Rome 1983), 225–30. Cf. Tamm, op. cit. (above note 19), 148–82, on apsidal halls in the first centuries B.C. and A.D., and their various uses. I confine my discussion to examples where the presence of a *stibadium* is clearly indicated by physical remains or by the layout of the mosaics.

73. *Ep.* 5.6.36–37; cf. Salza Prina Ricotti (1987), 137–38, with a reconstruction; ead., *Cronache Pompeiane* 5, 1979, 102–4.

74. Soprano (1950), 306–7, quoting F. Mazois, *Les Ruines de Pompéi* (Paris 1824–30), II, 50, pl. XII, figs. 1–2 (*non vidi*); Thédenat, op. cit. (above note 13), 84, fig. 50.

75. Salza Prina Ricotti (1987), 175–77; S. Aurigemma, *Villa Adriana²* (Rome 1984), 100–33. Ricotti's further suggestions for the adaptation of the Canopus to huge imperial banquets depend upon the use of movable furniture, and therefore cannot by their nature be proved. Another open-air *stibadium* with masonry couch in Hadrian's Villa in front of the Sala dei Pilastri Dorici: Salza Prina Ricotti, *MemPontAcc* 14, 1982, 33, pl. IV E.

76. A. Carandini, A. Ricci, M. de Vos, *Filosofiana. La Villa di Piazza Armerina* (Palermo 1982), 175–87, fig. 94, pl. XXIV, 53; first half of fourth century A.D.

77. P.E. Arias, *ASAtene* 24–26 (n.s. 8–10), 1946–48 (1950), 310-13, 322–26, fig. 2, pl. XXVI; probably mid-fourth century A.D.

78. D.B. Spanel, in R.A. Fazzini, R.S. Bianchi, J.F. Romano, D.B. Spanel, eds., *Ancient Egyptian Art in the Brooklyn Museum* (New York 1989), no. 100; A. Adriani, *Divagazioni intorno ad una coppa paesistica del Museo di Alessandria*

(Rome 1959), 13–14, pl. XV, 43; K. Weitzmann, ed., *Age of Spirituality. Late Antique and Early Christian Art, Third to Seventh Century* (New York 1979), 250–51, no. 230; fifth century A.D.

79. Mins. XXVII–XXX: R. Bianchi Bandinelli, *Hellenistic-Byzantine Miniatures of the Iliad* (Olten 1955), 67, 69, 103, figs. 190–91.

80. Tran Tam Tinh, *Catalogue des peintures romaines (Latium et Campanie) du musée du Louvre* (Paris 1974), 71–72, no. 50, fig. 57; probably beginning of third century A.D.

81. E. Jastrzebowska, "Les scènes de banquet dans les peintures et sculptures chrétiennes des IIIe et IVe siècles," *Recherches Augustiniennes* 14, 1979, 38–39, no. XXV, with earlier refs.; second half of fourth century A.D.

82. G. Koch, *ASR XII, Die mythologische Sarkophage 6, Meleager* (Berlin 1975), 48–50, 125–29; B. Andreae, *ASR I, Die Sarkophage mit Darstellungen aus dem Menschenleben 2, Die römischen Jagdsarkophage* (Berlin 1980), 102–3; N. Himmelmann, *Typologische Untersuchungen an römischen Sarkophagreliefs des 3. und 4. Jahrhunderts n. Chr.* (Mainz am Rhein 1973), 23–28, 57–66; L.B. van der Meer, "Eine Sigmamahlzeit in Leiden," *BABesch* 58, 1983, 101–15; R. Amedick, "Zur Motivgeschichte eines Sarkophages mit ländlichem Mahl," *RömMitt* 95, 1988, 205–34; Jastrzebowska, op. cit. (above note 81), 40–58.

83. Jastrzebowska, op. cit. (above note 81), 3–90, with refs. to the extensive earlier literature; esp. F. Gerke, *Die christliche Sarkophage der vorkonstantinischen Zeit* (Berlin 1940), 110–50. The arguments over the significance of the theme in Christian art are outside the limits of my topic, but cf. J. Engemann, "Der Ehrenplatz beim antiken *sigma*mahl," *Jenseitsvorstellungen in Antike und Christentum. Gedenkschrift für Alfred Stuiber* (*JAC* Ergbd. 9, 1982), 248–50, for a recent summary.

84. W. Jobst, "Das 'öffentliche Freudenhaus' in Ephesos," *ÖJH* 51, 1976–77, 73–82; probably late third-early fourth century A.D.

85. E. Rosenthal, *The Illuminations of the Vergilius Romanus* (Zürich 1972) 54–58, pl. IX: fol. 100v; O. Mazal, *Kommentar zur Wiener Genesis* (Frankfurt am Main 1980), 121, 154–55, pl. 34: fol. 17v.

86. Naples MN 120029, 120031, 120030: P. Gusman, *Pompei* (Paris 1899), 352–54, with figs.; Reinach *RPGR* (1922), 256, nos. 3, 6, 7; J. Ward-Perkins and A. Claridge, *Pompeii. A.D. 79* (London 1976), nos. 259, 260. MN 120030 is very poorly preserved.

87. W. Helbig, *Wandgemälde der vom Vesuv verschütteten Städte Campaniens* (Leipzig 1868), 360, no. 1481; T. Schreiber, *Kulturhistorischer Bilderatlas I, Altertum* (Leipzig 1888), pl. LXXVII, 5; Reinach *RPGR* (1922), 256, 4; Åkerström-Hougen, op. cit. (above note 52), 116, fig. 73 (after F. and F. Niccolini, *Le case ed i monumenti di Pompei disegnati e descritti 2, Descrizione generale* [1854–96] pl. 3). Here too there is a confusion in the perspective, especially in the drawing of the righthand edge of the couch, which (if not due to the engraver), raises the possibility that a *triclinium* rather than a *sigma* may be intended.

88. Helbig, op. cit. (above note 87), 148–50, nos. 757, 759, 760 = Reinach

RPGR (1922), 93, 3–4; 401, 2; illustration in Jashemski, op. cit. (above note 23), 97, fig. 153.

89. G. Spano, "La tomba dell'edile C. Vestorio Prisco in Pompei," *Atti della Reale Accademia d'Italia, Memorie della classe di scienze morali e storiche* ser. 7, 3, fasc. 6, 1943, 277–85, fig. 11; J.-M. Dentzer, "La tombe de C. Vestorius dans la tradition de la peinture italique," *MEFR* 74, 1962, 547–49.

90. E.g., from Pompeii VIII.6.6 or VIII.5.24: Gusman, op. cit. (above note 86), fig. p. 420; Reinach *RPGR* (1922), 162, 8; J.-P. Cèbe, *La Caricature et la Parodie dans le monde romain, des origines à Juvenal* (Paris 1966), 353, pl. XVIII, 7. A fragmentary one, with pygmies under an awning in a semicircle, but the lower part of the figures destroyed: Helbig, op. cit (above note 87), 379, no. 1533 = Reinach *RPGR* (1922), 161, 4; Cèbe, op. cit., 353, pl. XIV, 4. One from Stabiae (fig. 33): A. Allroggen-Bedel, "Die Wandmalereien aus der Villa in Campo Varano (Castellamare di Stabia)," *RömMitt* 84, 1977, 74, pl. 42, 4 (Helbig, op. cit., 379, no. 1532; Reinach *RPGR* [1922], 162, 5).

91. A. Maiuri, *Le Pitture delle Case di "M. Fabius Amandio", del "Sacerdos Amandus" e di "P. Cornelius Teges"* (*Monumenti della Pittura Antica*, sez. 3, *Pompei* II, Rome 1938), 24, no. IV, pl. IV, 1; 25, no. IX, pl. V, 2; Maiuri wrongly speaks of *media kline* of the second group, where in fact there seems to be a continuous semicircular cushion. Cf. also H. Whitehouse, *BSR* 45, 1977, 63–64; Cèbe, op. cit. (above note 90), 353, pls. XIII, 4; XIV, 2. For the *triclinium,* see above, note 26.

92. G. Bendinelli, *Le Pitture del Columbario di Villa Pamphili* (*Monumenti della Pittura Antica*, sez. 3, *Roma* V, Rome 1941), 7–8, pl. II, 1.

93. G. Rizzo, *Le Pitture della Casa di Livia* (*Monumenti della Pittura Antica*, sez. 3, *Roma* III, Rome 1936), 46, pls. V, IX (Wall IIIa, 1st intercolumniation); 48, fig. 33 (Wall IVb, 1st intercolumniation); ?another pl. VI, IX (Wall IIIa, 2nd intercolumniation). Another group of banqueters reclined in a semicircle on the ground on the lost stuccos of a tomb from Cumae, possibly early Augustan (K. Dunbabin, *JdI* 101, 1986, 239–40, fig. 49, with earlier refs.); and three figures recline under an awning among Egyptianizing scenes on a Campana relief: Adriani, op. cit. (above note 78), 28–29, pl. 42, 123.

94. *De R.R.* 3.5.9–17. Among many discussions and attempts at reconstruction, cf. Ch. des Anges and G. Seure, "La Volière de Varron," *RPh* 6, 1932, 217–90; G. Fuchs, "Varros Vogelhaus bei Casinum," *RömMitt* 69, 1962, 96–105; F. Coarelli, "Architettura sacra e architettura privata nella tarda repubblica," in *Architecture et Société de l'Archaisme grec à la fin de la République romaine* (Rome 1983), 206–15, who singles out the reconstruction of des Anges and Seure as the most convincing.

95. E.g., Plato *Rep.* 2.372B; Theocr. 7.67–68. Cf. Poland, *RE* 3A.2 (1929), 2481–84, s.v. *stibadeion, stibas;* Ch. Picard, "Un type méconnu de lieu-saint dionysiaque: le *stibadeion,*" *CRAI* 1944, 127–57 (the question whether Picard is correct in his identification of a special architectural form of Dionysiac *stibadeion* is outside

the scope of my discussion here); C. Weber-Lehmann, "Spätarchaische Gelagebilder in Tarquinia," *AthMitt* 92, 1985, 19–44, on "Gelage zu ebener Erde."

96. Cf. other accounts of luxurious late Republican picnics, such as those of Hortensius in the midst of his wild game park (Varro, *De R.R.* 3.13) and Lucullus in his aviary (ibid. 3.53): these and other references in A.R. Littlewood, "Ancient Literary Evidence for the Pleasure Gardens of Roman Country Villas," in E.B. MacDougall, ed., *Ancient Roman Villa Gardens* (Washington, D.C. 1987) 9–30. Cf. also Amedick, op. cit. (above note 82), 214–19, 227–29; E. La Rocca, in M. Cima and E. La Rocca, *Le Tranquille Dimore degli dei. La residenza imperiale degli horti Lamiani* (Rome 1986), 20–22.

97. F. Matz, *ASR* IV, *Die dionysischen Sarkophage* 3 (Berlin 1969), 328–39. Sometimes the outline of the rock shapes itself into a natural *sigma*, but there is a marked contrast with the regular rendering of the cushion on the later sarcophagi with hunters' picnics discussed above, note 82.

98. Suet. *Nero* 31.2; the parallel between this room and Varro's aviary is drawn by Coarelli, op. cit. (above note 94), 213. Cf. also Y. Perrin, in E. Lévy, ed., *Le Système palatial en Orient, en Grèce et à Rome,* Actes du Colloque de Strasbourg, 1985 (Leiden 1987), 390–91, on the octagon of the Domus Aurea as "une variation impériale du *stibadeion.*"

99. J. Engemann, op. cit. (above note 83), 239–50, who suggests that this rule, first attested by Juvencus ca. A.D. 330, replaced an emphasis on the middle of the *sigma* as the place of honor, which can be seen on numerous monuments of the third and fourth century.

100. H. Blanck, "Ein spätantikes Gastmahl: das Mosaik von Duar-ech-Chott," *RömMitt* 88, 1981, 329–44, pls. 142–49, with earlier refs. The date ca. A.D. 310–30 suggested by Blanck (342) is too early; the rendering of details such as the eyes, nose, and the folds of the drapery associates the mosaic with the group discussed in K. Dunbabin, "A Mosaic Workshop in Carthage around A.D. 400," in J.G. Pedley, ed., *New Light on Ancient Carthage* (Ann Arbor 1980), 73–83, and with the Mosaic of Dominus Julius (most recently W. Raeck, *"Publica non despiciens,"* *RömMitt* 94, 1987, 295-308, with refs.). I would therefore revise the date "around 350," which I proposed in *Mosaics of Roman North Africa* (Oxford 1978), 124, and suggest rather the last quarter of the fourth century.

101. Cf. above note 29. The third-century sarcophagus-relief quoted as a parallel for the type of seat by Blanck, op. cit. (above note 100), 334, pl. 148, 2, shows a tavern scene.

102. As suggested by Blanck, op. cit. (above note 100), 343–44. A relief of the first century A.D. from Amiternum represents two groups each of six banqueters on what appears to be an official occasion; one group reclines at a *triclinium,* the other is seated: A. Giuliano, "Rilievi con scene di banchetto a Pizzoli," *Studi Miscellanei* 10, 1963–64, 33–38, pls. XIII–XVIII. Giuliano suggests that the scene may be a banquet of *seviri* and/or *Augustales;* but the reason for the two different manners of dining is not clear. The group is seated on low stools around a small

three-legged table, in a manner quite different from the diners on the Carthage mosaic; it may well show the survival of local Italic tradition.

103. See J. Rossiter, below, 205–8.

104. The handful of other parallels for this type of seated dining (all slightly later than the mosaic) quoted by Blanck, op. cit. (above note 100), 334–35, all show abnormal occasions (Circe's metamorphosed victims dining outside her palace, in the Vatican Vergil; Abraham entertaining the three angels, in S. Maria Maggiore and S. Vitale; and Nestor entertaining Machaon in his tent in the Ilias Ambrosiana); they do not therefore have the specific social reference that the mosaic has. Blanck further points out that several take place in the open air; there are no indications of setting, indoors or out, on the Carthage mosaic.

The Symposium in Roman Elegy

John C. Yardley

"Whereas . . . so much Greek amatory poetry of both the archaic and the Hellenistic periods has a clear and specific sympotic setting, the *convivium* plays a much less prominent role in Roman erotic elegy. This poem (sc. Ovid, *Amores* 1.4) and its companion piece (*Amores* 2.5), are, in fact, the only Augustan elegies to make substantial use of such a context." This is the judgment of J.C. McKeown in the most recent volume of his fine edition of Ovid's *Amores*,[1] and it is one which, while essentially accurate (sympotic contexts *are* more prevalent in Greek poetry), calls for some comment. The symposium (a term which I shall use in preference to the Latin *convivium*) is, in fact, an important theme of Augustan elegy. For "substantial use" of a sympotic context, [Tibullus] 3.6 seems to be a good candidate, for Lygdamus' musings throughout are to be seen against the background of the symposium, to which he constantly harks back.[2] It is also likely that the background to *Am.* 1.7, the *rixa*, is to be seen as the symposium. The address to *si quis amicus ades* (1.2) and especially the line *quis mihi non "demens" quis non mihi "barbare" dixit* (1.19) reveal that the *rixa* took place in a gathering, and where else are we to assume this to be but the symposium, given that this is the standard venue[3] for such scenes? Moreover, large sections of elegies by all three poets, especially Ovid, are consecrated to the dinner party, and especially to the sympotic setting in which we find the "triangle" of lover, girl, and the *vir*.[4] To this situation we shall return.

Before we turn to these passages, however, it is also worth noticing that in Propertius, at least, we find an abundance of references to the symposium, which the poet evidently regards as an integral part of "the life of love" (to use Jasper Griffin's term). For Propertius the symposium is practically synonymous with the love affair: *laeserunt nullos pocula nostra deos* (2.15.48). It can represent success in a love affair; when the praetor is in town, received by Cynthia, and Propertius is rejected, his complaint is: *nunc sine me plena fiunt convivia mensa* (2.16.5). Indeed, when we first meet Cynthia in person, as it were, in 1.3, the poet purports to have come to her in a drunken state, garlanded and carrying apples.[5] He has been at a symposium without Cynthia, and Cynthia assumes that the night has been spent with another woman: *namque ubi longa meae consumpsti tempora noctis* (1.37). One might add that our first meeting with Corinna, too, in a specific setting—for she is certainly the poem's addressee[6]—is in *Am.* 1.4, the symposium.[7] So while it is indeed less pervasive a theme than in Greek erotic poetry, the symposium is nonetheless an important one in Augustan elegy.

Even so, it is clear that the poets are little interested in its details. As Jasper Griffin has pointed out, we find no reference to food, except in very general terms, and hardly any reference to vintage wines—a marked contrast to what we find in the *Odes* of Horace.[8] The various games and entertainments which, as we know from Pollux and Athenaeus,[9] were associated with the symposium, are almost entirely absent (exceptions are Prop. 4.8.41ff., the alfresco symposium held by Propertius with the two girls during Cynthia's absence, and *Ars* 3.353ff., where Ovid advises women on party games). In short, the symposium appears in Augustan elegy only in very general terms as one of the venues for the lovers.

This is also true of the extended sections on the symposium in the elegists; details of the background are omitted, and the poets focus on the players. And the players are almost invariably the girl, the lover, and a third person—the rival, but a rival who has some rights over the girl, so that lover and girl must communicate without his being aware of it. The best example of this is, of course, *Am.* 1.4, in which Ovid gives instructions to Corinna on what she should do to communicate furtively with him at a dinner that she is to attend with her *vir*,[10] and at which Ovid will also be present. But Ovid clearly found it an attractive theme, since he reworked it no less than six times elsewhere: *Am.* 2.5 and 3.11.23–24, where Ovid himself is the cuckolded party; *Ep.* 16.217ff. and 17.75ff., where the triangle is the mythical one of Paris, Helen, and Menelaus; *Ars* 1.565ff., where Ovid advises the lover on how to communicate with the girl in the presence of the *vir;* and finally *Trist.* 2.451ff., where the poet cites it as a theme of Tibullus' elegies. And indeed it is a theme found in Tibullus, at 1.6.15ff., where the *coniunx* of the *fallax puella* (Delia) is given advice on keeping her out of trouble, and Tibullus recalls his own experience of making contact with Delia at a symposium at which the *coniunx* was also present.

The example in Propertius, 3.8, is not without its difficulties. The poem begins with an expression of joy at a *rixa* that occurred between the poet and Cynthia the previous evening. Since Cynthia's weapons included a table (1.3) and full goblets (1.4), one must assume the setting to be a symposium. Propertius concludes that her violent behavior is really a sign of her love for him, a common theme of erotic poetry both Greek and Roman.[11] Then Propertius says (3.8.23–26):

> aut in amore dolere volo aut audire dolentem
>   sive meas lacrimas sive videre tuas,
> tecta superciliis si quando verba remittis,
>   aut mea[12] cum digitis scripta silenda notas.

The passage is obscure, but reference is surely being made to the situation that we have been discussing. "The lovers are in company at dinner and cannot communicate openly," comments Richardson,[13] "therefore they resort to subterfuge." One can go further; given the other instances of this scene in elegy, the subterfuge is necessary because Propertius visualizes a symposium at which Cynthia's *vir* is present.

So we have a theme that occurs in all three elegists, and several times in Ovid. Within these passages that theme is obviously highly stylized, embodying a number of repeated motifs or topoi. It will suffice to illustrate just three of these:

1. Secret signals, which are meant to pass undetected between lover and girl without the rival noticing.[14]

2. Wine-writing: the girl, or the lover, traces letters in wine on the table.[15]

3. Cup-kissing: the lover contrives to have the cup pass from the girl to himself so that he can put his lips to that part of it from which she has just drunk herself. In elegy this occurs only in Ovid, but on three occasions.[16]

These are but three of the recurring topoi of the sympotic "triangular" context: others include the lover admiring the girl's ring so he can touch her hand, and the husband put to sleep by wine;[17] but they suffice to demonstrate that we are dealing with a highly stylized situation. It may well be that there is literary influence at work here. Ovid knew the elegies of Propertius and Tibullus; indeed, he even refers to the symposium section of Tib. 1.6 in *Trist.* 2.454 and he was perhaps indebted to them,[18] but it is also clear that such a situation is by no means divorced from the realities of life in Augustan Rome. "The banquet had acquired a reputation for offering incitements to and opportunities for adultery," observes McKeown, and an excellent illustration of this is the story, told by Plutarch in the *Amatorius,* of Maecenas and the *gelotopoios* Gabba. Gabba had noticed Maecenas flirting with his wife at a dinner Gabba was giving in the great man's honor, and so he pretended to be asleep. Thereupon one of his slaves slipped into the room and proceeded to help himself to some wine, at which an irate Gabba shouted out: "Damn you! Don't you know that it's only for Maecenas I'm asleep?" (*Amator.* 760A) The same story is told by Festus of a husband called Cipius, who was nicknamed Pararhenchon. Festus quotes from Lucilius the expression *non omnibus dormio* and comments: "The proverb apparently originated with a certain Cipius who was called Pararhenchon because he would pretend to be asleep so his wife could fool around (*moecharetur*) with impunity."[19] So when Horace talks about the *matura virgo* seeking "junior adulterers" *inter mariti vina* (*Odes* 3.6.25ff.) this is not to be taken merely as a "literary" theme. Other relevant passages are Plin. *H.N.* 14.141, Juv. 1.55ff., Suet. *Aug.* 69.1, *Calig.* 25.1 and the second distich of the famous *triclinium* graffitto from Pompeii, which tells guests to keep their eyes off other men's wives.[20]

But to return to elegy. In fact, the situation is not confined to that genre, nor indeed to Latin literature. Lover and girl (*hetaera*) at a symposium, sometimes with rival present, is of course a common theme in later Greek literature, especially in the genres derived from comedy, such as Lucian's *Dialogi Meretricii*.[21] But sometimes, too, we find the topoi that we have observed in the elegiac examples discussed above. In Achilles Tatius (2.9) we have the rare example of a woman who is not a *hetaera* at dinner with her lover, and the two indulge in some surreptitious cup-kissing. Leucippe, the woman, is Cleitophon's cousin, and she and her brother are temporarily residing with Cleitophon and his parents. Cleitophon, the lover, has a wife marked out for him by his father, and so, although Leucippe is a free, unmarried girl, they cannot be seen to be flirting at family meals. However, Satyrus, the dependable slave in whom Cleitophon has confided his feelings, helps out by exchanging the lovers' cups so that they can each drink from the part of the cup touched by the other's lips. This is not, of course, the "comic" sympotic scene of the type we have seen above, but there is no doubt that that is the source from which Achilles Tatius drew the topos.[22] We can also parallel the theme of secret signals between the lovers.[23]

Since we find this sympotic situation and its various topoi recurring in Roman elegy and later Greek erotic literature, we can with some confidence trace it back to Greek comedy, to descriptions of symposia attended by the young lover and a *hetaera*. But there also seems to me good reason to believe that the elegists were directly influenced by Roman comedy, now more and more accepted as one of the important sources for Roman elegy.[24] The important play in this case is Plautus' *Asinaria*, a work that Ovid, at least, appears to have known and that seems to have influenced *Am.* 1.6.[25]

In the play Diabolus, the rival of the *pallidus amans*, Argyrippus, drafts his terms for the *lena* so that he can have exclusive rights to the *meretrix* Philaenium for an entire year, and at 755ff. these terms are read back to Diabolus by the parasite, who is going to take them to the *lena*. Among the terms are the following: the girl is not to look at anyone (770); she is not to accept a drink from anyone but Diabolus, evidently to avoid cup-kissing[26] (771–73); she is not to make secret signals (784: *neque illa ulli homini nutet, nictet, annuat*) or use ambiguous language (792). Clearly we have the sympotic love triangle of elegy, with the topoi of cup-kissing and secret signals included.

Reference to a similar scene occurs in a fragment of Naevius' *Tarantilla* (fr. 75R), which is cited by Isidore of Seville (*Orig.* 1.26.2). Isidore gives us no context, simply asserting that it is Naevius *de quadam impudica*, but clearly the background is a symposium, and the girl in question is doing exactly what Diabolus forbids Philaenium to do in the *Asinaria*:

> Quasi pila
> in choro ludens datatim dat se et communem facit.
> alii adnutat, alii adnictat, alium amat alium tenet.
> Alibi manus est occupata, alii pervellit pedem;
> anulum dat alii spectandum, a labris alium invocat,
> cum alio cantat, at tamen alii suo dat digito litteras.

Indeed, the resemblances between this and Plaut. *Asin.* 770ff. are strong enough to suggest that Plautus was influenced by Naevius: cf. Naev. 3 *alii adnutat, alii adnictat*, Plaut. *Asin.* 784 *ulli homini nutet, nictet, annuat*;[27] Naev. 5 *anulum dat alii spectandum*, Plaut. *Asin.* 778 *spectandum ne cui anulum det*.[28] In Naevius we find one element that does not appear in Plautus: *alii suo dat digito litteras* (l. 6). This is interpreted by Warmington as "writes words (in the air) with a finger,"[29] but one wonders whether it might not be a reference to wine-writing.

In sum, like so much else in Roman elegy, the sympotic love triangle, with lover, girl, and rival, and the topoi which recur in this scene, appear to derive ultimately from comedy, where the situation would have involved lover, rival, and *hetaera*. This must have occurred in Greek comedy, because we find it, and the topoi associated with it, in later genres of Greek literature that were derived from comedy. But it also occurred in Roman comedy, two examples of it surviving in Naevius and Plautus. The latter was probably as influential, if not more influential, for the elegists as the former.[30]

NOTES

1. J.C. McKeown, *Ovid: Amores: Text, Prolegomena and Commentary* (Liverpool 1989), II.76.

2. At 1–12, 22, 31, 37, 58, 62–64.

3. Cf. Theoc. 14.29ff.; Lucian, *Dial. Mer.* 15; Alciphron 4.8.3; Tib. 2.5.101ff.; Prop. 3.8.1ff. Cf. also Alciphron 3.9, 3.12.3 (nonerotic).

4. Cf. Prop. 3.8.23ff.; Tib. 1.6.15ff.; Ov. *Am.* 1.4, 2.5.13–28, 3.11.23ff.; *Ep.* 16.217ff., 17.75ff.; *Ars* 1.229ff., 569 ff., and 2.549ff. (?). Again, given the fairly consistent association of the *rixa* with the symposium, we are probably expected to assume a sympotic background.

5. Prop. 1.3.9, 21, 24.

6. See McKeown (above note 1) 77.

7. Other references to the symposium in Propertius: 2.3.17ff.; 2.9.21; 2.15.51ff.; 2.33.25ff.; 2.34.22, 57; 3.5.21ff.; 3.10.21ff.; 3.25.1ff.; 4.6.71ff.; 4.8.35ff., 51ff. Perhaps, too, the setting of 1.10 is to be understood as the symposium, as Richardson's note on line 9 ("What P. seems to have in mind is not so much leaving the party as letting himself fall asleep") seems to suggest: L. Richardson, Jr., *Propertius, Elegies 1–4* (Norman, OK 1977). In Tibullus: 1.2.1ff., 2.5.95ff. In Ovid: *Ep.* 1.1.31ff.; *Am.* 2.11.47ff., 3.1.17; *Ars* 2.549ff. (?), 3.349ff., 3.749ff.; *Rem. Am.* 146.

8. *Latin Poets and Roman Life* (London 1985), 67.

9. Pollux 6.107ff., Athen. 1.19ff., 13.607C, etc. Cf. also Plato *Smp.* 176E, *Prt.* 347D. Still a valuable account of such entertainments in the Augustan period is W.A. Becker's *Gallus*, F. Metcalf, trans. (London 1907) 499ff.

10. Surely, in view of 64 *iure coacta dabis*, he is her husband, despite McKeown's reservations; 2.5.29ff., where Ovid is referring to his "moral rights" to the girl, is not really parallel. The best explanation of the status of the elegiac *domina* still seems to me to be that of Adrian Hollis (*Ars Amatoria: Book I* [Oxford 1977], p. VI), who attributes the fluctuating status of the girl to the various sources on which elegy draws.

11. E. Fantham, *Phoenix* 40, 1986, 45ff.

12. So Barber ad. loc., in H.A. Butler and E.A. Barber, *The Elegies of Propertius* (Oxford 1933, reprint Hildesheim 1969, 280). But possibly *tua* should be retained, in which case Propertius (like Ovid in *Am.* 2.5) is perhaps to be seen as the cuckolded party (so J.C. Marr, *Mnemosyne* 31, 1978, 270).

13. Richardson (above note 7) on line 25.

14. Ov. *Am.* 1.4.17ff., 2.5.15ff., 3.11.23–24; *Ars* 1.574, 2.549ff.; *Ep.* 16.258, 17.81 ff.; *Trist.* 2.453; Tib. 1.6.19, Prop. 3.8.25; cf. also Maximianus 3.26, Juv. 6.140. Add Pichon, *Index Verborum Amatoriorum* (Paris 1902), s.v. *nutus.*

15. Ov. *Am.* 1.4.20, 2.5.17ff.; *Ars* 1.571–72; *Ep.* 17.87ff.; *Trist.* 2.454; Tib. 1.6.19–20; Prop. 3.8.25 as interpreted by M. Rothstein, *Die Elegien von Sextus Propertius* (Berlin 1920) and Richardson (above note 7) ad loc.: others (e.g., Camps,

Fedeli) take line 25 to refer to gestures, but *scripta* seems to tell against this ("schriftliche Mitteilungen," observes Rothstein).

16. *Am.* 1.4.31–32; *Ep.* 17.80; *Ars* 1.575ff. Cf. also *Ep.* 16.255ff.

17. Lover admires girl's ring: Tib. 1.6.25ff.; Plaut. *Asin.* 778. Husband put to sleep by wine: Tib. 1.6.27; Ov. *Am.* 1.4.51ff., 2.5.13ff. Cf. also 1.9.25, correctly interpreted by Barsby as "the traditional practice of making the husband sleepy with wine at a party in order to carry off the mistress": J. Barsby, *Ovid, Amores Book 1* (Oxford 1973), ad loc.

18. But he is *not* indebted for the cup-kissing topos of *Am.* 1.4.17, 2.5.16, and *Ars* 1.571–72, for which there is no parallel in Propertius and Tibullus; it does occur elsewhere in this situation, as we shall see. On Ovid's relationship to Propertius, see K. Morgan, *Ovid's Art of Imitation: Propertius in the Amores* (Leiden 1977), esp. 34–36 for imitation of Prop. 3.8. For imitation of Tib. 1.6 in Ovid, see Zingerle's *index locorum* under Tib. 1.6 (A. Zingerle, *Ovidius und sein Verhältnis zu den Vorgängern* [Innsbruck 1871], III 65).

19. Festus 173 M. Cf. also Cic. *Ad Fam.* 7.24.1, for the same story.

20. *CIL* 4.7698. See also D. Balsdon, *Life and Leisure in Ancient Rome* (London 1969), 50ff., McKeown (above note 1) 76–77, E. Courtney, *A Commentary on the Satires of Juvenal* (London 1980), on 1.55ff.

21. *Dial. Mer.* 2.3, 3.1–3, 6.3, 11.1, 12.1, 15.1; Aristaenetus *Ep.* 1.25; *Theoc.* 14.21ff. (an idyll influenced by comedy: A.S.F. Gow, *Theocritus* (Cambridge 1965), II.246: "slight reminiscences of the Middle Comedy"); Alciphron 2.14, 3.2, 4.8.3, 4.10.2, 12–13; Philostratus *Ep.* 33; Ach. Tat. 2.9.

22. Other examples of cup-kissing: Aristaenetus *Ep.* 1.25; Philostr. *Ep.* 33; Lucian *Dial. Deor.* 8.2, 9.2, *Dial. Mer.* 12.1; *A.P.* 5.261 (Agathias); Longus 3.8 etc.; McKeown (above note 1) on Ov. *Am.* 1.4.31–32 and E. Rohde, *Der Griechische Roman*[3] (Leipzig 1914, reprint Darmstadt 1960), 175, n. 3.

23. Lucian *Dial. Mer.* 12.1; Ach. Tat. 1.10.4; *A.P.* 5.262.1 (Paulus Silent.) etc.; G. Kölblinger, *Einige Topoi bei den lateinischen Liebesdichtern* (Vienna 1971), 24ff., and K. Kost, *Hero und Leander, Abh. zur Kunst- Musik- und Literaturwiss. LXXXXVIII* (Bonn 1971) on Musaeus 102.

24. Most recently, see Griffin (above note 5), 198ff.

25. See *PCPhS* 213, 1987, 182ff.

26. Another Plautine reference to cup-kissing seems to be *Pers.* 775–76: *hoc mea manus tuae poclum donat, ut amantem amanti decet.*

27. See Kölblinger (above note 23) 24.

28. This particular topos occurs only in comedy and Tib. 1.6.25–26.

29. Warmington, *Remains of Old Latin* (London 1936), II. 101, n. a; so, too, Kölblinger (above note 22).

30. I should like to thank my colleague of the Winter term, 1990, Niall Rudd, for his comments on this paper.

Symposia and Deipna in Plutarch's Lives and in Other Historical Writings

George Paul

In Greco-Roman historiography accounts of symposia and *deipna* often have a cautionary or admonitory effect. The incidents related may range from the merely disquieting to the murderously dire but their effect is to disturb and dissipate the atmosphere of ease and joy that the ideal symposium or dinner is expected to create. Naturally this discordancy is not present in every instance, but it occurs frequently enough—probably in the majority of cases—to warrant some reflection. The symposium in Greek and later in Roman society is one manifestation of that refinement in manners that results from a sense of style in living and from the leisure to devote time, effort, and reflection to interpersonal relations.[1] As such it has a peculiar interest for Plutarch, not only as biographer but also as essayist, especially in the six books of *Symposiaka*. For Plutarch, the dominant characteristic of the symposium is friendship: the *trapeza* is *philopoios*,[2] and the guest comes not only to share in the food and the wine, but also in the conversation, the entertainment, and the *philophrosyne* that ends in *eunoia*.[3] Few of the drinking parties or dinners he records in the *Lives* are like that, however, and the same is largely true of those recorded by other historical writers.

A review of the whole Greco-Roman historiography, even in respect of this one type of incident, would transgress the limits of a short chapter. So in order to set reasonable bounds to the discussion and because of Plutarch's special interests, his *Lives* will be cited as principal source but their evidence will be supplemented by instances drawn from other historical writers. Plutarch, as is well known, claims to be writing not *historiai* but *bioi*,[4] but though this distinction is a valid and important one for some purposes, in the present context we should note that the subjects of his *Lives* are politicians and generals, his subject-matter draws on a wide range of historical writing, and, as a recent writer points out, the *Lives* "contain a high proportion of historical narrative."[5] A concentration on Plutarch, therefore, should not lead to false conclusions about the presentation of symposia and *deipna* in historiography, particularly if evidence from the historians is cited as well from time to time as a control.

Before the discussion proper, however, three preliminary points should be made. The first concerns a problem in the ancient evidence, namely that writers do not always distinguish clearly in their accounts between *symposion* and *deipnon*, or they use terms such as *synousia* or *convivium* where the meaning is not clear-cut; in some cases what is called by one writer a *deipnon* will be described by another as a *symposion*. No doubt this is partly due to the fact that the distinction that obtained in the Classical period between *deipnon* and *symposion* began increasingly to be blurred in Hellenistic and Roman times, and also because even in earlier times *deipnon* and *symposion* could form successive parts of a single entertainment, governed by similar codes, the drinking of wine being a common element. Such uncertainty as exists, therefore, is perhaps not of great moment, for both dinner and drinking party were expected to provide similar social pleasures and any breach of their codes of manners was likely to be similarly regarded.

The second point is that we tend to think of such entertainments as being universally enjoyed, but there were notable exceptions. According to Plutarch,[6] Pericles consistently declined invitations to dinner and all such *philophrosyne* and *synetheia*. The only exception he made was for the wedding feast of his cousin, Euryptolemos, and he left that when the libations were poured, that is, at the start of the symposium. Plutarch's gloss is that *philophrosyne* and *synetheia* are dangerous to reserve and dignity. Nicias, on the other hand, avoided dinners and similar social occasions because he was so afraid of informers, rather spending all day at the Generals' office or at the *boule*.[7] Sertorius refrained from heavy drinking (*methe*) even when he was at leisure.[8] Such exceptions to the general enjoyment of drinking parties or dinners are rare, however, and indeed it is because of the importance of the symposium in particular as a central social institution that its treatment in historical writings deserves to be considered.

The third point is that though questions may arise from time to time about the historicity of the various reports, such questions are not a major concern of the present discussion. The aim is rather to illustrate the fact that historical writers regard symposia and *deipna* as significant and revealing elements in their narratives, and that they have a particular interest in some of the darker aspects these entertainments may manifest from time to time.

Though in Greek and in Roman society many symposia and *deipna* were no doubt unexceptionable, it will perhaps occasion little surprise that those described by historical writers frequently commemorate discordant behavior of one kind or another; the historian is seldom concerned with the events of ordinary life, being drawn more to record the unusual, extraordinary, or outrageous. Four types of discordant and even extreme behavior, jarring with the ideal of friendliness and pleasure, are well represented in Plutarch's *Lives* and in other historical narratives of symposia and *deipna*. While there is no intention to deny the existence of others, it is these types that are here presented (in a scale of increasing violence) as the most common, namely (1) disorderly or unmannerly conduct, (2) displays of excess and extravagance, (3) treachery and plotting, and (4) murder and decapitation.

Disorderly Conduct

We should hardly need to be told, though Plato does tell us,[9] that a certain amount of rowdiness was not uncommon in symposia, but some kinds of disorderliness called for special comment. The behavior of the Centaurs at the wedding of Peirithous and their brawl with the Lapiths may be regarded as a classic representation in myth of such disorder;[10] attempts to prevent actual disorderly conduct in a banquet setting are attested by various regulations for *collegia*.[11] At the earliest symposium (other than mythical ones) reported in a historical source, the one held by Cleisthenes of Sicyon and reported by Herodotus,[12] the dancing of Hippocleides caused increasing offense culminating in his standing on his head on a table and beating time with his legs. Dancing perhaps encouraged the display of uncongenial talents: Polybius tells us that when Deinocrates of Messenia was visiting Rome in 184 B.C. he was seen by Flamininus at a drinking party in a drunken dance and wearing long (i.e., women's) robes and was rebuked for it the next day.[13] In the very same year, however, as we shall see, Flamininus had to deal with the consequences of a much graver breach of the rites of the table by his brother, Lucius. One of the offenses attributed to Alcibiades was to turn up late, in a drunken *komos,* at a dinner given by his lover, Anytus, and—without even entering the *andron*—to order his slaves to carry off half of Anytus' gold and silver cups.[14] The other guests were outraged, but Anytus himself was more complacent, for Alcibiades, he said, might have carried off all the cups. The emperor Claudius was likewise lenient, though he responded more pointedly in the face of theft at the table, for when T. Vinius stole a golden cup from the emperor's table (the story is told by Tacitus as well as Plutarch[15]), the emperor, who was aware of the theft, invited him back the following day and ordered the servants to provide Vinius alone with an earthenware service. According to Plutarch's reports, Macedonian entertainments were frequently the locus of jarring incidents, ranging from quarrelsome disputes among the scholars attendant on Alexander[16] to the brawl at the wedding of Philip and Cleopatra: Alexander threw a skyphos at Attalos, and Philip drew his sword against Alexander, but fortunately he tripped and fell.[17] One of the most celebrated stories told how Alexander, inflamed at a symposium by the impassioned speech of the *hetaera,* Thais, led out his companions in a *komos* and set fire to Persepolis.[18] Demetrius, the presumptuous freedman of Pompey, created offense by reclining at table in a slovenly manner while Pompey was still receiving the other guests.[19] Yet even unmannerly behavior might sometimes be tolerated: Favonius, who prided himself on his "Cynic" boldness and frankness, gate-crashed a party given by Cassius and attended by Brutus and, when directed to the uppermost couch, forced his way past the servants and reclined on the middle one; nonetheless, says Plutarch, over the wine there was *paidia* that did not lack grace or philosophy.[20] Gate-crashing, however, was a potential source of disorder: according to Polybius, Antiochus Epiphanes frequently broke up parties by his gate-crashing.[21]

Displays of Excess

"In ritual and mythology there is obviously a no to every yes, an antithesis to every thesis, order and dissolution, inside and outside, life and death."[22] To offset the strife of Centaurs and Lapiths on the west pediment of the Temple of Zeus at Olympia there stands in the center Apollo, figure of order and peace. This aspect of Apollo is frequently associated with the symposium.[23] For Plutarch certainly, refined order and simplicity in the conduct of *deipnon* or symposium is an ideal, a mark of humane living. The emphasis on *kosmos* and *taxis* is well brought out in a saying attributed to Aemilius Paulus. When the Greeks marvelled at his courtesy and attention to detail, he responded to the effect that the same spirit was required both in marshalling a line of battle and in presiding at a symposium.[24] References to simplicity in entertainment constitute a topos in the *Lives*: Dion of Syracuse was modest at his table as if dining with Plato in the Academy;[25] Agesilaos made no innovations in his dining habits when he returned to Sparta from abroad;[26] Cleomenes usually dined in modest state, though when ambassadors or *xenoi* were present, the dishes were more generous and the wine *philanthropoteros*, and at the ensuing symposium the chief entertainment was conversation.[27] Moreover, Crassus generally invited ordinary people to his entertainments, which were marked by refinement and *philophrosyne* rather than extravagance;[28] Cicero in his province entertained daily with generosity but without extravagance;[29] Ti. Gracchus kept a simple and inexpensive table, but Gaius by comparison was extravagant and overfastidious and was blamed for purchasing silver dolphins, presumably as a table ornament, at a price of 1250 drachmae per pound;[30] an anecdote contrasts Pompey's simplicity at table with the luxury of Lucullus;[31] Caesar's indifference to food is contrasted with the offensive extravagance of Valerius Leo, who had myrrh rather than olive oil poured on his guests' asparagus.[32]

Greek myth and folktale recount gross and horrible stories of excess in meals, especially the presentation of children, killed and cooked, as a meal to their unsuspecting parents or others. Famous examples included Thyestes' children, Pelops son of Tantalus, and Itys son of Tereus. The motif enters historiography with the story of Astyages and Harpagus' son;[33] Thucydides reports the story of Tereus as if it were a series of actual happenings.[34] Such stories, whatever else they mean, serve to define the limits of proper human behavior. Generally, of course, the entertainments narrated by the historians do not include events so gross, though as we shall see some reported incidents come close to them in their contempt for human life. In Plutarch, reports of simplicity, good order, and refinement at dinner or at drinking parties are more usually offset by his (and other writers') accounts of excess and extravagance; these too are types of behavior unacceptable or unwelcome in normal human society. In the eighth century B.C. the prophet Amos inveighs against the luxury and excess attendant on the *marzeah,* a Middle Eastern precursor of the symposium.[35] In the Greek world, where it originated in aristocratic circles, the symposium perhaps by its very nature lent itself to luxury and the display of wealth; reclining at table, it has been argued, was itself a symbol of luxury[36] and is one of the objects of Amos' wrath. From the day he learned of the defeat at Pharsalus, Cato the Younger, in token of mourning, adopted a sitting posture at table and refused to recline except when sleeping.[37] The introduction or at least rapid spread of drinking parties among the young nobles at Rome is linked by Polybius with the extravagance and dissoluteness acquired during the war against Perseus.[38] Plutarch inveighs against the vulgarity of introducing silver-footed couches, purple coverlets, gold cups, and similar extravagances into a simple and common house: he reports an anecdote of the elder Leotychidas, reared in Spartan simplicity, who when dining at Corinth and gazing at the expensive, coffered ceiling, asked his host if trees grew square in that country.[39] Excess and extravagance at entertainments took many forms, most obviously in the consumption of wine itself. Phocion's son, Phocus, was notorious for *asotia*. According to Plutarch, when Phocus won a victory at the *Panathenaea* and Phocion was invited to the victory celebration, he found that *footbasins* of spiced wine were being carried round to the guests as they entered.[40] The Macedonians in particular were reputed to be heavy drinkers. Alexander, returning from the funeral pyre of Calanus, invited many of his friends and officers and proposed a contest in the drinking of unmixed wine. The winner, Promachos, drank as many as four choes, but he died three days later. Chares, Alexander's court usher, reported that forty-one other guests died of a chill consequent on their drunkenness.[41] Plutarch is interested in Alexander's drinking habits[42] and the version of his death the biographer prefers attributes it to the combination of heavy drinking and fever following upon a splendid entertainment and *komos*.[43] Sulla the Dictator would spend all day on couches drinking along with actresses, kithara players, and theatrical people, and spent lavishly on symposia.[44] Demetrius Poliorcetes and Antony, whose *Lives* form a pair in Plutarch's scheme, were notorious for their excessive drinking and the extravagance of their parties.[45] Demetrius' mistress, the *hetaera* Lamia, prepared a *deipnon* for him so widely renowned for its extravagance that it was written up by Lynceus of Samos (the brother of Duris),[46] while Cleopatra's increasingly lavish generosity on one occasion is described by Socrates of Rhodes, a historian probably of the first century B.C.[47] who calls it a *basilikon symposion*. Sallust describes the excessive and extravagant setting and rare foods provided for a *cena* in honor of Metellus Pius in Spain, at which a statue of Victory was lowered to place a wreath on Metellus' head.[48] Descriptions of luxurious *deipna* and symposia were now, it seems, established as a historiographical motif. Plutarch also makes biographical capital out of the anecdotes that circulated about the luxury and extravagance of Lucullus' dining arrangements.[49] Not only the parties but even the halls in which they were held are described in grander and more extravagant terms: Agathocles' Hall of Sixty Couches was said to have incurred the wrath of the gods,[50] while Alexander, it is reported, had a tent prepared to hold a hundred couches that he took with him on his expedition and used for the lavish entertainment associated with the weddings of the Persian women.[51]

Treachery and Plotting

As Circe ensnared the men of Odysseus, preparing them "a mixture of cheese, barley-meal, and yellow honey flavoured with Pramnian wine" into which she introduced "a powerful drug,"[52] so in historical writers symposia and *deipna* frequently appear as a cover for plots and treachery. The ease and enjoyment, harmony and fellow feeling at which symposia and *deipna* aimed, made them a welcome cloak for deception by the unscrupulous. The only entertainment of this kind to appear in the pages of Thucydides is the one at which the Athenian envoys are hoodwinked about the extent of Segestan wealth. In fact in this instance Thucydides may incautiously have accepted a popular tale, for Dover notes some of the difficulties in the report, and Aly points to similarities between this account and a popular *Wandermotiv* concerning deceptive displays of wealth.[53] On Plutarch's evidence one of the most pressing reasons for declining an invitation to a party might well have been the hope of circumventing the plots of one's fellow diners or symposiasts. A saying attributed to Epaminondas declares that (simple) meals such as he provided offered no scope for treachery.[54] Yet any meal or symposium with the traditional aims might be exploited as a cover for dark deeds. According to Plutarch, Aratus, when plotting the overthrow of Nicocles, threw the tyrant's spies off the scent by making public and obvious preparations for a symposium.[55] Pompey when a young man concealed his knowledge of a plot against his father and himself by acting with *philophrosyne* towards and drinking more freely with the plotter, Terentius, at supper.[56] When Sex. Pompey was entertaining Antony and Octavian on shipboard at Misenum, at the height of the revelry his lieutenant, Menas, offered to cut the cables and secure the mastery for Sextus; the story is also told by Appian and Dio.[57]

Plots in some cases led to killings. When Pelopidas and his companions undertook to dispose of the Theban tyrants, one of their associates proposed a symposium for the tyrants to throw them off guard, and the plotters turned up with women's clothes over their armor and wearing garlands of pine and fir.[58] Alexander, the son of Cassander, plotted to kill Demetrius Poliorcetes over the wine, but the plot was forestalled and he himself became the victim of Demetrius' counterplot as he left the dinner table.[59] Cleomenes had four of the ephors killed while they were dining.[60] Parysatis, the mother of Artaxerxes II, poisoned the king's wife, Stateira, at dinner after a supposed reconciliation; Plutarch derives his account from Ctesias and Dinon.[61] The plot against the life of Sertorius in Spain culminated in a banquet at which the plotters first tried to provoke the restrained and decorous Sertorius by dissolute behavior and then killed him, the signal for the attack being the dropped wine cup.[62] Diodorus tells the story of the murder of the younger Agathocles at a sacrificial banquet, followed by the poisoning of the king at dinner by his slave, Menon, who handed him a poisoned toothpick; Justin's quite different account of the king's death makes no mention of a banquet.[63] Plots of this kind seem to be peculiarly appropriate to entertainments within royal courts or family gatherings: there are several examples in Josephus; Phakeas (Pekahiah) is "treacherously murdered *in a symposium with his friends*" where the words emphasized are Josephus' addition to the narrative of 2 *Kings;*[64] in his rendering of an incident from Jeremiah, the words "and those who reclined with him in the symposium" are also Josephus' addition to the biblical account.[65] For Josephus at least, treacherous murder at a symposium is a topos that may be used to flesh out a spare narrative. The Hasmonaean High Priest, Simon, dies at the hands of his son-in-law "after a plot against him in a symposium";[66] Malichus bribes Hyrcanus' wine pourer to poison Herod's father, Antipater;[67] Herod responds by having Malichus killed under cover of an invitation to a *deipnon*.[68] According to one account, Herod has Hyrcanus strangled after ensnaring him at a symposium;[69] Herod's brother, Pheroras, is said to have been poisoned at dinner.[70]

Murder and Decapitation

The fact or belief that a murder had been committed at a symposium or banquet added to the horror of the act. In the case of the killing of Clitus by Alexander, that it was carried out in a banquet setting, though not stressed by Plutarch, is underlined by other elements of the tradition and by moralizing commentators such as Seneca.[71] The cruelty of the deed in such a setting was enough to turn it into an exemplum.[72] Alexander had acted in a drunken rage; other killings at symposia or *deipna* reported in the historical tradition were more cold-blooded. Agathocles is said to have slaughtered his enemies, "five hundred in number," at a banquet after previously learning their real opinion about his rule while they were under the influence of wine,[73] while Alexander Jannaeus reputedly, as he feasted in a conspicuous place with his concubines, ordered "about eight hundred" of his Jewish enemies to be crucified, slaughtering the wives and children of his still-living victims before their eyes, "a deed," says Josephus, "most cruel of all."[74] One of the most notorious killings at a symposium, though it concerns only a single victim, was an action by L. Quinctius Flamininus, for which he was expelled from the Senate. There are various versions of the story, some of them intended to palliate L. Flamininus' offense, but Livy's version claims to be based on a speech of Cato the Censor giving the reason for Lucius' expulsion. According to this Lucius, while on campaign in Gaul, in order to gratify a young male favorite, had executed by his own hand, *inter pocula atque epulas*, a Boian chieftain who had come seeking Roman protection.[75] Examples of similar cruelty at symposium and *deipnon* continue to be reported from later days. The Roman knight Vedius Pollio, while entertaining Augustus, would have had a slave who had broken a prized crystal cup thrown to the *muraenae* to be torn to pieces, had not Augustus intervened.[76]

According to Suetonius, the emperor Gaius not only conducted judicial examinations by torture while dining or drinking but had an expert headsman on hand for the execution of prisoners.[77] Later emperors are alleged to have watched displays of gladiators, criminals, and wild beasts just before or during dinner.[78] Nicolaus of Damascus refers to the Roman practice of introducing two or three pairs of gladiators as an after-dinner entertainment, and Strabo attributes this practice to the Campanians.[79] The assassins sent by Nero killed Faustus Sulla when he was reclining at supper; Sulla's severed head was brought back to Nero, who mocked it as he did that of Rubellius Plautus.[80] The display of a severed head at a banquet or drinking party constitutes a motif in itself. The *locus classicus* is the presentation of the head of John the Baptist at the birthday feast of Herod Antipas; Josephus in his report of the Baptist's death makes no mention of the feast or of Salome's request, while the Gospel accounts contain folktale elements, e.g., the rash oath and the boon at a banquet.[81] Plutarch recounts that after the Roman defeat at Carrhae, the head of Crassus was brought to the Parthian king, Orodes (Hyrodes), as he was banqueting with the Armenian Artavasdes. When the tables had been removed, Jason, a tragic actor, was about to sing the scene from Euripides' *Bacchae* in which Agave enters with the head of Pentheus; at that point the head of Crassus was thrown into the midst of the company and picked up by Jason, who substituted it for the mask of Pentheus and recited Agave's lines:

> We bring from the mountain
> a tendril fresh-cut to the palace,
> a wonderful prey.[82]

The historian Appian, surely in this case a victim of Augustan propaganda, reports the allegation that Antony placed the head of Cicero before his table at meals until he was satiated with the evil sight.[83] Even earlier, Seneca—no historian—had descanted on how the heads of *principes civitatis* were brought to Antony as he dined, and how in the midst of the most elaborate banquets and royal luxury he had examined the faces and hands of the proscribed.[84]

The foregoing makes no pretension to provide an exhaustive list of symposia and *deipna* in the historical writers, but enough has been said to illustrate how Plutarch and other writers frequently choose to record, as caution or admonition, aspects of symposium or *deipnon* that offended against the code of ease and friendliness. Certain motifs recur and point to exaggerations, distortions, and even sheer inventions in the record. Though much of the material has been drawn from Plutarch, he himself was heavily dependent on earlier historical writings; the evidence of surviving works proves the interest of historians in symposia and *deipna* as important social institutions, especially perhaps in those incidents that offend against the social code governing these institutions. The appearance of disturbing symposia and *deipna* in myth may suggest that these institutions were seen or felt to be bastions of civilization in a war against barbarism that constantly threatened to overwhelm it. Likewise, since such entertainments may be seen as a microcosm of society, the orderly conduct of symposium or *deipnon* may be held to reflect the good order and discipline of *polis* or *respublica*. Whether such ideas remained uppermost in ancient thinking or sank from recollection, the readiness of historians to report examples of discordant behavior at symposia and *deipna* and the moral outrage that frequently colors their reports attest the strength of their conviction that a properly conducted symposium or *deipnon* was an index of civilized behavior.

NOTES

1. Cf. A. Dihle, *Studien zur griechischen Biographie*[2] (Göttingen 1970), 43 ff.
2. Cf. *Mor.* 612D; *Cat. Ma.* 25.4. Note the emphasis on *koinonia*, *Mor.* 643B.
3. *Mor.* 660B; cf. 660A fin.
4. Plut. *Alex.* 1.2.
5. A. Wallace-Hadrill, *Suetonius: The Scholar and His Caesars* (London 1983), 8 and n. 13.
6. *Per.* 7.5 ff.
7. Plut. *Nic.* 5.1.
8. Plut. *Sert.* 13.2.
9. Plato, *Lg.* 2.671A, 3; cf. 1.640A, 1.
10. Cf., e.g., Hom. *Od.* 21.295ff.; Ov. *Met.* 12.210ff.
11. E.g., *ILS* 7212, pag. II.25—Lanuvium; *SIG*[3] 1109.73ff—Iobacchi.
12. 6.130.
13. Polyb. 23.5.7–13; cf. Plut. *Flam.* 17.6.
14. Plut. *Alc.* 4.4–6; Athen. 12.534E-F (with additional detail).
15. Tac. *Hist.* 1.48; Plut. *Galba* 12.4 (silver cup); Suet. *Claud.* 32 (without naming Vinius).

16. *Alex.* 52.8–9; cf. Nero's enjoyment of the wrangles of philosophers *post epulas,* Tac. *Ann.* 14.16.

17. *Alex.* 9.6–14; Athen. 13.557D (Satyros).

18. *Alex.* 38; Cleitarchus, *FGrH* 137 F 11 (= Athen. 13.576D-E); Strabo 15.3.6, 730C (no mention of Thais); Arrian's account is altogether more sober, omitting the romantic element, 3.18.11–12.

19. Plut. *Pomp.* 40.7.

20. Plut. *Brut.* 34.8.

21. 26.1.4; cf. Diod. 29.32; Athen. 10.439A.

22. W. Burkert, *Greek Religion,* trans. J. Raffan (Cambridge, MA 1985), 248.

23. Cf. W.J. Slater, *ICS* 6, 1981, 205ff.

24. Plut. *Aem.* 28.9; *Mor.* 615E-F; Polyb. 30.14; Liv. 45.32.11; Diod. 31.8.13.

25. Plut. *Dio* 52.3; cf. 13.3: after Plato's arrival in Sicily, the *aidos symposiōn* at the court of Dionysius led the citizens to entertain hopes of a change for the better; but at the beginning of the reign Dionysius was alleged to have had a drinking party for ninety consecutive days, and at the court in this period drunkenness and jesting and music and dancing and buffoonery held sway, ibid., 7.7.

26. Plut. *Ages.* 19.6; cf. Xen. *Ages.* 8.7.

27. Plut. *Cleom.* 13.4–7.

28. Plut. *Crass.* 3.2.

29. Plut. *Cic.* 36.3

30. Plut. *Tib. Gr.* 2.4; Plin. *H.N.* 33. 147; Tacitus, however, dates the spread of *luxus mensae* to the century after Actium, *Ann.* 3.55; cf. Friedländer, *Sittengeschichte* 2[10], 284ff.

31. Plut. *Pomp.* 2.11–12; cf. 1.4; *Luc.* 40.2.

32. Plut. *Caes.* 17.9–10.1 (from Oppius?); cf. Suet. *Caes.* 53 (= Oppius fr. 7 P), taking *conditum* from *condire.*

33. Hdt. 1.107–20.

34. 2.29.3

35. 6.4–7; see the important discussion by Philip J. King, *Amos, Hosea, Micah— An Archaeological Commentary* (Philadelphia 1988), 137ff.

36. Cf. J.-M. Dentzer, *RA* 1971, 215–58. On luxury and extravagance at table see, in general, Athenaeus, bk. 4.

37. Plut. *Cat. Mi.* 56.7, 67.1; App. *BC* 2.98, 407.

38. 31.25.4ff.

39. Plut. *Lyc.* 13; 607; *Mor.* 227C; also told of Agesilaus in Asia, *Mor.* 210D.

40. *Phoc.* 20.3; Athen. 4.168F gives a somewhat different version.

41. Plut. *Alex.* 70.1–2; Chares, *FGrH* 125 F 19b; 19a (= Athen. 10.437A-B); Ael. *VH* 2.41.

42. *Alex.* 23.1; *Mor.* 623E-F.

43. *Alex.* 75.4–5; cf. Diod. 17.117; Justin, 12.13.7; Arr. 7.24.4ff.

44. Plut. *Sull.* 36.1, cf. 2.4; *Comp. Lys. et Sull.* 3.5.

45. *Demetr.* 19.4, 7; Diod. 20.92.4; Plut. *Ant.* 9.5–6; Cic. *Phil.* 2.61; Dio

45.28.1–2; note esp. Antony's association with Cleopatra, Plut. *Ant.* 28.2–6; 71.4–5.

46. Plut. *Demetr.* 27.3; cf. Athen. 3.101E, 4.12A-B.

47. *Ant.* 26.6; Socrates, *FGrH* 192 F 1 (= Athen. 2.147E–148B): cf. I. Becher, *Das Bild der Kleopatra in der griechischen and lateinischen Literatur* (Berlin 1966), 143–45, on the doubtful aspects of Socrates' description.

48. Sall. *Hist.* 2.70 M, *ultra Romanum ac mortalium etiam morem curabant;* Plut. *Sert.* 22.3 (with embellishments).

49. Plut. *Luc.* 40–41.

50. Diod. 16.82.2.

51. Diod. 17.16.4; Athen. 12.538C, 539D.

52. Hom. *Od.* 10.234–236, Penguin trans. E.V. Rieu (Harmondsworth 1946).

53. Thuc. 6.46; A.W. Gomme, A. Andrewes, and K.J. Dover, eds., *A Historical Commentary on Thucydides* vol 4. (Oxford 1970), 313; W. Aly, *Volksmärchen, Sage und Novellen bei Herodot und seinen Zeitgenossen,* 2nd ed. by L. Huber (Göttingen 1969), 35.

54. Plut. *Lyc.* 13.6.

55. *Arat.* 6.4–5.

56. Plut. *Pomp.* 3.2.

57. Plut. *Ant.* 32.3–8; App. *BC* 5.73, 308–11; Dio 48.38.

58. Plut. *Pel.* 9.4–11; *Mor.* 594E–597C; Xen. *HG* 5.4.4–7.

59. Plut. *Demetr.* 36.4–12; cf. the plotting and counterplotting of Neoptolemos and Pyrrhos at dinner, *Pyrrh.* 5.7–14.

60. Plut. *Cleom.* 7–8; cf. the attack of Damon and his associates on the magistrates of Chaeronea, *Cim.* 1.5.

61. Plut. *Art.* 19.107; Dinon, *FGrH* 690 F 15b; Ctesias, *FGrH* 688 F 29b.

62. Plut. *Sert.* 26.7–11.

63. Diod. 21.16.3–5; Justin 23.2.3–12.

64. *AJ* 9.233–234; cf. 2 *Kings* 15.25.

65. *AJ* 10.168–69; cf. *Jer.* 41.1–2.

66. *BJ* 1.54; cf. *AJ* 13.228, 20.240.

67. *BJ* 1.226; *AJ* 14.281.

68. *BJ* 1.233–34; *AJ* 14.291–92.

69. *AJ* 15.174–76.

70. *AJ* 17.62.

71. Plut. *Alex.* 50–52.7; Curt. 8.1.20–2.12; note esp. 8.1.51, 8.2.3, 8.6, 8.8; Justin 12.6.1–16, esp. 6.3, .6, .12, Arr. 4.8.1–9.4; Sen. *Ep.* 83.19; *De Ira* 3.17.1.

72. Lucian *Hist. Conscr.* 38; Homeyer ad loc. cites Ps.-Aristid. *Rhet.* A 162 (*Rh. Gr.* 5.61.13 Schmid).

73. Diod. 20.63.6.

74. *AJ* 13.380.

75. Liv. 39.42.5–43.5; Cato *ORF*³ fr. 71; Plut. *Cat. Ma.* 17.1–6; *Flam.* 18–19.5; Cic. *De Sen.* 42; Auct. *De Vir. Ill.* 47.4; Val. Max. 2.3. Valerius Antias and

"many others" (Plut.) had given versions of the story. For discussion see A.E. Astin, *Cato the Censor* (Oxford 1978), 79ff. A line from a much-quoted passage of Ennius' *Telamon* (*scen.* 314V[3]) points the contrast between *epulae* and *mortiferum bellum*.

76. Dio 54.23.1–4; Sen. *De Clem.* 1.18.2; *De Ira* 3.40.2–4.

77. Suet. *Cal.* 32.1.

78. *SHA: Verus* 4.9; *Elagab.* 25.7.

79. Nic. Dam. *FGrH* 90 F 78; Strabo 5.4.13, 250C.

80. Tac. *Ann.* 14.57.4, 14.59.3; Dio 62.14.1; [Sen.] *Oct.* 437.

81. *Ev. Marc.* 6.14–29; *Ev. Matt.* 14.1–12; Jos. *AJ* 18.119. For other examples see reports of Marius' dealings with the orator Antonius, Plut. *Mar.* 44.1–7; App. *BC* 1.72, 333–35; Val. Max. 9.2.2; Flor. 2.9.14; cf. also Diog. Laert. 9.10.58.

82. Plut. *Crass.* 33.1–7 (Eur. *Bacch.* 1169); Polyaen. 7.41. I should like to thank Dr. Eric Csapo for helpful discussion of the passage in Plutarch.

83. App. *BC* 4.20.81.

84. Sen. *Ep.* 83.25; cf. Sen. *Suas.* 6.7; Dio 47.8.1–2.

Slaves at Roman Convivia

John H. D'Arms

Dining room slaves, the human props essential to the support of upper-class Roman convivial comforts, are the subjects of this chapter. I welcome the opportunity to attempt to connect the functions of this group of household slaves to factors that are essentially noneconomic, namely upper-class values and attitudes. In what follows, based primarily on selected passages from literature and inscriptions of the principate, I offer a brief conspectus, first, of the service that dining room slaves were typically expected to perform in the houses and villas of the Roman rich; second, of the benefits they gained, and of the human indignities to which they were typically subjected, in the line of duty. In conclusion, stimulated by comparative evidence from the antebellum south, I advocate a more critical approach to what is typically taken for granted in modern discussions of Roman private life: namely, that conditions of urban domestic slaves were always preferable to those of slaves elsewhere in economy and society.

At the outset, two methodological points should be made explicit. First, I exclude from this survey persons of servile status whose primary function was to provide entertainment, since this topic is discussed by C.P. Jones elsewhere in this volume.[1] (In so doing, I recognize, of course, that the boundaries between providing service and providing entertainment are not always clear-cut, as will be seen shortly, when we consider wine servers.) Secondly, I shall not always specify whether the conditions described apply to formal banquets (*epulae*, and *cenae rectae*), or to the smaller private dinners (*convivia*), even though the servile apparatus required for mounting large-scale feasts was obviously more elaborate than was that at private *convivia*. The Romans themselves were well aware of differences between these two fundamental forms of commensality: as the Younger Seneca once observed, "no one judges himself to be the *hospes* of an innkeeper, or the dinner guest [*conviva*] of a man giving a banquet."[2] But let us be clear: the Roman propertied classes numbered their household slaves in dozens, sometimes in hundreds (see below); in this chapter, it is large households like these that occupy the foreground.

In our texts, Roman writers rarely distinguish the kinds of service performed by slaves in the *triclinium*, referring merely to *ministri* or *ministratores*. Inferring the specific tasks assigned to these menials is thus not always an easy matter, nor are we aided very reliably by Martial's epigram on the disreputable Zoilus.[3] That man employed five dining room attendants to cater to his idiosyncratic needs: a catamite with feathers to induce vomiting; a concubine to cool him with a fan; a slave boy to shoo away flies with a sprig of myrtle; a shampooer to massage his limbs; and a eunuch to help him urinate. But in less esoteric settings, and in general terms, the service functions group themselves into three main categories: supervisory duties, gate keeping, and guest control; the various food services; and the duties of the wine staff. Each of these categories deserves attention.

First, the prerogative to issue invitations, and to assign places at table, was not the host's alone: a *vocator* had authority to do both. Given the scale of the emperor's dinners, delegating responsibilities like these would have been essential, and thus it is hardly surprising to find that, in order to secure an invitation to one of Caligula's *convivia*, a rich provincial paid the *vocator* HS 200,000.[4] More unexpectedly, the *vocator* had comparable influence at private dinners as well, and indeed, even served as scapegoat when invitations went awry: in one of Martial's epigrams, we discover a host refusing to acknowledge that he overlooked the inviting of a particular guest and blaming the *vocator* instead.[5] *Nomenclatores*, too, seem sometimes to have controlled lists of dinner guests, and they had responsibility (as did lictors, on occasion) for arranging and announcing the presents (*apophoreta*) that often were bestowed upon departing guests.[6] To the *vocator* also fell the more sinister task of surveillance, *convivarum censura*, as Seneca once labels it:[7] he is to watch out for guests' *adulatio*, or *intemperantia aut gulae aut linguae*, since these will serve as the basis for tomorrow's invitations. Who gave overall directions to the dining room staff? Possibly the same *vocator*, though Fortunata seems to have played this role at Trimalchio's feast, and *ianitores* too were figures of consequence in many houses; and, in imperial households, *tricliniarchae* are attested for emperors beginning with Claudius.[8]

Second, the food service. The empress Livia had a freed *obsonator* in her household, who Treggiari thinks planned menus and laid in provisions.[9] *Obsonatores* turn up also at private *convivia*, where their knowledge of the subtleties of their masters' palates helped to stimulate appetites and to promote high hogging.[10] At given signals (by the host?) the meal's several courses (at least three, seldom more than six) were carried in by a crowd of waiters (*turba ministratorum, agmina exoletorum*); the emperor Claudius is reported to have brought his own supply to others' dinners.[11] The culinary specialists, cooks, bakers, and carvers of game birds, occupied privileged positions on the dining room staff. They are so often singled out as a "prestige" group in the dining literature that we may reasonably conclude that they were exempt from the multiple forms of dining room tasks to which the other slaves were subject—the *Digest* is explicit that household slaves might do double duty *in triclinio*.[12] Cooks, bakers, and carvers can hardly have been expected to sweep up the diners' spit-out food (*sputa*), or to gather up the leftovers (*analecta*), both of which were standard parts of the typical waiter's job.[13] Among the comic distortions we encounter in Trimalchio's dining room, the highly specialized duties of the slaves make a specially strong impression: *ministri*, usually designated merely as *pueri*, make no fewer than thirty-five separate entrances, pouring out snow-cooled water (31), spreading coverlets (40), sprinkling the room with saffron and vermilion-colored sawdust (68), carrying round bread (35), or towels (40), or hot water (68); anointing the diners' feet with ointment and winding garlands around their ankles (70); singing (34), or clapping (36), or dancing (36) in a troupe as they moved fantastic foods theatrically in and out of the room.

One of the emperor Tiberius' meals was served by naked girls.[14] Food waiters, normally, were male, and a host took some pains—excessive pains, in the case of Horace's Nasidienus[15]—to have them properly attired and neat for waiting on table. But it was wine waiters to whom the real prestige attached in the dining rooms of the powerful, and for them, far more than good grooming was essential. They were routinely expected to be young, smooth-shaven (but long-haired), and sexually attractive. They also bore Greek names: it is noteworthy that the only slave called by a name (other than in jest) by Trimalchio is Dionysus, a grape-bearing *puer speciosus*.[16] In setting out the laws for feasts in his *Saturnalia*, Lucian advocates stern reprisals against rich men whose wine servers are meager with their portions: "pray that their pretty, long-haired pages, whom they call Hyacinthus or Achilles or Narcissus, just as they are handing their masters the cup, suddenly go bald and have their hair fall out and grow a pointed beard."[17] Wine waiters might be assigned to specific guests, with whom, however, flirtation was not permitted. When the guest Cleodemus tried to pass two drachmas to a smiling boy with the wine cup and was caught out, his host tactfully and silently sent the boy away, substituting for him, in Lucian's words, "an older, sturdier slave, a muleteer or a horse groom."[18] If the guest was an emperor, he probably brought his own cupbearer with him to private dinners, the *a cyatho* attested in inscriptions[19]—just as, as we have seen, he brought his own waiters. Augustus is even said to have sent his freedmen ahead of him to the villas of his country hosts to select the wines for dinner.[20]

In Tacitus' account of the consular Petronius' last hours on earth—a splendid parody of a Stoic death scene—the condemned man, we are told, "treated some of his slaves to gifts, others to beatings."[21] We need next to consider the rewards and punishments for service at the tables of the powerful, and then, in conclusion, to draw up some provisional kind of balance sheet.

Examples of signal slave service, for which perpetrators are rewarded, are occasionally attested and commended in the sources; these range from acts of culinary skill—Trimalchio's cook, whose efforts earned him a silver crown and a drink, the cup handed to him on Corinthian plate[22]—to acts of moral courage, as by the loyal slave who alertly slipped his master's senatorial ring, engraved with a portrait of Tiberius, off his finger when the senator was on the verge of urinating into a chamber pot at table, thus saving the senator from prosecution for *maiestas*.[23] Table service in great houses brought other benefits: witness the *licentia* displayed by Trimalchio's slaves at the end of the *Cena,* when they are allowed to crowd onto the couches and to displace the guests; and if that be thought fanciful, their access to the leftover food and drink is not.[24] Slaves, it would seem, routinely had access to such remains at *convivia;* according to Plutarch, they greatly preferred such leftovers to a *cena* provided apart;[25] Apuleius' ass Lucius brilliantly confounded two slaves, a cook and a baker, by pilfering and stuffing down the leftover delicacies that they had been sequestering for their own suppers.[26]

Last, let us not underestimate a more intangible reward from slaving at the tables of the rich: in Roman society, an attendant to the proud and powerful got ample opportunity to display pride and to exercise power on his own. *Maxima quaeque domus servis est plena superbis:*[27] Juvenal's maxim points to one of the most common topoi in the dining literature, that of the haughty slave who reserves the choicest foods and wines for the master and other grandees, and distributes scraps and dregs to others— lesser *amici,* clients, lowly dependants of other guests, *umbrae.*[28] If we think that in showing such preferential treatment slaves were doing no more than carrying out their masters' wishes, we need to notice that Caesar severely punished his baker for deceitfully passing worse bread to guests than to himself, and that Hadrian devised a scheme for detecting *obsonatores* who cheated in this way;[29] if we suppose that slaves took no personal satisfaction from such patronizing behavior, Lucian's description of the dining room slaves in *De Mercede Conductis* and many other texts proves precisely the opposite.[30]

Gratifications, though, such as eating the rich man's leftovers and humiliating guests of lowly status, like other forms of tokenism within the framework of slavery, are as nothing when set against one fundamentally degrading condition that slave status imposed: a slave's obligation to answer to an owner with his or her body for any and all offenses, including his unrestricted availability in sexual relations.[31] Brutally bizarre punishments, disproportionate to the nature of the crimes, seem the more grotesque when the settings are convivial: for instance, the cupbearer who broke a crystal goblet and whom P. Vedius Pollio commanded to be thrown to the lampreys in his fish ponds; or the slave who stole a silver plate during one of Caligula's public feasts: with his hands cut off and hung around his neck across his chest, he was forced to parade among the diners, preceded by a placard that proclaimed his crime; or the freedman of Domitius Ahenobarbus, father of Nero, who was killed for refusing at dinner to drink as much as he was ordered; or finally the cook in Apuleius who lost an expensive ham of a stag when a dog got at it, and anticipating his master's blows and further torture he hanged himself by the neck.[32]

Texts like these reveal that when slaves were murdered, mutilated, or thrown into chains, they had usually stolen (or destroyed) extremely valuable objects, or had seriously deceived their masters. But beatings could be inflicted on the slightest pretext. Most attested instances arose out of clumsy service or from petty theft. Did a slave drop a cup? —then box his ears.[33] Steal sweetmeats off the platter he was passing? —then inflict a blow.[34] Did he pinch two napkins? —then scald him with burning iron.[35] Is he slow with the hot water? —then give him three hundred lashes.[36] Is the game underdone, or the fish improperly seasoned? —then strip and beat the cook,[37] or downgrade him to harsher forms of service.[38] Did he spill food on the guests or floor? —then throw him into the water, or have the *tortores* strip him for flogging.[39]

At the baths on his way to dinner, Trimalchio urinates, calls for water to wash his hands, and then wipes them on a slave's head.[40] The episode takes us past the corporal punishments meted out for inadequate service and leads us to the other degradations to which slave bodies were unrestrictedly subject. Direct sexual exploitation of slaves by their masters is of course the dehumanizing device par excellence, and in *triclinia,* as was already suggested, the focus was upon the wine service; we saw that *pueri*.

speciosi were sternly forbidden to flirt with guests, but owners' rights were another matter. I am prepared to let Seneca have the last word on this group of slaves:

> the server of the wine has to dress like a woman and to wrestle with his advancing years; he can't get away from his boyhood, but is continually dragged back to it. His body hair is plucked away, and he is kept beardless; he is forced to keep awake all night, dividing his time between his master's drunkenness and his lust.[41]

One compensation for slaving at feasts is generally thought to be the fixed occasions—holidays—when Roman masters arranged feasting for slaves; conspicuously, the *Saturnalia,* which was supposed to represent a kind of Liberty Hall for slaves, with the chief emphasis on feasting.[42] From our scattered sources we can recover two different ways of bridging the social gulf at this festival. The rarer form was that of full-scale social transformation: masters and slaves reversed their respective roles, and the former waited upon the latter.[43] More commonly, a temporary grant of equality enabled slaves and masters to participate together in a common meal.[44] Yet despite modern emphasis upon "la suspension de toute differ-entiation sociale" at the *Saturnalia,*[45] ancient sources are remarkable primarily for revealing the ways in which the Romans successfully continued to keep their slaves at a distance even on this occasion. In one of our pertinent texts, Roman children—not Roman masters—are made to entertain and wait upon the slaves at dinner;[46] in another, the slaves' feast precedes that of their owners;[47] in still another, slaves simply get the privilege of donning their masters' clothes during the festival.[48] When Cicero fed Caesar and his entourage during the *Saturnalia* of 45 B.C., the humbler freedmen and the slaves had their meal in a separate dining room, segregated from the luxuries offered to the grander members of the party.[49] A casual remark of the Younger Pliny, passing the *Saturnalia* at his villa near Ostia, makes it clear that he managed to avoid the spirited revelling of his slave *familia* altogether.[50] Thus, whereas we may grant that the function of the festival was to enforce social control through occasional rewards or incentives, I conclude, from these and other passages, that slaves during the Roman *Saturnalia* experienced far less than the *tota licentia* claimed by Macrobius;[51] Ganymede in the *Cena Trimalchionis* comes closer to social reality with his bitter remark "it's upper class jaws which are keeping carnival—at the Saturnalia and all year round."[52]

It is time now to attempt the balance sheet provided above. In a careful study of the household slaves of Livia, based primarily on inscriptions and published in 1975, Treggiari concluded that Livia's slave staff was large; that its structure was highly organized, with a recognizable chain of command among the slaves; and that there was a high degree of specialization within the household.[53] In general terms, the evidence discussed above—a mixture of the literary and epigraphic, and most of it derived from texts later than those exploited by Treggiari—largely corroborates her own main findings. To her emphasis on organization we might add that Trimalchio's arrangement of his household slaves into gangs, or *decuriae*,[54] makes nonsense if it did not reflect actual social arrangements to at least some recognizable degree. On specialization, it needs to be remembered that highly differentiated slave households were signs of status: as Saller observes, "the Roman aristocrat who had to use female servants in front of guests or to have one servant fulfill two household functions was regarded as déclassé."[55] The size of slave households, finally, when visualized in the particular context of the dining practices of the Roman rich, evokes a powerful and unsettling image, one that is normally ignored in discussions of Roman private life. We should try now to bring this into sharper focus.

That the numbers of slaves in the dining rooms of the powerful were considerable is in itself hardly surprising, given the Roman upper-class obsession with *existimatio, liberalitas, munificentia,* and the conspicuous consumption that is one of the by-products of these. After all, "owning many slaves" ranks high in any list of the desires of a would-be *dives;* not one in ten of his slaves knew Trimalchio by sight; the city prefect L. Pedanius Secundus had 400 in his household *familia* in Rome in A.D. 61.[56] More striking than mere numbers, however, are these three features: the crowds of slaves often outnumbered the diners; they were typically expected to stand; they were also under strict orders to remain silent throughout the proceedings: what are we to make of this silent standing mass of servile humanity? Seneca points to the "crowd of standing slaves" (*stantium servorum turba*) by which masters are customarily surrounded at their dinners; he goes on to add that "their slightest murmur is repressed by the rod; they pay a huge penalty for the slightest breach of silence; all night long they have to stand around, hungry and dumb."[57] In the *Cena,* each guest has his own table, Trimalchio explains, "so these filthy slaves won't make us so hot by crowding past us."[58] In a remarkable aside, the Elder Pliny once contrasts contemporary with earlier times. "Nowadays," he writes,

> our food and drink need to be protected from the crowds of dining room slaves [*mancipiorum legiones*]. How different from the past, when a single slave of a Marcus or of a Lucius [*Marcipor,* or *Lucipor*] took all his meals with the family in common; nor did one need to

keep watch on one's slaves. Today we acquire sumptuous fare only to have it stolen, and we are afraid that the masses of our slaves will pilfer the masses of our food and drink.[59]

It is granted that the authors of moralistic utterances like these tend to exaggerate social troubles so as to counterattack them more effectively. Even so, in the interests of more fully unravelling the structures of meaning in these passages, questions such as the following might be asked: how did Roman slaves react to being made to stand while masters reclined (a bitter source of resentment by slaves in the antebellum South)?[60] In the rosy past described by the Elder Pliny, how far could a man without a name of his own (*Marci puer* or *Luci puer*) actually feel himself to be a participant in the household's communal meal? And does not Pliny, by conceiving so narrowly the grounds for later adversarial tensions between diners and the mute mass of mealtime slaves, serve merely to trivialize them? How frequently was food pilfering a petty, day-to-day form of slave resistance, and how frequently the result of underfeeding?[61] In my view, passages like these evoke an atmosphere of social tension, even recalling Proust's observation about domestic servants: they are bound to act in a manner abhorrent to their upper-class employers, since "they live in a situation inferior to our own, and add to our wealth and our weaknesses imaginary riches and vices for which they envy and despise us."[62] To be sure, art historians could object to this somewhat sinister vision of the *triclinium*, pointing out that such an atmosphere does not seem to be corroborated by known representations of Roman dining scenes. But is that not because the artist's eyes were on the diners, not the slaves, and because when slaves are included, status differences are usually represented through hierarchic scaling?[63]

In Roman *triclinia*, the late J.P.V.D. Balsdon asserted, slaves typically "enjoyed themselves as much as the guests. There [was] plenty of good food and drink to be consumed outside the dining-room; there [were] tips, and there [was] the immense pleasure of watching the indecorous conduct of your betters."[64] That will not do, nor does the assertion by Veyne—in a new volume intended to provide a state-of-the-art discussion of Roman private life—that the slave's master "punished paternally" and "commanded with love," mark much of an improvement.[65] Such conclusions, of course, follow naturally enough from the assumption that Roman household slaves were always well treated in comparison to their counterparts in agriculture, mining, or manufacturing. If that was always and everywhere true, then it is easier (though still far too sanguine) to claim that, in large and wealthy households under the empire, "a quick and bright young slave had the possibility of a really exciting future."[66]

Of course, the common assumption has a good deal to recommend it. Slaves' working conditions in the mines were notoriously grim, and on the land they fairly typically implied chains.[67] Domestic slaves, unlike their agricultural counterparts, had direct access to owners and would on occasion be able to exploit that opportunity to their own advantage; they were also extremely expensive, and it was thus in the owners' interests to treat them well. Such slaves, finally, will have enjoyed comparative advantage, too, in being able to build families and to achieve manumission.[68] It is thus hardly surprising that we find in the sources instances of pampered and ill-behaved urban slaves being threatened with deportation to the country as punishment.[69]

But the plain fact is that domestic service in a grand urban house did not guarantee an easier life for slaves; and whether it did more often than not remains problematic. Dining room slaves' proximity to owners could bring punishment, as well as privilege, as we have seen; so also agricultural slaves drew benefits, and not only hardships, from being removed from their masters' constant surveillance. That slaves in the fields were not to be beaten except as a last resort is a fair inference from Varro's advice to the *vilicus;*[70] and rural slaves did not typically have to suffer the arbitrary acts of brutality and other indignities that masters, their inhibitions loosened by drink, brought down upon slaves in the *triclinium*. Aesop's master became enraged at dinners; Aesop paid the price with thrashings.[71] The hypothesis that Roman domestic slaves enjoyed conditions more favorable than rural slaves or those in manufacturing calls out for proper investigation, for it has never been established, and it needs careful testing.[72]

Here, we can but begin to outline what such a test might require. We would need to review the known instances of brutality inflicted on all kinds of domestic slaves—the scribe, for instance, whose angry master struck him in the eye with a reed pen; or the slave of Augustus whose legs were broken because he took a bribe; or the bath attendant, ordered by the twelve-year-old Commodus to be thrown into the furnace, when the future emperor found the *calidarium* too hot.[73] Psychological factors too would have to be part of such a test, and, along with others, this question especially suggests itself: from the slaves' point of view, how far did proximity to the tables of the powerful increase their sense of superiority over fellow slaves, and how far did it serve merely to accentuate the distance between their own condition and that of their owners, the privileged consumers of the luxuries and comforts that the slaves dispensed? The Roman evidence in and of itself is, of course, unlikely ever to provide a satisfactory answer to that question, but comparative evidence from slavery in the New World is suggestive. Consider this excerpt from Frances Anne Kemble's journal of her residence on a Georgian plantation in 1838–39.

> The house servants have no other or better allowance of food than the field laborers, but have the advantage of eking it out by what is left from the master's table—if possible, with even less comfort in one respect, inasmuch as no time whatever is set apart for their meals, which they snatch at any hour and in any way that they can—generally, however, standing or squatting on their hams round the kitchen fire; the kitchen being a mere outhouse or barn with a fire in it. On the (plantation) where I lived . . . they had no sleeping rooms in the house; but when their work was over, they retired like the rest to their hovels, the discomfort of which had to them all the additional disadvantage of comparison with their owners' mode of living. In all establishments whatever, of course, some disparity exists between the accommodation of the drawing rooms and best bedrooms and the servants' kitchen and attics; but on a plantation it is no longer a matter of degree. The young women who performed the offices of waiting and housemaids, and the lads who attended upon the service of their master's table where I lived, had neither table to feed at nor chair to sit down upon themselves; the "boys" lay all night on the hearth by the kitchen fire, and the women upon the usual slave's bed—a frame of rough boards, strewed with a little moss off the trees, with the addition perhaps of a tattered and filthy blanket.[74]

Fannie Kemble, with her strong antislavery bias and penchant for the dramatic, is something less than fully reliable as witness. But as the two Genoveses have well shown, her voice, when taken together with those of slaves themselves, casts serious doubt on the common assumption that high prestige and superior creature comforts were standard features of domestic service in the great houses of the antebellum south. Historians of American slavery are coming to replace the legend promulgated by owners of plantations and of town houses in Charleston, Natchez, and Mobile, with a more balanced, realistic estimate, one in which many house servants are discovered living in torment, chafing under the ceaseless scrutiny, impossibly high expectations, and cruelty of their masters, and actually preferring, for these and other reasons, work in the fields.[75] *Mutatis mutandis,* these revisionist tendencies, generated by historians of slavery in the New World, could open profitable avenues of inquiry too for historians of Roman society and culture.

NOTES

I gratefully acknowledge the friendly aid of Anka Begley and Benjamin Victor, and I am indebted to fellow symposiasts, very especially to Keith Bradley, for helpful criticism.

1. See below, pp. 185–98.
2. Sen. *De Ben.* 1.14.
3. Mart. 3.82.
4. Suet. *Calig.* 39.2.
5. Sen. *De Ira* 3.37.4. (*vocator* and private dinners); Mart. 7.86; cf. also *CIL* VI.3975 (*invitator*).
6. Sen. *Ep.* 19.11 (*nomenclatores* controlling guest lists); Petr. *Sat.* 56 (lictors); Suet. *Tib.* 72.3.
7. Sen. *Ep.* 47.8.
8. Petr. *Sat.* 67 (Fortunata); Apul. *Met.* 1.15–16 (*ianitor*); *CIL* VI.9083ff. (*tricliniarchae*).
9. S. Treggiari, *PBSR* n.s. 30, 1975, 51; *CIL* VI. 8945.
10. Sen. *Ep.* 47.8. *Praegustatores* are apparently attested only for emperors (Suet. *Claud.* 44.2; *CIL* VI.5355; *CIL* X.6324).
11. Suet. *Aug.* 74 (courses); Sen. *Ep.* 95.24 (waiters); Suet. *Claud.* 35.1 (Claudius).
12. Sen. *Ep.* 95.24, 47.6; Petr. *Sat.* 68; Apul. *Met.* 10.13–14; *Dig.* 33.7.12.32.
13. Mart. 7.20.17 (*analecta*); Sen. *Ep.* 47.5.
14. Suet. *Tib.* 42.2.
15. Hor. *Sat.* 2.8.69–70.
16. Petr. *Sat.* 41.
17. Lucian, *Sat.* 17.24.
18. Lucian, *Symp.* 15.
19. *CIL* VI.8817 (Antonia).
20. Plin. *H.N.* 14.72.
21. Tac. *Ann.* 16.19.
22. Petr. *Sat.* 50.
23. Sen. *De Ben.* 3.26; Suet. *Tib.* 58.
24. Petr. *Sat.* 70 (*licentia*), 64, 67, 74 (access to leftovers); cf. also Hor. *Sat.* 2.6.66ff.
25. Plut. *Quaest. Conv.* 7.4.5.
26. Apul. *Met.* 10.13–14.

27. Juv. *Sat.* 5.66.

28. Plin. *Ep.* 2.6.2; Juv. *Sat.* 5.125–27; cf. J.H. D'Arms, "The Roman *convivium* and the Idea of Equality," in O. Murray, ed., *Sympotica* (Oxford 1990), 318.

29. Suet. *Caes.* 48; *SHA Hadr.* 17.4.

30. Lucian, *De Merc. Cond.* 14, 26, 27.

31. See M.I. Finley, *Ancient Slavery and Modern Ideology* (New York 1980), 95ff.; K.M. Hopkins, *Conquerors and Slaves: Sociological Studies in Roman History I* (Cambridge 1978), 118ff.; K.R. Bradley, *Slaves and Masters in the Roman Empire: A Study in Social Control* (Oxford 1987), 113–37.

32. Sen. *De Ira* 3.40.2, cf. *De Clem.* 1.18.2, Dio 54.23.1–4, Plin. *H.N.* 9.77 (Vedius Pollio); Suet. *Calig.* 32.2 (Caligula's slave's parade); Suet. *Ner.* 5.1 (*libertus* of Ahenobarbus); Apul. *Met.* 8.31, Lucian, *Lucius* 39 (Apuleius' cook).

33. Petr. *Sat.* 34.6.

34. Juv. *Sat.* 9.5.

35. Juv. *Sat.* 14.15–22.

36. Amm. Marc. 28.4.16.

37. Mart. 3.13, 3.94, 8.23; *Life of Aesop* 62.

38. Petr. *Sat.* 47.

39. Lucian, *Sat.* 1.4; Petr. *Sat.* 49.

40. Petr. *Sat.* 27.

41. Sen. *Ep.* 47.7.

42. See the good discussion by Bradley (above note 31), 40–45.

43. Lucian, *Chronos* 18.

44. Sen. *Ep.* 47.2.14; *SHA Ver.* 7.5; Macrob. 1.11.1, *exaequato omnium iure.*

45. M. LeGlay, *Saturne Africain: Histoire* (Paris 1966), 471.

46. Athen. 14.639.

47. Macrob. 1.24.23.

48. Dio 60.19.

49. Cic. *Ad Att.* 13.52.2.

50. Plin. *Ep.* 2.17.22.

51. Macrob. 1.7.26.

52. Petr. *Sat.* 44: *isti maiores maxillae semper Saturnalia agunt.*

53. S. Treggiari, "Jobs in the Household of Livia," *PBSR* n.s. 30, 1975, 48ff., esp. 60; for additional inscriptional evidence from the early Julio-Claudian period cf. also J. Griffin, "Augustan Poetry and the Life of Luxury," *JRS* 66, 1976, 105.

54. Petr. *Sat.* 47.11.

55. R.P. Saller, "Slavery and the Roman Family," *Slavery and Abolition* 8, 1987, 71.

56. Lucian, *Sat.* 1 (would-be *dives*; cf. Sen. *De Vita Beata* 23.1, 25.1); Petr. *Sat.* 37 (Trimalchio's slaves); Tac. *Ann.* 14.43 (Pedanius Secundus). For upper-class attitudes towards wealth see in general J.H. D'Arms, *Commerce and Social Standing in Ancient Rome* (Cambridge, MA 1981), 152–55, 169–70.

57. Sen. *Ep.* 47.3.

58. Petr. *Sat.* 34.

59. Plin. *H.N.* 33.26.

60. See, e.g., E.D. Genovese, *Roll, Jordan, Roll: The World the Slaves Made* (New York 1974), 334.

61. Ibid. (above note 60), 602–3, on the distinction between stealing and taking in slave societies.

62. M. Proust, *Remembrance of Things Past. Volume I, Swann's Way,* trans. C.K. Scott Moncrieff and T. Kilmartin (New York 1981), 389.

63. Finley (above note 31), 96, citing N. Himmelmann, *Archäologisches zum Problem der griechischen Sklaverei, AAWM* 1971, 13 (Wiesbaden 1971).

64. J.P.V.D. Balsdon, *Life and Leisure in Ancient Rome* (New York 1969), 52; cf. also 110.

65. P. Veyne, ed., *A History of Private Life. Volume 1, From Pagan Rome to Byzantium,* trans. A. Goldhammer (Cambridge, MA 1987), 51, 65, on which see R.P. Saller, *AHR* 94, 1989, 705–6.

66. Balsdon (above note 64), 111.

67. Diodorus 5.38 (Spanish silver mines); Strab. 12.3.40 (realgar mines); Plin. *Ep.* 3.19 (emphasizing his avoidance of chained gangs, and implying that his practice was exceptional). See in general Hopkins (above note 31), 118–19.

68. Rightly noted by Bradley (above note 31), 123.

69. Hor. *Sat.* 2.7.118; Juv. *Sat.* 8.179ff., cf. Plaut. *Bacch.* 365, *Asin.* 341ff.; Bradley (above note 31), 120.

70. Varr. *R.R.* 1.17.5.

71. *Life of Aesop* 58, 77a.

72. The issue does not even surface in Veyne (above note 65); for pointers in the right direction see Bradley (above note 31), 123.

73. Galen, *De Anim. Morbis* 17–18 (scribe); Suet. *Aug.* 67 (slave of Augustus); *SHA Comm.* 1.9 (bath attendant).

74. Frances Anne Kemble, *Journal of a Residence on a Georgian Plantation in 1838–1839* (Athens, GA 1984), 361; cf. also 101.

75. E.D. Genovese (above note 60), 331–33; Elizabeth Fox-Genovese, *Within the Plantation Household* (Chapel Hill 1988), 172–91, 308–33.

Dinner Theater

Christopher P. Jones

In this chapter I want to consider the visual entertainment that hosts in antiquity offered to their guests over dinner, or more precisely in the drinking stage that followed dinner, the symposium. I shall call this phenomenon "dinner theater," understanding by it both that which is specifically intended to be watched, as opposed to being heard, but also that which is appropriate to the public spaces of the theater and to a lesser extent of the amphitheater. Thereafter I want to consider something about which we know much less, public banquets given in these same two places at which those present were entertained by artists such as pantomimes: we may call this phenomenon "theater-dinner." After juxtaposing these two I conclude with some general observations on ancient benefaction. My evidence is mainly verbal (literature and inscriptions), and I am very conscious of my unfamiliarity with the pictorial and archaeological remains.

For dinner theater my prime exhibit will be Petronius' Trimalchio. Much of Petronius' novel gives so realistic an impression that one readily forgets it is not a document of social history, a slice of ancient life. Still, fiction, if carefully used, can sometimes give us access to social life no less directly than documents; thus a study of Victorian family planning has a whole chapter on the question whether Anthony Trollope can be used as a source, and it concludes that he can.[1] We must therefore use Petronius discreetly, testing what he says against what we can learn from elsewhere, but we must not disqualify him as a witness of fact merely because he is a writer of fiction.

The overwhelming impression that we receive of Trimalchio's dinner is its visual variety, what we may call its theatricality. Petronius draws attention to this element soon after the narrator, Encolpius, and his friends have reclined. Noticing that the servants sing even as they perform the most menial of functions, cutting toenails, serving drinks, and so on, Encolpius comments that "one would have thought it the chorus of a pantomime, not the dining-room of a respectable householder"—*patris familiae triclinium* (31.3–7). The pantomime was a solo dancer in a mythological ballet, supported by a chorus singing the libretto, so that Encolpius' allusion immediately prepares us for the element of display and staginess that will mark the whole meal, down to its tragicomic ending. Part of this display is expressed in incidentals or in the author's turns of phrase. In the early stages of the dinner, Encolpius several times notices the orchestra that strikes up at important moments, for example at the entrance of Trimalchio (32.1; cf. 34.1, 36.1, 36.6). The two African slaves who wash the guests' hands in wine are compared to those who scatter sand in the amphitheater (34.4). The carver who carves a dish in time to music is compared to an *essedarius* fighting to the strains of an organ (36.6): the *essedarius*, as the commentators note, was not a racing driver but a type of gladiator, so that again the allusion is to the amphitheater. Twice Encolpius uses the word *automatum* of a surprise effect: once when the host has staged a little scene that ends with the presentation of a stuffed pig and again when the narrator wrongly anticipates a similar trick (50.1, 54.4). The appearance of this unusual word in Suetonius (*Claud.* 34.2) to describe a theatrical contrivance shows that Petronius is again thinking of the theater. Late in the meal there occurs what the narrator calls "a new round of games"—*nova ludorum commissio* (60.5): fruits and cakes are brought in which, when touched, squirt the diners with saffron. Again, the commentators note that such showers of saffron were a feature of the theater.[2] The main course of Trimalchio's dinner, if such a meal can be said to have a main course, consists of a huge boar. Before it is carried in, the servants put up tapestries depicting nets and all the paraphernalia of hunting; then Spartan hunting dogs bound among the tables; finally the creature itself is brought in, with little baskets (*sportellae*) filled with dates hanging from its tusks. The carver is dressed as a huntsman and cuts the boar up with a hunting knife (*venatorio cultro*); out fly thrushes, which are caught by bird-catchers; Trimalchio has these distributed to each of the diners, and then the slaves take up the baskets and distribute the dates (40).

This scene, we may suspect, is not so much meant to recall hunting in the wild as hunting in the guise in which it was most familiar to the citizen of a Greek or Roman city of the period, what in Latin is called *venatio* and in Greek *kynegion* or sometimes *theatrokynegion* or *theatrokynegesion*. This was a spectacle akin to, but yet distinctly different from, the duels called in Latin *munera* and in Greek *monomachiai*.[3] Such spectacles usually took place, as the Greek name implies, in the theater, most ancient cities not having the luxury of an amphitheater: when nowadays we see theaters such as that of Dionysos in Athens modified for so-called gladiators, these modifications are in fact for *venationes*, where the use of animals made them essential.⁴ The décor could include trees, either specially planted or produced by stage machinery. That dogs were used is known from Martial and other sources; among the many varieties of animals killed, boars are frequently mentioned.⁵

At Trimalchio's dinner, the boar is followed by dessert, and so begins the drinking and the conversation, the symposium as opposed to the *deipnon*. This being Trimalchio's dinner, however, the conversation is interrupted when three white pigs, decorated with bells, are led on leashes into the dining room. Encolpius comments thus: "I thought acrobats [*petauristarii*] had come in and pigs which were going to do tricks [*portenta*] as they do for crowds [*in circulis*]"; he finds instead that the meal is continuing and that one of the pigs is to constitute the next course (47.9).

Petronius' *petauristarii* are the performers called by other authors *petauristae*. The Greek *peteuron* means "shelf," "plank," "perch," but as used in this compound has been variously interpreted as "trapeze," "trampoline," or "seesaw." The question is not of great importance here, but the word must have designated some kind of device whereby a person could be catapulted into the air to do somersaults, fly through hoops, and the like. The grammarians derive the word from the Greek *petesthai*, "fly," and the usual translation, "acrobats," is no doubt the best: as with the modern word, however, which in this sense is not ancient, we should allow for a certain fluidity of meaning, and not suppose that every *petauristarius* necessarily used a *peteuron*.⁶

Encolpius' language does not make it quite clear whether he expects the supposed *petauristarii* to perform in conjunction with the pigs, or whether he uses the word simply in the sense of "animal trainer." As for his description of the pigs, the word *portenta* exactly renders the Greek *thaumata*, the standard word for tricks and displays of every kind, juggling, conjuring, puppetry, and so on. We hear much about performing animals in antiquity, for example elephants walking the tightrope, but this seems the only reference to performing pigs.⁷

Shortly after, Encolpius' expectations are fulfilled and the acrobats do come in. "A thoroughly boring lout [*baro*] stood with a ladder [*cum scalis constitit*] and ordered a boy to go up the rungs and to dance to a sung accompaniment at the top, then to jump through burning hoops and to pick up a jar with his teeth" (53.11). A *baro* is not necessarily a strong man, but like "oaf" or "lout" in English the word tends to imply brawn without brains: in its one other occurrence in Petronius it refers to a Cappadocian slave who "could lift a raging bull" (63.5). I am inclined to think that the "lout" here merely stood holding the ladder; so also a print of

nineteenth-century acrobats in Paris shows a mustachioed strongman
steadying a contraption on which a lighter acrobat performs.[8] We hear of
stunts performed by strongmen in antiquity that are much more spectacular
than the one in Petronius. Louis Robert has cited a passage from the
fourteenth-century polymath, Nicephoros Gregoras:[9] "one man balanced
on his forehead a long pole, not less than three *orguiai* [about 5.5 meters
or 18 feet], around which was wrapped a rope from top to bottom resembling rungs [we would say a rope ladder]; a boy climbed up these rungs,
grasping them with hands and feet, passing one hand over the other until
he had reached the top, and then came down again, while the man constantly walked around keeping the pole on his forehead." Closer in time to
Petronius is a passage at the very beginning of Apuleius' novel, in which
the author makes a fantastic blend of such a balancing act and a quite
different type of stunt, sword-swallowing: "a mountebank buried a hunting-
spear just where it threatens extinction [we would say, "by the point"] in
the bottom of his innards. Whereupon, a beautifully sensuous boy climbed
up [the shaft], and twisting sinuously performed a dance without bone or
muscle . . . You would say that a beautiful serpent was clinging with slippery
embraces to the staff of the healing god" (Apul. *Met.* 1.4). To return to
Petronius, "jumping through hoops" was a noted feat of *petauristarii,* and
Manilius, who gives us one of the clearest descriptions of this type of
performer, mentions their "limbs shot through flames and burning hoops"
(5.442).

As he watches the acrobats, Trimalchio muses that they and trumpeters
(*cornicines*) are the only types of performer he really enjoys; "I had bought
comedians too, but I preferred them to act farces [*Atellanae*], and my choral
flautist I ordered to play to a Latin text" (53.12–13). We shall return to
the subject of actors, but for the moment we may note the implication that
Trimalchio owns, and has not merely hired, the acrobats: there is ample
evidence for wealthy Romans owning troupes of such entertainers, as for
example the old Ummidia Quadratilla in the Younger Pliny owns a troupe
of pantomimes (*Ep.* 7.24). In Petronius, this social fact explains the immediate sequel: the boy-acrobat causes an unexpected scene by falling on top
of the host, but the outcome is that, instead of being punished, he is given
his liberty (54).

Petronius talks of *circuli,* groups standing in a circle, as the venue for
such performances, and anyone who has stood, for example, outside the
Musée Pompidou in Paris to watch the fire-eaters knows what such circles
are like. It might therefore be thought that the acrobats at Trimalchio's
dinner are not to be classed among theatrical performers, but that would
be to overlook a development observable in the history of the Hellenistic

and even more the Roman theater. Inscriptions of Delphi from the imperial period honor performers of different kinds: one is among other things a rope-walker; one is a strong man; another is a "dancer and trick-artist." It is a secure inference that all three performed in the theater, just as we are told by Athenaeus that the Eretrians put up a statue of a conjuror in their theater.[10] An unpublished graffito from the theater of Aphrodisias, which was begun in the late first century B.C., is a charming sketch of a rope-walker.

After further talk at Trimalchio's dinner, a new act comes on: these are the *Homeristai,* who act a mythological scene in Greek. Trimalchio's account of the myth is comically confused, but it must have involved the mad Ajax, since at the conclusion the hero attacks a boiled calf with his sword and divides the slices among the guests. The latest English commentary observes, "instead of the old rhapsodists who merely recited passages from Homer these *Homeristai* combined to give theatrical performances,"[11] but this does less than justice to Petronius' humor. The *Homeristai* were mime actors who specialized in imitations of Homeric combat. The dream interpreter Artemidorus, in a chapter of his work that is full of information about ancient performers, tells of a surgeon who dreamed that he was a *Homeristes* and wounded many people; the result in waking life was that he performed a large number of operations. Artemidorus explains that "the *Homeristai* wound and draw blood, but do not mean to kill, and surgeons are the same."[12] These wounds and blood, we may suspect, are probably stage devices: some will recall the scene in Achilles Tatius when Leucippe undergoes a sham death by means of a dagger with a retractable blade and of a pouch of blood concealed in her clothes. The dagger had belonged to "one of those persons who make verbal display of Homer in the theaters [*ton ta Homerou toi stomati deiknuonton en tois theatrois*]," that is, a *Homeristes,* and the trick with the blood may also come from the theater (Ach. Tat. 3.20). This cultural context explains the scene in Petronius: *Homeristai* mimed Homeric combats with stage weapons, and Trimalchio's *Homeristes* plays the role of Ajax in order to carve up a calf.

Trimalchio's dinner ends, at least for Encolpius, with a scene that explicitly fuses the public and the private spheres, and indeed has the effect of mediating between the two by allowing the narrator and his two companions to escape from their confinement in Trimalchio's house to the outside world. The symposium is now in its last stages, and Trimalchio orders a "new act [*novum acroama*], trumpet players" (78.5); he proceeds to stage his own mock-funeral, and the noise made by the trumpeters brings in the fire brigade. Here again the cultural context illuminates the narrative. *Novum* here cannot surely mean "novel" or "strange," but as the Loeb rightly understands, "new" or "fresh." That *cornicines* were not novel is already clear from Trimalchio's earlier declaration that they and acrobats are the only acts he really likes (53.12). Trumpet players were indispensable to public entertainments of every kind. A tradition that can be traced from the late Hellenistic period to the second century of the Roman Empire ordained that musical and theatrical contests begin with the competitions of trumpeters and heralds;[13] but trumpeters were also necessary for gladiatorial shows and regular stage plays. It is characteristic of the topsy-turviness of Trimalchio's household that an act that normally serves to open public displays closes his.

We cannot measure exactly how far Petronius' account of Trimalchio's dinner corresponds to real life. We can be sure, however, that dinner theater has a long tradition in ancient literature, though as with Petronius we have always to test the literary accounts against what we know about actual practice. The classic text is the *Symposium* of Xenophon, which purports to describe a dinner given by the wealthy Athenian Callias in 422. The dramatic time covers both the dinner and the symposium, though the latter occupies much the larger part of the work. After dinner is finished and the tables are removed, a Syracusan enters with a troupe of three entertainers: a woman piper (*auletris*), a dancing girl "of the kind that can do tricks" (*ton ta thaumata dynamenon poiein*), and "a very handsome boy who played the cithara and danced very well." Socrates reacts appreciatively: "I swear, Callias, you're giving us a perfect dinner. You have served us with a superb meal, and now you're providing the most agreeable entertainments for eye and ear [*kai theamata kai akroamata hedista*]" (2.1–2). We should note what Socrates does not say; there is no hint that the show put on by Callias is novel or strange, simply that it is pleasurable to see and to hear. We may infer that by the early fourth century and perhaps already in 422, dinner theater was a familiar form of entertainment, at least at dinners of the rich.

The acts that the artists perform, at least the two dancers, have many echoes in later literature and documents. The first trick is something that we still see in the modern circus: as the piper plays, the girl dancer begins to dance, and the boy hands her hoops up to the number of twelve, "and as she took them she simultaneously danced and threw them spinning into the air, watching how high she should throw them in order to catch them in rhythm" (2.8). This act is perhaps what Artemidoros calls by the verb *trochopaiktein*.[14]

The girl's next act is to turn somersaults in and out of a circle of upright swords (2.11). This trick is mentioned by Artemidoros in the very same sentence as that just cited, "playing with hoops or whirling around knives" (*machairais peridineisthai*). Another of her feats is to write or read (presumably aloud) while perched on a potter's wheel as it turns (7.2–3). Finally, both boy and girl dance a mime of Dionysos and Ariadne (9.2–7). This, it has long been recognized, is an early form of that entertainment already mentioned in connection with Trimalchio's household, pantomime.[15] In the Roman period it is still called "dancing" (*orchesis*), though its performers were frequently also called in Greek *pantomimoi,* or in Latin *histriones.*

Given the loss of so much Hellenistic literature, we cannot hope to trace the history of dinner theater between Xenophon's time and the beginning of the principate. One text, however, gives us a tantalizing glimpse of what might happen. It is from the early Hellenistic period, a letter preserved in Athenaeus and written by a certain Hippolochus to describe the wedding feast of a Macedonian grandee called Karanus.[16] The description may be exaggerated, but it beggars Encolpius' account of Trimalchio. To mention only the entertainers, there were female pipers (just as at Callias' symposium), musicians (again probably female), and women *sambuca*-players (the *sambuca* was a stringed instrument particularly associated with indecency).[17] Hippolochus comments on this "all-girl orchestra," "they looked naked to me, but some said they had undergarments on" (129A). At a later stage there enter mummers, then ithyphallic dancers, persons called *skleropaiktai* whose act is unknown,[18] and naked women who "somersaulted over swords [exactly as in Xenophon] and blew fire from their mouths": these are clearly what we now call "fire-eaters" (129D). Later on the wedding hymn is sung by a chorus one hundred strong, while dancing girls perform dressed as nymphs and nereids (130A): we are reminded of the mythological ballet in Xenophon.

When we come to the imperial period, the evidence for dinner theater becomes abundant, and at last we can begin to feel confident that we are dealing with history and not fiction, however close that fiction may be to real life. Let us begin at a level above that of Trimalchio, that of the wealthy littérateurs on whom we depend for so much of our knowledge of the social life of the empire. Here a very important text is one of Plutarch's *Convivial Questions* (OC 7.8, 711Aff.), devoted to the topic, "What are the best kind of entertainers [*akroamata*] to have during dinner?" A Stoic philosopher of the severer kind asserts that most should be reserved for the stage and the orchestra, but he praises a fashion, recently introduced into Rome, whereby slaves act out some of the lighter dialogs of Plato. Another Stoic of the company claims to have intervened to have this desecration stopped, and Plutarch is our only source for it. A third speaker then enumerates other kinds of performance that should be eliminated (*perikoptea*); the word "eliminated" must imply they were all in vogue in the author's time (711Eff.). The first is tragedy, which is said to be too painful for the symposium: we shall see later that tragedy was performed at the table of Hadrian, and so not long after Plutarch was writing. The same speaker then discusses *orchesis* in the specialized sense already considered, pantomime. Appealing to the testimony of Xenophon, he approves the kind of pantomime founded by the notorious Bathyllus in the reign of Augustus, a simpler variety that represented the dance of Echo, Pan, or a Satyr and Eros. By contrast, he rejects the type of pantomime associated with Bathyllus' rival Pylades, which was in fact much more popular: this is the type that borrowed its subjects from classical tragedy and required the chief dancer, who was usually solo, to change masks in rapid succession for each role that he played. The speaker then turns to comedy. Old Comedy is rejected as being too heterogeneous, serious in the *parabaseis,* in other parts scurrilous and indecent. "New Comedy, however, can have no critics: for it is so bound up with symposia that you could more easily regulate the drinking without wine than without Menander" (712B). The speaker proceeds to praise the suitability of the plots; there is no pederasty, when girls are raped or seduced they usually end up married, when the leading man has an affair with a *hetaera* it is either broken off, if the girl is "bold and fast," or else there is some kind of happy ending. I will return to these descriptions of comedy in a moment, but first let us finish Plutarch's catalog of entertainments. The author himself now takes up the subject (712Eff.). He begins by discussing mime. This, quite different from pantomime, was a kind of farce or low comedy extremely popular throughout classical antiquity and beyond. Plutarch then turns to musical entertainment, the cithara, the pipe, and the lyre, which he allows if they accompany texts, for instance the poems of Anacreon and Sappho. These two poets are also mentioned as dinner entertainment by Aulus Gellius (19.9.4).

Of these entertainments, the most widely approved, at least in the first two centuries of our era, seems to have been comedy. We recall Trimalchio's claim that he had bought *comoedi* but ordered them to act Atellan farces; clearly Petronius means to suggest the gesture of a *nouveau riche* towards his idea of superior culture. The Younger Pliny several times mentions *comoedi* as one of the entertainments to be expected at his and his friends' dinners: thus at one table of ostentatious simplicity, "the dinner is frequently enlivened by *comoedi,* so that even pleasures may be seasoned with learning"

(3.1.9, cf. 1.15.2, 9.17.3, 9.36.4). Since Friedländer the view persists in commentaries and handbooks that what was offered was merely excerpts, or recitals by a single author. While this may sometimes have been true, we saw that Plutarch, as he weighs the suitability of Old and New Comedy, considers the plays in their entirety, commenting on the heterogeneity of the first and the improving plots of the second. It is surely to be inferred that whole plays were sometimes performed, so that when modern scholars ask whether the Romans were accustomed to seeing Menander they should not underestimate the elaborateness of dinner performances.[19]

We should not imagine that even in cultivated circles dinner theater was always so decorous as a reading of Plutarch or Pliny might imply. Even Pliny teases a friend allegedly for turning down one of his own invitations for a table at which *Gaditanae,* dancing girls from Cadiz, may be seen (1.15.3). Lucian anticipates that a Greek philosopher hired by a wealthy Roman may soon find himself outshone by others such as the *orchestodi-daskalos,* the owner of a troupe of dancing girls (*De Merc. Cond.* 27).

When we come to the top of the social pyramid, the emperors, for whom wealth and power allowed an almost limitless range of self-display, we should expect a wide variety of dinner entertainments. Augustus is praised by Suetonius for the excellence of his dinners, "with three courses or at the most six"; and the biographer (*Aug.* 74) tells us that "he exhibited performers [*acroamata*], pantomimes [*histriones*], or even common players from the circus, and very often story-tellers [*aretalogos*]." The implication is that this is modest fare: we may suspect that contemporaries of Augustus, not to mention hosts under his immediate successors, would have offered very much more. Caligula liked his dinners or symposia to be enlivened either by torture or by decapitations performed by a particularly expert soldier (*Cal.* 32.1). Hadrian's tastes, as we might expect, correspond closely to those of men like Plutarch and Pliny, his older contemporaries, though with a dash of that *varietas* for which this emperor was famous. "Over dinner," says his biographer, "he put on tragedies, comedies, Atellan farces, *sambuca*-players, readers, poets, always as the occasion dictated" (*SHA Hadr.* 26.4). The three theatrical entertainments that head the list are all in effect considered by Plutarch, since the Atellans were the Italian equivalent of mime; of the other entertainments, we saw *sambuca*-players at the feast of the Macedonian Karanus. Both Lucius Verus and Elagabalus are credited with watching gladiatorial shows at dinner (*SHA Verus* 4.8–9, *Elag.* 25.7). Curiously, this is a revival of a practice often held up as proof of Campanian decadence in the time of the Middle Republic (Liv. 9.40.17; Strab. 5.4.13, C.250; Sil. Ital. 11.51–54); Nicolaus of Damascus, writing under Augustus, claims that it had been a Roman practice too (Athen. 4.153F-154A = FGrH 90 F 78).

So far I have argued that in Greco-Roman culture theatrical entertainment in the broad sense was an accepted part of the banquets of the wealthy. I now want to turn to what I earlier called "theater-dinner," meals given in theaters and similar buildings and accompanied by visual entertainment.

The fullest account of such an occasion is found in one of Statius' *Silvae* (1.6), where the poet describes a banquet given by Domitian in Rome on a first of December: commentators take the setting to be the Colosseum. The day begins with a *sparsio* of a simpler kind, nuts, dates, plums, et cetera, showered on the diners from above (9ff.). Later in the day there is a set banquet (28ff.).

> Along all the seats climbs a second crowd, conspicuous in beauty and finely dressed, no less in number than the crowd sitting down. These carry baskets, white napkins, and elegant dinners; others dispense drowsy wines; you would think them so many servants from [Mount] Ida. . . . Every order dines at a single table, children, women, plebs, knights, senate; liberty sets reverence aside . . . Why even you [Statius is addressing the emperor] join with us in friendly banquet—what god could issue such an invitation or make such promises? Now everyone, whoever he is, rich or poor, boasts of being our ruler's guest. Amid this din and this unexampled luxury the pleasure of the spectacle escapes unnoticed. . . .

The poet goes on to describe the various performers—female gladiators, dwarf gladiators, prostitutes, Lydian flute-girls, Gaditane dancing girls with their tamborines, and so on. Next he describes another hail of *missilia*, this time consisting of exotic birds like pheasants and guinea fowl (75ff.). The day ends with a primitive sort of fireworks (85ff.).

This occasion is really a dinner on an Olympian scale, and most of the entertainment has its domestic analogs. We have seen dates distributed at Trimalchio's dinner table; dancing girls were frequent at dinners, to the discomfort of moralists like the Younger Pliny (*Ep.* 5.3); the mock blood sports of female and dwarf gladiators correspond to Trimalchio's *Homeristai.* Yet in so entertaining the people of Rome Domitian was at the same time following a pattern of public munificence well established in the Greek East, just as his Capitoline games were modeled on the Greek contests of the day.

A passage of Dio Chrysostom (64.8–10), which may actually have been written under Domitian, gives a satirical view of this type of munificence. Dio is comparing the tribulations of the ambitious politician (*philodoxos*). with the comparatively easy lot of the pederast (*philopais*).

> Who would not admit that it is easier to manage the most difficult youth than the most moderate *demos?* . . . The [politician] has to buy much food and wine, he has to assemble pipers, mimes, cithara-players, mountebanks [*thaumatopoioi*], and in addition boxers, pan-cratiasts, wrestlers, runners and other such types if the feast he plans to give to the mob is not to be a mean one . . . Pederasts consider themselves very lucky in comparison with city-lovers. They hunt out quails, a cock, a nightingale, while they watch the other having to hire Amoebeus and Polus [respectively a citharode of the third century and an actor of the fourth], or hire some Olympic victor for five talents.

I cannot find any example of athletic entertainment such as that implied by Dio, and indeed among the many inscriptions referring to public banquets there are very few that mention the entertainment at all. I take two, one from the late Hellenistic period and the other from the first century of our era.

One of the long decrees honoring the benefactor Zosimus of Priene says as follows (I translate the text as supplemented by Louis Robert):

> After the war [probably the First Mithridatic War], as *stephanephoros* he gave a notable feast to the whole people, the only person to do so, using the (meat) from the sacrifices for the reception . . . And desir-ing to provide what conduced not only to pleasure but also to amuse-ment, he hired performers from abroad, including the pantomime Ploutogenes, who was able to beguile by his art, and he exhibited him for three days, making the occasion participate in this kind of enjoyment too.

The word here translated "pleasure" is *hedone* while "amusement" is *apate;* the first represents the pleasure of the senses, the second the pleasure of the intellect.[20] We should surely assume that the banquet took place in the theater and that Ploutogenes danced as the public was eating; and since pantomime dancing involved a full chorus and orchestra, we should probably also imagine that he arrived with a troupe of goodly size. We are a long way from the three young artists who entertained Callias' symposium with the myth of Dionysos and Ariadne.

My second inscription is another long decree, this time for the benefactor Epaminondas of Acraiphia in Boeotia about A.D. 40. Among his many generosities is one that concerns a "thymelic" contest, that is, a musical and theatrical one.

> In the spectacles which occurred during the thymelic [contest] [that is, as the contestants were performing] he gave a collation [*eglykisen*] in the theatre to the spectators and to those who had arrived from the [neighboring] cities, and threw out large and extravagant gifts [*rhimmata*] so that his expenditures were heard of also in the cities round about.[21]

This *glykismos,* which following Robert I have translated as "collation," is as its name implies essentially a serving of sweet wine, no doubt accompanied by some food such as dates.[22] The word *rhimmata* was read on the stone by M. Feyel, where previous editors had restored [*pe*]*mmata*. Though it is otherwise unattested in this sense, Robert saw that it must be equivalent to the *missilia* of Latin inscriptions, objects thrown to the crowd: we recall the objects thrown out at Domitian's banquet in Rome.

I would draw a few conclusions. The host of a dinner is essentially a benefactor, though on a comparatively small scale. No doubt a man who aspired to fame was obliged, as is still true, to offer both private and public munificence, lavish dinners at home as well as gifts to the crowd. For related reasons, those who had the means to own or to hire performing artists could exhibit them both in private and in public: the old lady Ummidia Quadratilla in the Younger Pliny watches her troupe of pantomimes at home, but also exhibits them on the stage. There is an inevitable link between dinner theater and theater-dinner: they are complementary aspects of the same system of benefaction. More importantly, dinner theater and theater-dinner are linked by their theatricality, the visual display that was a large part of life for the citizens of the Greek or Roman city. We hear much nowadays about public and private space, but in many periods of history the private acts of certain individuals have been very much public events. In modern Europe, we think of the court life of the *ancien régime,* under which the king's getting up and going to bed, not to mention other parts of his daily routine, were matters of the most elaborate ceremonial. In the ancient city the very appearance in public of a wealthy man was an occasion: he was marked off by clothing (for Roman citizens, by white in contrast to the gray of the *pullati*), and his movement in public, accompanied by bearers, nomenclators and the like, was already a veritable procession. When such a person entertained, his status was marked not only by the house, furnishings, and utensils, but equally by the splendor of the visual entertainment he could offer his guests; indeed the performers were often his own property. On the public level, to offer the public both food and spectacle was to make one's generosity as conspicuous as it could be. If that public included visitors from elsewhere, the effect was to make the citizenry as well as its benefactor a spectacle to its neighbors. Dinner theater and theater-dinner are part of the larger theater constituted by the ancient city itself.

NOTES

1. J.A. Banks, *Prosperity and Parenthood: A Study of Family Planning among the Victorian Middle Classes* (London 1954), chap. 8.

2. E.g., Mart. 5.25.7–8; *Oxford Latin Dictionary* s.v. *crocum* I a.

3. On this fundamental distinction, L. Robert, *Les Gladiateurs dans l'Orient grec* (Paris 1940), chap. 5. On the *venatio* see also G. Ville, *La Gladiature en Occident*, BEFAR 245 (Rome 1981), esp. 51–56.

4. Cf. Robert (above note 3), 34–35.

5. Trees: Robert (above note 3), 327–28. Dogs: e.g., Mart. 11.69, with the commentary of N.M. Kay, *Martial, Book XI: A Commentary* (London 1985), 215–19. Boars: Robert (above note 3), 314; Kay, 218–19.

6. G. Lafaye, in Daremberg-Saglio s.v. *petaurum* (emphasizing the fluidity of the term); Kay (above note 5) on Mart. 11.21.3.

7. H. Blümner, *Fahrendes Volk im Altertum,* SBMünchen 1918, 6, 22, and n. 162.

8. *Enciclopedia dello Spettacolo* 1 (Rome 1954), 63.

9. L. Robert, *Opera Minora Selecta* 2.895 n. 4 (*BCH* 1928, 424), citing Nic. Greg. *Hist.* 8.10.4.

10. Rope-walker (*kalobates*): Robert, *Opera Minora Selecta* 2.896 n. 2 (= *BCH* 1928, 425). Strongman (*ischuropaiktes*): Robert, op. cit. 893–96 (*BCH* 1928, 422–25). Dancer and trick-artist (*orchestes kai thaumatopoios*): Robert, op. cit. 1.221–22 (= *REG* 1929, 433–34). Conjuror (*psephokleptes*): Athen. 1.19A-B; Robert, op. cit. 1.225 (*REG* 1929, 437).

11. M.S. Smith, *Petronius: Cena Trimalchionis* (Oxford 1975), 164. For a good discussion of this passage see R.J. Starr, *Latomus* 46, 1987, 199ff.

12. Artemid. 4.2, p. 245 Pack; cf. J. and L. Robert, *Bull. Ep.* 1983.475, p. 184.

13. M. Wörrle, *Stadt und Fest im kaiserzeitlichen Kleinasien* (Munich 1988), 229–31.

14. Artemidorus, *Oneirocr.* 1.76, p. 82 1. 27 Pack. Cf. Robert, *Opera Minora Selecta* 1.224 n. 8 (*REG* 1929, 436).

15. O. Weinreich, *Epigramm und Pantomimus,* SBHeidelb. 1944/48, 1, 128–35.

16. Athen. 4, 128C–130D. On Hippolochus (not in *RE*), F. Susemihl, *Geschichte der griechischen Litteratur in der Alexandrinerzeit* I (Leipzig 1891), 487 n. 8, 881–82.

17. J.G. Landels, *JHS* 86, 1966, 69.

18. Cf. Robert, *Opera Minora Selecta* 1.894 n. 2 (*BCH* 1928, 423).

19. Cf. R.E. Fantham, *TAPA* 114, 1984, 299–309; I hope to return to this subject elsewhere.

20. *Inschriften von Priene* 113, lines 63–67 as restored by Robert, *Opera Minora Selecta* 1.662–65 (*Hermes* 1930, 114–17); Robert, *Hellenica* XI/XII (Paris 1960), 9–11.

21. *IG* VII. 2712, lines 75–78, with the discussion of Robert, *Arch. Eph.* 1969, 34–39.

22. On *glykismos,* see the bibliography in Robert (above note 21), p. 35 n. 4.

Convivium and Villa in Late Antiquity

Jeremy Rossiter

In a recent study of the architecture of the great fourth-century Roman villa at Piazza Armerina in Sicily, William MacDonald has argued that the villa should be viewed conceptually as a microcosm of Roman city planning: "Its plans and dispositions are . . . best explained as the results of adapting imperial town-making to private purposes on an ample scale."[1] The analogy is a useful one, at least in so far as it encourages us to think of Roman villas in terms of their component parts, for villas were generally designed to accommodate a wide range of economic and social activities, each requiring its own purposefully built environment. Not only was the villa normally the center of a working farm (this might not always be the case of course—some seaside and suburban villas were built more for pleasure than for profit), it was also a recreational retreat, a place for leisurely study, for physical exercise, and for entertaining guests. All this required careful planning. It involved the integration of numerous component buildings, the range and scale of which reflected both the economic status of the villa's owner and the social fashions of the age.

Among the major architectural components of any rich villa were the public rooms built to accommodate guests on the occasion of a dinner party or *convivium*. The great importance attached to such occasions in the social life of the Roman aristocracy is apparent from the frequent accounts of dining and entertaining at villas that appear in Roman aristocratic literature from the time of Cicero onward.[2] By the period of the Later Roman Empire, the role of the villa as a place for social interaction among the landowning classes was well established. In the late fourth century the villas of rich aristocratic families like the Symmachi, the Valerii, or the Ausonii were constantly thronged with house guests. Symmachus talks of "crowds of friends" (*catervas amicorum*) descending upon his villa at Baiae. At other times he is at his villa near Praeneste, welcoming numerous relatives and friends—men and women of the same privileged class, who came to the country to relax, to hunt, to debate, and, above all, to share the pleasures of their host's dinner table.[3]

Yet the precise relationship between design and social function in Late Roman villas has not always been well understood. In studies of villas, rooms have been variously labeled "reception rooms" or "audience halls" or "dining rooms" without a clear understanding of the social protocols which dictated the design of domestic buildings of the age. Furthermore, fashions of entertaining and dining change, and with them the architectural environment created to support them. In late antiquity this process of change demands careful observation. For how long, we may wonder, did the aristocratic dining rituals of the Late Roman upper classes continue to influence the social customs of their post-Roman descendants? For how long did buildings designed to accommodate specific Roman dining customs continue to be used and imitated by later generations? To answer these questions we need to look equally at the archaeological and the literary sources for the design and use of domestic buildings throughout the period of late antiquity. We will start with the literary evidence, with a look at two of the more revealing accounts of upper-class entertaining and dining left us by fifth-century writers. In both we find clues to the established social conventions that influenced the design of aristocratic houses and villas during the last century of the Roman Empire in the West.

In the mid-460s A.D. Sidonius Apollinaris records a visit he made to the villa of his friend Tonantius Ferreolus near Nîmes in southern Gaul.[4] Like Sidonius' own villa at Avitacum and the villa of his contemporary Leontius at Burgus, Ferreolus' villa was probably an old family property, dating back in large part to the more affluent years of the fourth century.[5] Sidonius indicates that renovations were under way in the villa's bathhouse, which we can perhaps take as a sign of the building's aging fabric.[6] Although Sidonius does not describe the villa in detail, he does give a detailed account of some of the social activities that highlighted his visit. In particular he tells of a gathering of the houseguests in one of the villa's rooms before lunch. From Sidonius' description of the scene inside this room, it is clear that this was the villa's library. The room was a large one, large enough to allow for segregated seating arrangements. Among the furnishings, Sidonius mentions chairs designated for the use of women in one part of the room, close to the *codices* thought appropriate for feminine digestion, and for men in another part of the room, where again suitable reading material was at hand.[7] Sidonius tells how some of the houseguests sat in one corner of the room and engaged in a debate on the subject of Origen's writings, while elsewhere in the library other guests amused themselves at gaming tables. Thus the guests passed their time in conversation and recreation, until a slave entered to announce that the meal was ready. Thereupon, the company adjourned to the villa's dining room for what Sidonius describes, with probable understatement, as a light but varied lunch: *multas epulas paucis parabsidibus* to be compared to the formal lunch party of *SHA Elag.* 28.5: *cum summos viros rogasset ad prandium*.

A comparable episode, in this case in an urban context, is described by Macrobius in the *Saturnalia*, a work written during the first half of the fifth century but set in the penultimate decade of the fourth century.[8] The occasion described is the feast of the *Saturnalia*; the setting is a house in Rome belonging to the aristocrat Vettius Praetextatus—almost certainly the ancestral House of the Vettii, traces of which have come to light on the Esquiline.[9] Macrobius describes how a dozen guests (this time all male) convened before dinner in one of the main guest rooms of the house, a room that is again identified as the library (*bibliotheca*). The room was evidently a large one (Macrobius uses the expression *tantum coetum*) and was undoubtedly elegantly furnished and decorated.[10] Here the predinner gathering continued for several hours, allowing for a lengthy debate among the guests on topics ranging from the kind of activities permitted on feast days to the proper treatment of slaves. The use of the library on this occasion for the staging of a protracted formal debate was hardly routine, however. More usually, as Praetextatus himself comments, the gathering of guests in the library before dinner was an occasion for games of backgammon and draughts.[11] As in Ferreolus' villa, the debate taking place in Praetextatus' library was eventually interrupted by an announcement from a slave (in this case the head slave, the *praesul famulitii*) that the dinner was ready to be served. The guests then proceeded from the library and took their place at table in the *triclinium*.

In both these fifth-century accounts of aristocratic hospitality, the social protocols observed are much the same. Two distinct stages of the *convivium* can be recognized: first, the reception and entertainment of the guests in the library before the meal, and then, following an announcement by a slave, the gathering of the guests in the *triclinium* for the dinner itself. The rooms used to accommodate this pattern of aristocratic entertaining can be identified in the excavated remains of many Late Roman villas. Among the numerous public and private apartments that make up their plans, it is usually possible to distinguish two rooms which, to judge from their exceptional size and decoration, were intended as the main public guest rooms.[12] We see this, for example, at Piazza Armerina, where the whole complex is dominated by two large and richly decorated halls built in a commanding position on the east side of the villa (fig. 1 30, 46).[13] The same is true at another Sicilian villa, the roughly contemporary villa at

Patti Marina, where again two greatly emphasized rooms can be identified (fig. 2 a, b), in this case both facing out onto adjacent sides of the villa's main peristyle.[14] A similar arrangement is found in the partially explored Late Roman villa at Almenara de Adaja in Spain (fig. 3 a, b), another peristyle villa with two large halls overlooking the courtyard.[15] On a somewhat grander scale, the Late Roman villa at Gamzigrad in Dacia, now identified as the villa built by Galerius for his planned retirement, offers a further variation on this same theme. To the north of the main residential block was a large apsidal room overlooking the peristyle; further south, but also connected to the same peristyle, was a second hall with a smaller apse (fig. 4 D, G). Both rooms are among the most richly decorated of the entire villa.[16]

Taken individually, some of these public rooms have been interpreted as multipurpose halls. The same room, it is supposed, may have served both as a dining room and as a reception room, or at another time as a room for conducting official business.[17] It is probably wrong, however, to consider the function of any of these rooms in isolation. As we can see from the accounts of aristocratic entertaining provided in the literary sources, the uses of the main public rooms of the villa were closely interrelated. The major social obligation of the Roman aristocrat in residence at his villa was to feed and entertain the crowds of family members and friends who came to the villa to share with him the pleasures of country life. To cater to these guests in the conventional way, the villa was provided with two major public rooms, which were used together on all important social occasions, one as a place to relax and receive guests during the morning or afternoon, the other for dining and entertainment at the appropriate hour.[18]

Among the different public rooms that can be identified in Late Roman villas, the rooms used for dining are usually the most architecturally distinctive. By the fourth century, the furniture most commonly associated with formal dining was the curved couch (*stibadium*) and small D-shaped or round table (*mensa, orbis*) around which the couch was set.[19] The shape of the *stibadium* lent itself naturally to the form of the apse and so in its simplest form, the formal dining room evolved as a combination of apse (often slightly more than a semicircle) and rectangular or square hall. This is the kind of dining room found in the villa at Almenara de Adaja (fig. 3 a) and also at Gamzigrad (fig. 4 G). Each component of this bipartite scheme served a distinct purpose, the apse to accommodate the *stibadium* on which the diners reclined, the hall to provide the necessary space for attendants and entertainers. *Stibadium* couches seem to have varied considerably in size, with room for anywhere from five to nine diners, although seven was perhaps the norm. This is the number often specified by Roman writers as the optimum number at a *convivium* and is also the number implied by the segmented pattern of the *stibadium* mosaic found in the Villa of the Falconer at Argos.[20]

To overcome the seating limitations of a single *stibadium*, dining rooms were often built with more than one apse. The most common formula was that of the triconch, a room composed of a central square flanked by three peripheral apses. Rooms of this design are a distinctive feature of many fourth-century villas, among them the villas at Piazza Armerina and Patti Marina in Sicily (figs. 1 46, 2 a), the villa at Ecija in Spain (fig. 5 A), and the partially excavated villa at Desenzano del Garda in Lombardy (fig. 6).[21] Although the dimensions of these halls vary slightly from one villa to another, in most examples the diameter of the apses approximates more or less to the six-meter width of the Villa of the Falconer dining room, indicating their potential for the placement of a similar seven-person *stibadium*.

The central square was used in part by those serving at the meal. It was here that servants stood in readiness to attend to each diner's summons, waiting to hurry forward with dishes of food for the table and with wine to replenish the guests' cups.[22] Other tasks included bringing bowls of water for the guests to wash their hands and fetching and trimming lamps during the evening meal.[23] The second important function of the central square of the triconch, the area defined in the sources as being "before the tables," was to provide space for entertainers.[24] This was where, on festive occasions, dancers, musicians, and actors were employed to provide after-dinner entertainment for the assembled dinner guests.[25] In this respect the dining room served virtually as a private theater, providing an intimate setting for a colorful assortment of entertainments, chosen by the host to suit the particular occasion.[26]

This theaterlike quality generally extended beyond the dining room itself. It was seen too in the ornamental gardens, pools, and porticoes that were laid out in formal fashion in front of the dining room. These open spaces may have served at times as a place for outdoor entertainments, but they were no doubt also enjoyed simply for the beauty and coolness that they gave to the setting of the *cena*.[27] In many villas the view of these gardens and peristyles was shared by a number of the villa's public rooms. (figs. 2, 3). Occasionally, however, a more exclusive arrangement existed, where the dining room was integrated architecturally with a separate peristyle court (figs. 1 41, 2F, 6). Nowhere perhaps is this more strikingly illustrated than in the villa at Piazza Armerina, where the doors of the triconch dining room opened onto an elliptical forecourt with curving porticoes, baroque fountains, and, at the far end opposite the dining room, a monumental nymphaeum.[28] A close parallel for this whole architectural composition can be found in Sidonius' account of the dining room of Leontius' villa in Gaul.[29] Here, we are told, those reclining on the *sigma*-couch could look out through the dining room's folding doors into a courtyard framed by curving colonnades *(porticus ampla curvata)* and equipped with a well-stocked fish pond *(pendente lacu)*. Beyond this lay a magnificent view of the Garonne valley and the surrounding hills.

Views like this were a much-prized feature of any villa dining room. Describing his villa at Laurentum, Pliny makes much of the fine view of the Latian coastline that could be seen from the *triclinium*.[30] Similarly, in the fifth century Sidonius boasts of the impressive lakeside setting of one of the dining rooms of his own villa at Avitacum, "which opens on to the lake and from which almost the whole lake is visible."[31] In such a setting the ceremonies of the dining room became part of a broader experience, one that involved a delicate interplay between the manmade world of the villa and the natural landscape in which it was set.[32]

The widespread popularity of *stibadium*-dining in the fourth century is indicated by the large number of houses and villas built at this date that included facilities designed specifically to accommodate this type of dining furniture. In architectural terms, the triconch hall is undoubtedly one of the most distinctive of these, but it was by no means the only purposefully built structure used for *stibadium*-dining. In summer, dining at an outdoor *stibadium* was a favorite ritual at the aristocratic villa. At times, this would involve little more than the setting-up of a *stibadium* cushion at an agreeable spot in the grounds of the villa, as we see depicted for example on the famous Small Hunt mosaic from the villa at Piazza Armerina.[33] For greater sophistication, rich villa owners might opt for a special type of building to accommodate these outdoor banquets. Pliny thus describes an elaborate outdoor dining pavilion that stood in the grounds of his villa at Tifernum.[34] In the fifth century, Sidonius provides a detailed description of a comparable summer *cenatiuncula* that formed part of his wife's ancestral villa at Avitacum.[35] The structure was open-fronted, affording the diners a broad vista of the estate and lake. It was perhaps unroofed, more strictly an open hemicycle than an actual room. Sidonius uses the word *area*—literally "an open space"—to denote the floor, not *pavimentum,* the more usual word for the floor of a room.[36] According to Sidonius, the hemicycle contained two features, a *stibadium* and a marble table, both presumably permanent fixtures. One of the great advantages of the outdoor *stibadium* was its potential size. In a conventional indoor setting, the *stibadium* could never be very large, because of the formidable problems involved in building an apse and dining hall of corresponding dimensions. Out of doors, however, in an unroofed hemicycle, could be set a single *stibadium* large enough to accommodate a substantial number of dinner guests, possibly as many as twelve.[37]

Archaeological evidence for this kind of summer *cenatiuncula* in Late Roman villas is relatively rare. One building that can probably be identified as such, however, is the "round room" that forms part of the villa at Almenara de Adaja in Spain (fig. 3 e). This was a roofed building but its use as a summer dining room seems certain. It was designed to contain a single *stibadium* from which the diners could enjoy a close yet shaded view of the villa's courtyard garden. Another possible summer dining facility can be recognized among the excavated features of the fourth-century villa at Montmaurin in Aquitania. Here the inner courtyard of the villa was flanked by two pillared hemicycles built around opposite garden apses (fig. 7 nos. 10, 24). The usual interpretation of these lateral hemicycles is that they contained ornamental gardens used to display plants and artworks.[38] But perhaps what was intended here was something more practical, a purposefully built facility for summer dining, where two *stibadia* could be placed facing one another in a secluded outdoor setting. Reclining here at dinner, guests to the villa could look down on the fish ponds in front of them, and be entertained by performers in the open-air square beyond.

Stibadium-dining was clearly in high fashion in the fourth century. But how long did this typically Roman, aristocratic style of dining survive? Certainly it appears to have remained popular among the Roman aristocracies of fifth-century Italy and Gaul, for we find a number of references to this type of dining arrangement in the written sources for this period. In mid-fifth-century Ravenna, Bishop Peter I "Chrysologus" (432–50) must surely be thinking of contemporary dining fashions when, in one of his sermons, he refers to Christ at dinner with the *publicani* with the words *discumbebat . . . sigmate.*[39] Moreover, his successor in office, Bishop Neon (450–52), is known to have rebuilt the episcopal palace with a great new dining room which later sources refer to as the *Quinque Accubita,* a room designed to accommodate five separate *stibadia.*[40] Not much later, Sidonius, in a letter written in A.D. 468, records a dinner given by Majorian at Arles on the occasion of the *ludi circenses.*[41] The guests at dinner, seven in all, reclined at the traditional *stibadium,* their places allocated according to rank and status. Sidonius does not specify the location of this dinner, but we may suspect that the house or villa in which it was hosted was, like so many of the other buildings mentioned by Sidonius in his correspondence,

an old Roman building, designed specifically for this kind of dinner ceremony in an earlier age.[42]

This link between *stibadium*-dining and "historic" architecture becomes
particularly noticeable in the sources relating to the post-Roman aristocracies of the Latin West in the later fifth and sixth centuries. When Roman
dining protocol is seen to survive under Gothic or Vandal rule, the context
(when specified) is very often revealed as a building of earlier Roman date.
Thus Procopius describes a dinner given by the Vandal rebel Guntharis in
Carthage in A.D. 546.[43] The dinner took place in the old Roman proconsul's
residence where, we are told, the dinner guests reclined at three *stibadia*,
which had been there "from olden times" (*ek palaiou*). It is difficult to
know exactly what Procopius means by this. Perhaps we are to imagine a
dining room filled with antique furniture. More probably, however, we
should suppose that these *stibadia*, like the *stibadium* of Sidonius' summer
cenatiuncula, were made of stone, and that the dinner described by Procopius took place in the open air.

Other illustrations of the survival of *stibadium*-dining in the sixth century
are found in Merovingian sources. Gregory of Tours gives an account of
a private dinner, in which the diners are said to be "reclining" (*discum-
bentes*); all, that is, except the host's wife, who was seated at a chair (*sellula*)
pulled up next to the *stibadium*.[44] Also in the late sixth century, Venantius
Fortunatus, bishop of Poitiers in Gaul, refers to his friend, Bishop Leontius
of Bordeaux, as "reclining at table" in his newly renovated villa on the
banks of the Garonne.[45] Again we may observe that the context is a "historic" house, almost certainly a surviving relic of old Roman Gaul. Once
more Roman custom survives, but in a building designed for this specific
ritual at an earlier age.

The reaction of the Gothic rulers of Italy and Gaul to Roman dining
practices seems to have been mixed. On the one hand there are some
indications of opposition to Roman customs. When Sidonius visited the
court of Theodoric the Visigoth (d. 466), he was surprised to find that the
king dined *simile privato*—i.e., sitting at table, without the familiar trap-
pings of the Roman dining room.[46] So too the Ostrogothic king Totila
refused an invitation to recline at dinner with Bishop Sabinus of Canosa.[47]
On the other hand, Theodoric the Ostrogothic king of Italy was by all
accounts a staunch supporter of the old Roman ways. In his great palace
at Ravenna, the Roman tradition of *stibadium*-dining was maintained in
a magnificent new setting. Such at least we may infer from what we know
of the architecture of the palace *triclinium*, which, according to the later
authority of Agnellus, was built with a central apse containing a mosaic

portrait of the king.[48] If Theodoric dined here in traditional Roman style, the same may well have been true at the villa which, according to the evidence of Paul the Deacon, Theodoric had built in the valley of the Bidente near Forli.[49] Several attempts have been made to identify this villa among the excavated remains of villas found in the region, but none of them is entirely convincing. One of these villas, however, did contain an apsed hall, with mosaics said to be of early sixth-century date.[50] The design of the apse mosaic was divided into nine segments, reminding us of the *stibadium* markings of the almost contemporary mosaic in the Villa of the Falconer at Argos.

In sixth-century Gaul and Italy, however, outside the Gothic court, there is little evidence for new investment in the kind of extravagant domestic architecture associated with the traditional dining ceremony of the old Roman world. There were, as we have seen, some who sought to maintain and renovate old Roman houses and villas, and who there continued to enact some of the social rituals of a bygone age;[51] but at the same time the sources tell of many an old Roman mansion fallen into disrepair and disuse: in Rome, the once-great house of the Sallustii was still in ruins in the mid-sixth century;[52] in Milan, the house of Boethius was in urgent need of repair;[53] later in the sixth century, Pope Gregory speaks of the sorry condition of one of Rome's former mansions; it was, he says, *parte detecta, parte diruta, parte igne . . . consumpta.*[54] The wealth (and perhaps too the skills) needed to restore these houses to their former glory seems now to have vanished. And as the means to maintain, or to reproduce, the flamboyant architecture of the Late Roman world waned, so too did the ability to preserve the social rituals and ceremonies for which that architecture was originally created. The domed halls and pillared courts that were once a familiar feature of the villas of the rich were now a thing of the past. A few excavated villas of late fifth-century date point to a new and more austere style of villa architecture, one which was unsuited to the social fashions of the Late Roman world. Buildings like those at San Giovanni di Ruoti in South Italy (fig. 8) and Galeata in the north, with their compact architecture and elevated apartments, speak of different social practices, far removed from the traditions of Rome.[55]

In contrast, in the eastern half of the old Roman Empire, the continued use of the *stibadium* for dining seems to have been maintained widely in aristocratic circles well into the sixth century. Procopius, in several accounts of dining among the aristocracy of mid-sixth-century Constantinople, refers to the *stibadium* as the normal furniture of the dining room.[56] Perhaps best known is his account of a dinner given in the house of Germanus, Justinian's nephew, an occasion on which a conspiracy against Justinian was detected thanks to a loyal agent who hid himself under the *stibadium* couch on which the dinner guests were reclining.[57] In urban contexts the continuing influence of this style of dining on the domestic architecture of the upper classes can clearly be seen in the large number of apsidal dining rooms found in the East in town houses that date to the fifth and early sixth centuries.[58] As late as A.D. 512 the bishop's palace at Bosra in Syria was built with a triconch dining hall, in direct imitation of earlier Roman practice.[59] Comparable evidence for fashions in villa architecture in the East during the post-Roman period is hard to find. Archaeology provides little evidence for new villa construction after the mid-fifth century. However, occasional mention of villa building and of life at villas in the East during the sixth century can be found in some of the written sources for the period. Procopius speaks often of new villas built by Justinian in the region of Constantinople, among them a coastal *suburbanum* that Justinian built for Theodora at Hiereia on the Bosporus.[60] In this same villa, some fifty years later, Bishop Theodore of Syceon was entertained to dinner by the emperor Maurice and his family.[61] In the contemporary *Life of St. Theodore* the guests at dinner on this occasion are said to have reclined at table (*anaklino*), presumably in a dining hall built specifically for this kind of ritual. Of much greater fame was the imperial villa at the Hebdomon, a villa whose foundation goes back to the fourth century, but which was rebuilt on a grand scale by Justinian.[62] According to Theophylact, the sixth-century villa here included among its many architectural components "a many-couched hall" (*oikia polystibas*), which surely must imply a multilobate dining hall designed for the furniture of traditional Roman dining.[63]

The rebuilding of the Hebdomon palace by Justinian in the mid-sixth century may be seen perhaps as the final chapter in the long history of Roman villa architecture. Here, in a suburban setting, was an imperial residence with all the amenities of the classic Roman villa, among them a banqueting hall in which the old rituals of *stibadium* and *spectaculum* could be maintained. Beyond the sixth century, it was only in the most exclusive of contexts, in the great imperial and papal palaces of the Early Middle Ages, that such traditions lingered on. Thus, in seeking to build a prestigious new banqueting hall at the end of the eighth century Pope Leo III turned again to the ancient formula of the Roman triconch.[64] As late as the tenth century, the emperor in Constantinople entertained visitors to the palace at a banquet held in full "Roman" style, complete with draped *stibadia* and musicians and entertainers. But by this date, what had once been a familiar scene in the houses and villas of the Late Roman aristocracy, was witnessed by one of the guests, the envoy Luitprand of Cremona, as a novel and eccentric imperial ritual, whose roots in the world of Roman high society some six or seven hundred years earlier were by now largely forgotten.[65]

NOTES

1. W.L. MacDonald, *The Architecture of the Roman Empire* II (New Haven and London 1986), 274.

2. A famous early example is Cicero's account of the dinner given to Julius Caesar and his entourage at a villa on the Bay of Naples in 45 B.C. (Cic. *Ad Att.* 13.52). For a useful survey of the literary evidence for the use of Roman villas, see A.R. Littlewood, "Ancient Literary Evidence for Pleasure Gardens of Roman Country Villas," in E.B. MacDougall, ed., *Ancient Roman Villa Gardens: Dumbarton Oaks Colloquium on the History of Landscape Architecture* X (Washington, D.C. 1987), 9–30.

3. Symm. *Ep.* 1.7, 1.14, 2.32, 8.18, 8.23; *V. Melaniae* I.18–20; Aus. *Ep.* 6, 10, 11, *Car.* 2; Paulinus of Pella *Euch.* 207–9. On Symmachus' villas: O. Seeck, *MGH.AA* 6.1 (Berlin 1883), xlv–xlvi; J.H. D'Arms, *Romans on the Bay of Naples* (Cambridge, MA 1970), 226–29; J.A. McGeachy, *Q. Aurelius Symmachus and the Senatorial Aristocracy of the West* (Diss. Univ. of Chicago 1942), 112ff. The villas of Valerianus Pinianus and his wife Melania the Younger are briefly discussed in E. Clark, *The Life of Melania the Younger* (New York 1987). On the villas of the Ausonii in Aquitania: R. Étienne, *Bordeaux Antique I* (Bordeaux 1962), 351–61.

4. Sidon. *Ep.* 2.9.5; C.E. Stevens, *Sidonius Apollinaris and His Age* (Oxford 1933), 64.

5. Cf. Sidon. *Ep.* 2.2.3; *Car.* 22.17–19, 142–43.

6. Sidon. *Ep.* 2.9.8: *balneas habebat in opere uterque hospes, in usu neuter.*

7. Sidon. *Ep.* 2.9.5.

8. *Sat.* 1.6.1. On the date, see A. Cameron, *JRS* 56, 1966, 25–38.

9. H. Jordan, *Topographie der Stadt Rom im Alterthum* (Berlin 1871–1907) bd. 1.3, 368; S.B. Platner and T. Ashby, *A Topographical Dictionary of Ancient Rome* (Oxford 1929), 197–98. For Praetextatus' career and family in general: A. H.M. Jones, J.R. Martindale, and J. Morris, *The Prosopography of the Later Roman Empire I* (Cambridge 1971), s. v. Praetextatus 1.

10. Macrob. *Sat.* I.7.4. On the need for spacious private libraries, cf. Vitruv. *De Arch.* 6.5.2. In late fifth-century Rome, the library in the house of the Boethii was decorated with rich wall mosaics: Boeth. *De Cons.* 1.5.

11. Macrob. *Sat.* 1.5.11: *sed vultisne diem sequentem, quem plerique omnes abaco et latrunculis conterunt, nos istis sobriis fabulis a primo lucis in cenae tempus . . . exigamus.*

12. See the comments by N. Duval in E. Lévy, ed., *Le système palatial en Orient, en Grèce et à Rome,* Actes du Colloque de Strasbourg, 1985 (Leiden 1987), 482. On the distinction between public and private spaces in Roman domestic architecture: Y. Thébert, "'Private' and 'Public' Spaces: the Components of the Domus," in P. Veyne, ed., *A History of Private Life. From Pagan Rome to Byzantium* (Cambridge and London 1987), 1353–81; A. Wallace-Hadrill, "The Social Structure of the Roman House," *BSR* 56, 1988, 43–97.

13. For recent comprehensive studies of this villa and its mosaics, with extensive bibliographies, see A. Carandini, A. Ricci, M. de Vos, *Filosofiana: la villa di Piazza Armerina. Immagine di un aristocratico romano al tempo di Constantino* (Palermo 1982); R.J.A. Wilson, *Piazza Armerina* (London 1983).

14. G. Voza, "Le ville romane del Tellaro e di Patti in Sicilia e il problema dei rapporti con l'Africa," in *150-Jahr Feier DAI Rom: Ansprachen und Vorträge, 4–7 Dez. 1979, MdI(R) Erg. H.* XXV (Mainz 1982), 202–09; idem, *Kokalos* 22–23, 1976–77, 572–74; and 30–31, 1984–85, 659–61.

15. G. Nieto, "La villa romana de Almenara de Adaja (Valladolid)," *BSEAA* 9, 1943–44, 192–243; J.-G. Gorges, *Les villas hispano-romaines. Inventaire et problématique archéologique* (Paris 1979), 437–38, fig. 53.

16. For a summary of recent work at the villa see D. Srejovic, A. Lalovic, and D. Jancovic, *Gamzigrad. Kasnoanticki Carski Dvorac* (Belgrade 1983), with an English summary. The villa is discussed at some length in J.J. Wilkes, *Diocletian's Palace, Split. Residence of a Retired Roman Emperor* (Sheffield 1986), 66–70.

17. E.g., Wilson (above note 13), 25, on the north hall at Piazza Armerina: "The hall was probably designed for receptions, parties and banquets; it may also have served as an audience-hall for hearing petitions from clients"; cf. L. Bek, "*Quaestiones Conviviales.* The Idea of the *triclinium* and the Staging of Convivial Ceremony from Rome to Byzantium," *AnalRom* 12, 1983, 81–106, who sees the same room (*ibid.* 93) as a probable combination of audience hall and dining room. Carandini (above note 13) calls it "a ceremonial audience-hall."

18. Cf. Thébert (above note 12), 373–74. It is hard to agree with Thébert, however, in his repeated use of the word *exedra* to refer to the principal reception room of the aristocratic house. Thébert bases much of his discussion on the evidence of Apuleius; but in Apuleius the word *exedra* is never used in this sense. In Pontianus' house in Oea, the room used to receive guests and in which the owner's valuable works of art were housed is identified, as in the Late Roman authors we have already cited, as the library or *bibliotheca* (Apul. *Apol.* 53–54).

19. For a full discussion of the evolution of *stibadium*-dining in the Roman world, see K.M.D. Dunbabin, above pp. 121–48. Other studies include J. Marquardt, *Das Privatleben der Römer,* 4th ed. rev. A. Mau (Leipzig 1886, repr. Darmstadt 1964), 306–9; G. Akerström-Hougen, *The Calendar and Hunting Mosaics of the Villa of the Falconer in Argos,* Skrifter Utgivna av Svenska Institutet i Athen, 4, XXIII (Stockholm 1974), 101–10.

20. Mart. *Ep.* 10.48.6: *septem sigma capit; sex sumus, adde Lupum;* Capit-

olinus, *SHA Verus* 5.1: *septem convivium, novem vero convicium.* For alternative numbers of diners, ranging from five to eight: Marquardt (above note 19), 307; Akerström-Hougen (above note 19), 104 and fig. 7. For an illustration of the mosaic from the Villa of the Falconer, see Dunbabin, above, fig. 21.

21. For the Ecija villa: Gorges (above note 15), 374–75, pl. XLVI.1; for the villa at Desenzano: E. Ghislanzoni, *La villa romana di Desenzano* (Milan 1962); E.A. Arslan, *Lombardia, Itinerari Archeologici* 9 (Rome 1982), 318–22; T. Ferro, *Villa romana e monumenti di Desenzano del Garda* (Bornato 1984). Other examples of villas with triconches are listed in I. Lavin, "The House of the Lord: Aspects of the Role of Palace *triclinia* in the Architecture of Late Antiquity and in the Early Middle Ages," *Art Bulletin* 44, 1962, 1–27. To these may now be added the villa at Saturo (Taranto) in Apulia: F. d'Andria, *Puglia, Itinerari Archeologici* 3 (Rome 1980), 134.

22. Sulpicius Severus, *V. Martini* 20: *eminus secundum famulantium disciplinam solo fixa constitit inmobilis.*

23. Sidon. *Ep.* 1.11.10; Amm. Marc. 16.8.9.

24. Macrob. *Sat.* 3.14.4; Olymp. *FHG* iv fr. 23.

25. For dancers: Macrob. *Sat.* 2.1.7, 3.14.4, 7.1.16; Ambrose *Ep.* 27.13; Amm. Marc. 14.6.20. For musicians: Jer. *Ep.* 107.8; Amm. Marc. 14.6.18; Claudian *De Cons. Stil.* 2.141–42. For actors: Olymp. *FHG* iv fr. 23.

26. Gaudentius *Serm.* 8.7 (*PL* 20 col. 890): *infelices illae domus sunt quae nihil discrepant a theatris;* cf. Joh. Chrys. *Hom. in Matth.* 48.6. For other references to after-dinner entertainment in late antiquity, see M. Bonario, "La musica conviviale dal mondo latino antico al medioevo," in *Spettacoli conviviali dall'antichità classica alle corti italiane del '400* (Viterbo 1983), 119–47.

27. For this theme, see especially Bek (above note 17), 91–96. Macrobius (*Sat.* 3.14.4) talks of dancers performing *ante triclinium,* which may mean "outside the dining room," although the meaning could also be "in front of the couches."

28. Carandini, Ricci, and de Vos (above note 13), 298–306, fogl. XLIV–XLV; Wilson (above note 13), 28–29.

29. Sidon. *Car.* 22.204ff. This idea of dining room and forecourt as two parts of a single architectural scheme appears in earlier writers too. It is implied, for example, by Pliny *H.N.* 36.60: *[columnas] ampliores XXX vidimus in cenatione;* also perhaps by Sen. *Ep.* 115.8: *ingentium maculae columnarum . . . porticum aliquam vel capacem populi cenationem ferunt.* For these and other references, see B. Tamm, *Auditorium and Palatium: Stockholm Studies in Classical Archaeology* 2 (Uppsala 1963), 195–96.

30. Plin. *Ep.* 2.17.5.

31. Sidon. *Ep.* 2.2.11: *cui fere totus lacus quaeque tota lacui patet.*

32. This point is developed at greater length by N. Purcell, "Town in Country and Country in Town," in MacDougall (above note 2), 187–203.

33. Carandini (above note 13), 178, fig. 94. A similar scene of outdoor banqueting is depicted on one of the pavements from the villa at Tellaro: G. Voza, "I

mosaici della villa del Tellaro," in *Archeologia nella Sicilia sud-orientale* (Naples 1973), 175–79, pl. 590. On changing fashions in outdoor dining during the Roman period, see K.M.D. Dunbabin, above pp. 121–48.

34. Plin. *Ep.* 5.6.36. For a discussion and reconstruction of this "water *triclinium*" see E. Salza Prina Ricotti, "The Importance of Water in Roman Garden triclinia," in MacDougall (above note 2), 135–84, fig. 1; K.M.D. Dunbabin, above p. 132.

35. Sidon. *Ep.* 2.2.11.

36. Cf. Sidon. *Car.* 22.150–51: *haec post assurgit duplicemque supervenit aream porticus ipsa duplex.* The reference here is to an open courtyard flanked by two curving colonnades.

37. On large *stibadia* in general, see Marquardt (above note 19), 307.

38. G. Fouet, *La villa gallo-romaine de Montmaurin: Gallia,* suppl. 20 (Paris 1983), 75–77; J.-M. Pellier, "Montmaurin: A Garden Villa," in MacDougall (above note 2), 218–19.

39. Petrus Chrysologus *Serm.* 29 (*PL* 52.283).

40. Agnellus *Lib. Pont.* 29; F.W. Deichmann, *Ravenna: Haupstadt des Spätantiken Abendlandes* II.I (Wiesbaden 1974), 194ff.; J.B. Ward-Perkins, *From Classical Antiquity to the Middle Ages* (Oxford 1984), 177; G. De Angelis D'Ossat, "Sulla distrutta aula dei *Quinque Accubita* a Ravenna," *Corsi di Cultura sull'Arte Ravennate e Bizantina* 25, 1973, 263–73.

41. Sidon. *Ep.* 1.11.10ff.

42. For other villas that were undoubtedly old buildings by the time Sidonius wrote about them: *Ep.* 2.2 (Sidonius' own villa at Avitacum, a property inherited by his wife); *Car.* 22 (Leontius' villa at Burgus, built by Leontius' grandfather Paulinus in the fourth century); *Ep.* 2.9 (Ferreolus' villa near Nîmes, evidently undergoing major rebuilding at the time of Sidonius' visit there: above note 5).

43. Procop. *Bell.* 4.28.1.

44. Greg. Tours *Miraculorum Liber 1 de Gloria Martyrum* (*PL* 71.776–77), quoted by Akerström-Hougen (above note 19), 103 n. 84. This kind of discrimination was nothing new. At one time the Roman aristocracy had widely regarded reclining at table as a strictly male prerogative: cf. Val. Max. 2.1.2: *feminae cum viris cubantibus sedentes cenitabant;* Isid. *Orig.* 20.11.9: *postea . . . viri discumbere coeperunt, mulieres sedere, quia turpis visus est in muliere accubitus.* A number of Late Roman mosaics from Antioch show dining scenes in which the male figures recline, while their female companions are seated: D. Levi, *Antioch Mosaic Pavements* (Princeton 1947), I.201–4, II, pls. XLVc-d.

45. Venantius Fortunatus *Car.* 1.19: *quo super accumbens celebrat convivia pastor.*

46. Sidon. *Ep.* 1.2.9.

47. Greg. Mag. *Dial* 2.3 (*PL* 77.225); *Acta Sanct.* Feb. 9, 326. The date of the building (presumably the episcopal palace in Canosa) in which this dinner took place is unknown. It may well, however, have dated back to the time of the city's

first bishop, Stercorius (mid-fourth century): A. Quacquarelli, "Sulle origini cristiane di Canosa di Puglia," *Atti del VI Congresso internazionale di Archeologia Cristiana* (Ravenna 23–30 Sett. 1962) (Vatican City 1965), 321–46.

48. Agnellus *Lib. Pont.* 94, *MGH Script. Rerum Longobard. et Italic. Saec. VI-IX,* 337. On this palace in general see Ward-Perkins (above note 40), 160–63.

49. Paulus Diaconus *V. Hilarii* 2.

50. S. Aurigemma, "Una villa del re Teodorico," *Le Vie d'Italia* (Nov. 1940), 1256–62; R. Olivieri Farioli, "Nota su di un mosaico pavimentale 'Ravennate' da Meldola," *Felix Ravenna* 42 [XCIII], 1966, 116–28. For another villa built by Theodoric, but noted only for its bathhouse: Agnellus *Codex Pont.* XXI (John I) 107–8; Ward-Perkins (above note 40), 213.

51. For renovations to Roman buildings in the sixth century: Cassiodorus *Var.* 2.39, 3.21, 4.51; Ennodius *Car.* 2.12; Venantius Fortunatus *Car.* 1.19.

52. Procop. *Bell.* 3.2.24; cf. Greg. Mag. *Dial.* 2.15 (*PL* 66 col. 162): *in hac urbe dissoluta moenia, eversas domos, destructas ecclesias turbine cernimus, eiusque aedificia longo senio lassata . . . videmus.*

53. Ennodius *Ep.* 8.31: *omnia aedificia eius sub neglegentia consenescunt.*

54. Greg. Mag. *Ep.* 14.3.

55. For the villa at Ruoti: M. Gualtieri, M. Salvatore, and A. Small, *Lo scavo di S. Giovanni di Ruoti ed il periodo tardoantico in Basilicata,* Atti della Tavola Rotonda: Roma 4 Luglio 1981 (Bari 1983); A.M. Small and J.Z. Freed, "S. Giovanni di Ruoti (Basilicata). Il contesto della villa tardo-antico," in A. Giardina, ed., *Società romana e Impero tardoantico III: Le Merci, gli Insediamenti* (Rome 1986), 97–129. For the villa at Galeata: G. Jacopi, *NSc* 4, 1943, 204–12; F. Krischen, *AA* 58, 1943, 459–72.

56. Procop. *Bell.* 3.12.5; *Hist. Arc.* 9.17. A similar picture of *stibadium* dining in mid-sixth-century Constantinople is found in John of Ephesus (*PO* 19.2, 92, 205), quoted by A. Cutler, *JRA* 2, 1989, 406 n. 16.

57. Procop. *Bell.* 7.32.35.

58. See, for example, J. Sodini, "L'habitat urbain en Grèce à la veille des invasions," in *Villes et peuplement dans l'Illyricum protobyzantin: CEFR 77* (Paris 1984), 341–97; R. Stillwell, "The Houses of Antioch," *DOP* 15, 1961, 45–57; J. Balty, "Notes sur l'habitat romain, byzantin et arabe d'Apamée: rapport de synthèse," in J. Balty, ed., *Actes du Colloque Apamée de Syrie. Bilan des recherches archéologiques 1973–1979* (Brussels 1984), 471–503.

59. Lavin (above note 21), 10–11 and fig. 11.

60. Procop. *Aed.* 1.11.16; *Hist. Arc.* 15.36; cf. R. Janin, "La banlieue asiatique de Constantinople," *Échos d'Orient* 22, 1923, 182–90.

61. *V. Theodori Syceonis* 97, trans. E. Dawes and J. Baynes, *Three Byzantine Saints* (Oxford 1948). The Greek text is found in T. Ioannu, *Mnemeia Hagiologica* (Venice 1884), 361–495.

62. Procop. *Aed.* 1.11; J.-B. Thibaut, "L'Hebdomon de Constantinople," *Échos d'Orient* 21, 1922, 31–44.

63. Theophylactus *Hist.* 1.1.2, ed. M. and M. Whitby, *The History of Theophylact Simocatta* (Oxford 1986), 19ff.

64. *Lib. Pont.* 2.3–4 (367). Lavin (above note 21), 12; Ward-Perkins (above note 40), 176.

65. Luitprand of Cremona *Antapodosis* VI.7–8 (*MGH Scriptores* 3.338). The dining hall that formed the setting of this banquet was the famous *Decanneacubita* or "Hall of the Nineteen Couches," for which see R. Krautheimer, "Die Decanneacubita in Konstantinopel. Ein kleiner Beitrag zur Frage Rom und Byzanz," in W. N. Schumacher, ed., *Tortulae: Studien zu altchristlichen und byzantinischen Monumenten: Römische Quartalschrift,* suppl. XXX (Freiburg 1966), 195–99.

Index

Plates

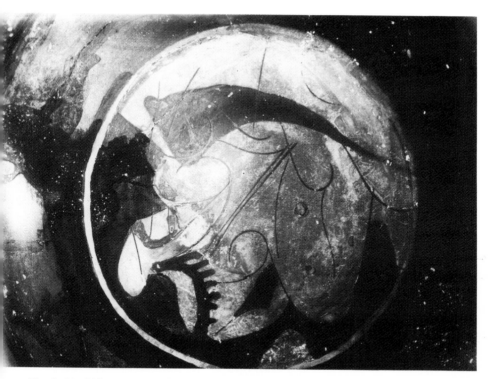

Fig. 1. #1. Pithos Painter: Rhodes Museum 13386, cup (I). T.A.P. Service.

Fig. 2. #2. Attic unattributed: Geneva, Collection Fondation Thétis, Zimmermann-Chamay 105, cup (I).

Fig. 3. #3. Colmar Painter: New York, The Metropolitan Museum of Art, Rogers Fund, 1916 (16.174.41), cup (A [B]).

Fig. 4

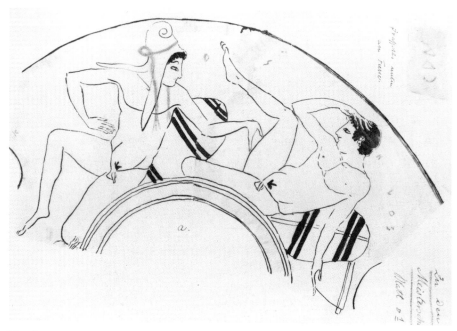

Fig. 5

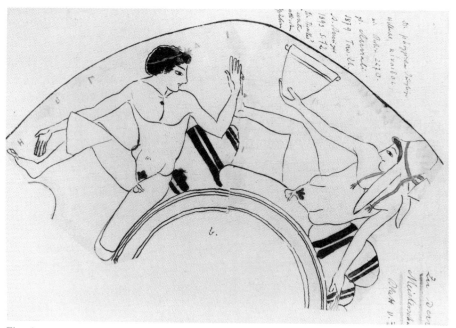

Fig. 6

Figs. 4–6. #4. Triptolemos Painter: formerly Leipzig, Museum des Kunsthandwerks 781.03.G, cup (I, A, B). After drawings in the Beazley Archive.

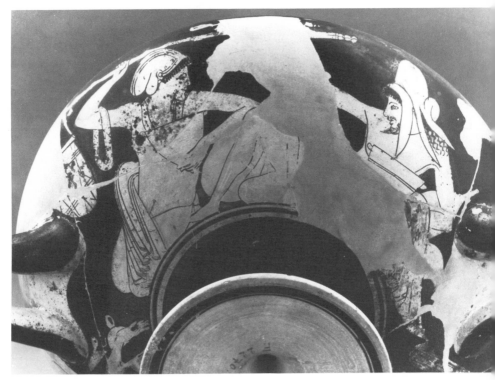

Fig. 7

Fig. 8

Figs. 7–8. #5. Thorvaldsen Group: Antikenmuseum Staatliche Museen
Preussischer Kulturbesitz Berlin F 2270, cup (A, B).

Fig. 9

Fig. 10. A detail

Figs. 9–10. #6. Brygos Painter (von Bothmer): The Cleveland Museum of Art, rhyton in the form of a ram's head. Purchase from the J. H. Wade Fund, 88.8.

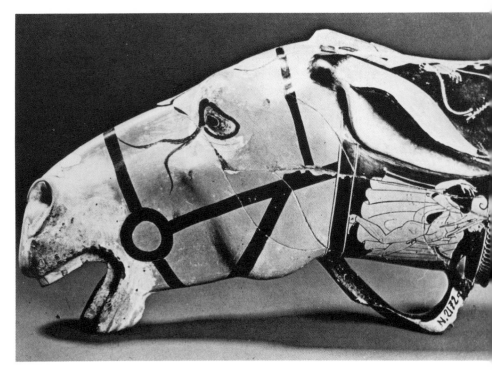

Fig. 11

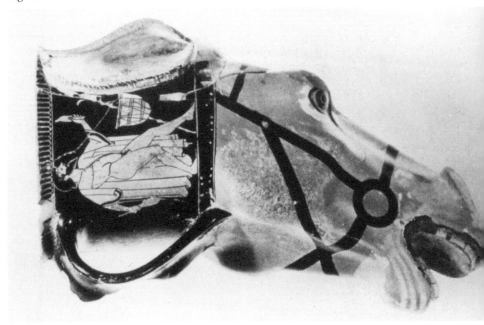

Fig. 12

Figs. 11–13. #7. Brygos Painter: Musee d'Aléria (Corsica), Jehasse 1902, donkey's-head cup. After Jehasse pls. 33, 35b, and museum postcard.

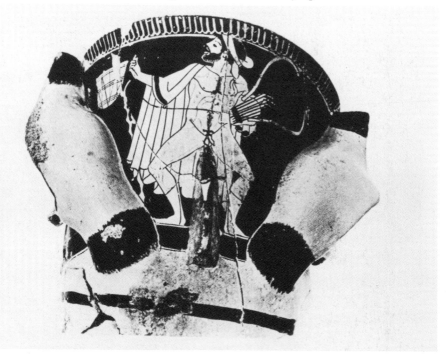

Fig. 13

Fig. 14. #8. Douris: Florence, Museo Archeologico 3922, cup (A).
Soprintendenza Archeologica per la Toscana-Firenze.

Fig. 15

Figs. 15–18. #9. Manner of Douris (Jucker): Collection Ebnöther Les Arcs, head kantharos (A, B, side). Foto Endrik Lerch Ascona.

Fig. 16

Fig. 17

Fig. 18

Fig. 19

Fig. 20

Fig. 21

Figs. 19–21. #10. Attic unattributed: London BM 95.10–27.2, stemless cup (I, A, B). Courtesy Trustees of the British Museum.

Fig. 22

Figs. 22–23. #11. Leningrad Painter: London BM E 351, pelike (A, B). Courtesy Trustees of the British Museum.

Fig. 23

Fig. 24

Figs. 24–25. #12. Nausikaa
Painter: Villa Giulia 3583, column
krater (A, B). DAI Negs. 80.224,
80.223.

Fig. 25

Fig. 26. Stieglitz Painter: Oxford, Ashmolean Museum 1966.688, cup (I).

Fig. 27. Stieglitz Painter: Bryn Mawr
College, Ella Riegel Memorial
Museum P-932, P-955, cup (I).

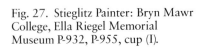

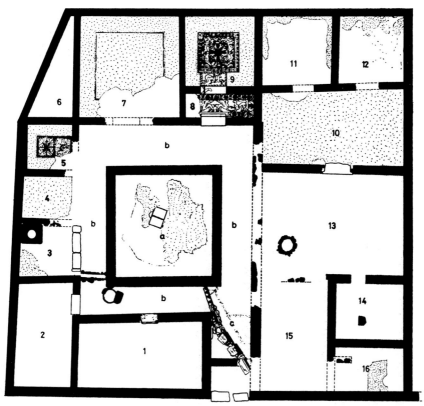

Fig. 1. Eretria, House of the Mosaics, plan. After P. Ducrey, *AntK* 22, 1979, 1, 5, fig. 2. Courtesy École Suisse d'Archéologie en Grèce.

Fig. 2. Olynthus, House of the Comedian, *andron*. After D. M. Robinson and J. W. Graham, *Excavations at Olynthus 8, The Hellenic House* (Baltimore 1938), pl. 17, 1.

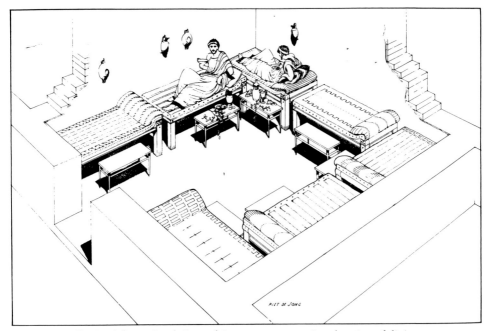

Fig. 3. Athens, South Stoa of Agora, reconstruction drawing of dining room. Photo courtesy American School of Classical Studies at Athens, Agora Excavations.

Fig. 4. Delos, House of the Trident, plan. After J. Chamonard, *Délos* VIII, *Le Quartier du Théâtre* (Paris 1922), 1, pl. XIII.

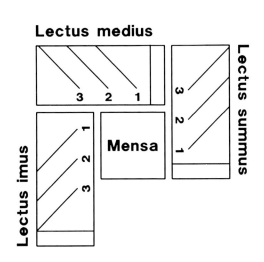

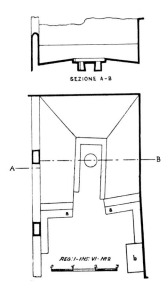

Fig. 5. Layout of Roman *triclinium*. After H. Thédenat, *Pompéi* (Paris 1910), fig. 44.

Fig. 7. Pompeii I.6.2–4, Casa del Criptoportico, *triclinium* plan. After Soprano (1950), fig. 30.

Fig. 6. Pompeii I.6.2–4, Casa del Criptoportico, *triclinium*. Photo KMDD.

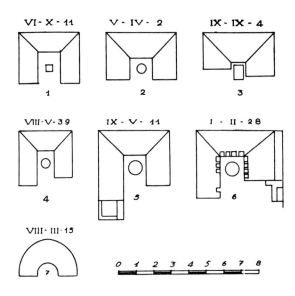

Fig. 8. Pompeii, plans of outdoor *triclinia*. After Soprano (1950), fig. 28.

Fig. 9. Pompeii III.vii, vineyard *triclinium*. Photo S. Jashemski, courtesy W. Jashemski.

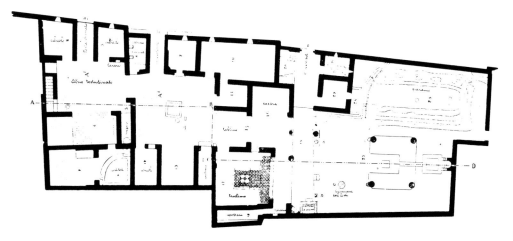

Fig. 10. Pompeii I.7.10–12, Casa dell'Efebo, plan. After A. Maiuri, *NSc* 1927, fig. p. 33.

Fig. 11. Pompeii I.7.10–12, Casa dell'Efebo, outdoor *triclinium*. After A. Maiuri, *NSc* 1927, pl. V.

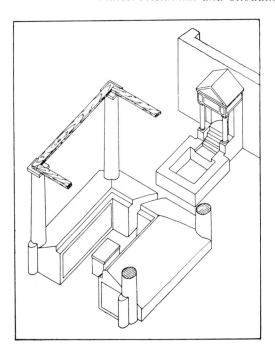

Fig. 12. Pompeii I.7.10–12, Casa dell'Efebo, outdoor *triclinium*. After Soprano (1950), fig. 31.

Fig. 13. Antioch, Atrium House, *triclinium* mosaic. Photo courtesy Department of Art and Archaeology, Princeton University.

Fig. 14. Antioch, House of Drinking Contest, *triclinium* mosaic. Photo courtesy Department of Art and Archaeology, Princeton University.

Fig. 16. Volubilis, House of Dionysus and the Seasons, *triclinium*. Photo KMDD.

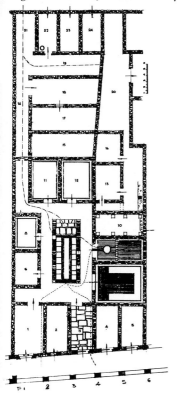

Fig. 15. Volubilis, House of
Dionysus and the Seasons, plan.
After R. Etienne, *Le Quartier
Nord-Est de Volubilis* (Paris 1960),
pl. VI.

Fig. 17. Thysdrus, House of the Months, *triclinium*
mosaic, drawing. After L. Foucher, *Latomus* 20,
1961, pl. XI.

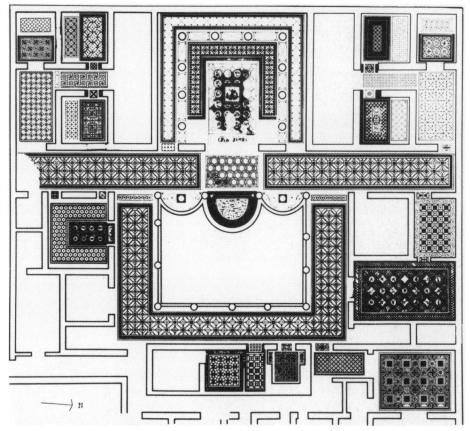

Fig. 18. Acholla, House of Neptune, plan. After S. Gozlan and A. Bourgeois, *BAC* n.s. 17B, 1981 (1984), pl. 2. Courtesy S. Gozlan.

Fig. 19. Complutum, Casa de Baco, cup bearers from corridor leading to *triclinium*. Photo courtesy D. Fernandez-Galiano.

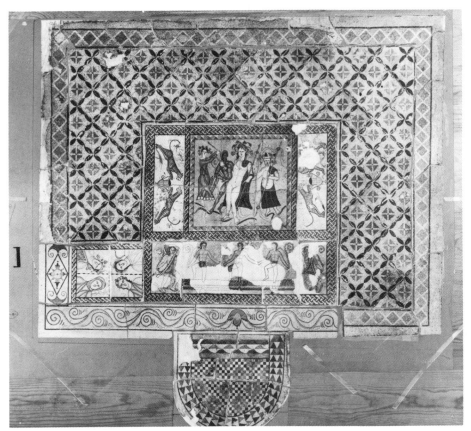

Fig. 20. Complutum, Casa de Baco, *triclinium* mosaic. Photo courtesy
D. Fernandez-Galiano.

Fig. 21. Dargoleja, room for
stibadium, drawing. After
J. M. Blazquez, *Mosaicos
romanos de Sevilla, Granada,
Cadiz y Murcia* (CMEsp IV,
Madrid 1982), fig. 9.

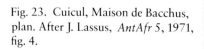

Fig. 22. Argos, Villa of the Falconer, mosaic of *stibadium*, drawing.
Courtesy G. Akerström-Hougen (drawing O. Söndergard).

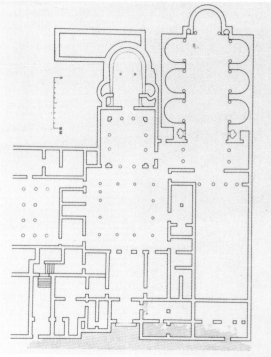

Fig. 23. Cuicul, Maison de Bacchus,
plan. After J. Lassus, *AntAfr* 5, 1971,
fig. 4.

Fig. 24. Antioch, House of Buffet Supper, general view. Photo courtesy
Department of Art and Archaeology, Princeton University.

Fig. 25. Antioch, House of Buffet Supper, detail of mosaic. Photo courtesy
Department of Art and Archaeology, Princeton University.

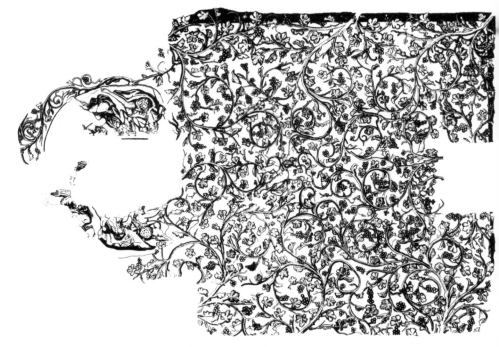

Fig. 26. Vienne, mosaic with Lycurgus and vine and Dionysiac banqueters, drawing. After J. Lancha, *Recueil général des mosaiques de la Gaule* III. *Narbonnaise* 2. *Vienne* (1981), pl. LXXVIII (drawing R. Prudhomme).

Fig. 27. Vienne, detail of Dionysiac banqueters from Lycurgus mosaic. Photo courtesy J. Lancha.

Fig. 28. Coptic textile, roundel of rustic feast; Brooklyn Museum acc. no. 44.143c. Photo courtesy Brooklyn Museum.

Fig. 29. Rome, *Hypogaeum* of Vibia, painting of Banquet of Blessed. After J. Wilpert, *Le pitture delle catacombe romane* (Rome 1903), pl. 132, 1.

Fig. 30. Leiden, sarcophagus lid with hunters' picnic; Rijksmuseum van Oudheden, Inv. Nr. H *8. Photo courtesy Rijksmuseum van Oudheden, Leiden.

Fig. 31. Pompeii V.2.4, Casa del Triclinio, painted panel from *triclinium* showing indoor banquet; Naples MN 120029. After M. Borda, *La pittura romana* (Milan 1958), 252.

Fig. 32. Pompeii IX.3.5, Casa di M. Lucretius, painting, Erotes and Psyches at outdoor banquet; Naples MN 9207. Photo S. Jashemski, courtesy W. Jashemski.

Fig. 33. Stabiae, Villa in Campo Varano, frieze with outdoor banquet of pygmies; Naples MN 9099. Photo DAI (Rome), Inst. Neg. 67.2369.

Fig. 34. Pompeii I.7.10–12, Casa dell'Efebo, frieze from outdoor *triclinium*, Nilotic landscape with banqueters. After A. Maiuri, *NSc* 1927, pl. VII.

Fig. 35. Rome, Villa Doria Pamphili, sarcophagus with Dionysiac *stibas* (Matz, *ASR* IV, 3, no. 194). Photo DAI (Rome), Inst. Neg. 76.88.

Fig. 36. Carthage, mosaic of banquet with seated diners; Tunis, Musée du Bardo A.162. Photo DAI (Rome), Inst. Neg. 63.356.

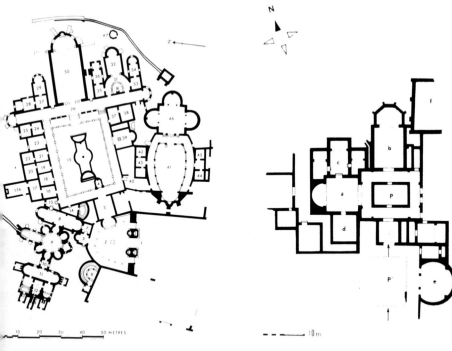

Fig. 1. Plan of the fourth-century villa at Piazza Armerina, Sicily (from Wilson 1983, fig. 1)

Fig. 3. Plan of the third/fourth-century villa at Almenara de Adaja, Spain (from Gorges 1979, pl. LIII)

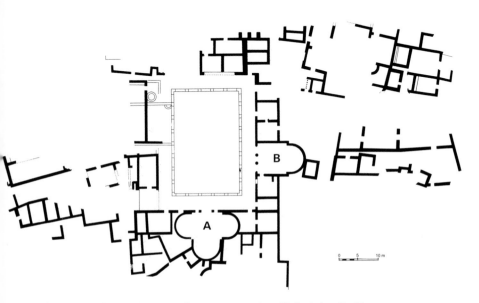

Fig. 2. Plan of the fourth-century villa at Patti Marina, Sicily (after De Voza 1982, fig. 1)

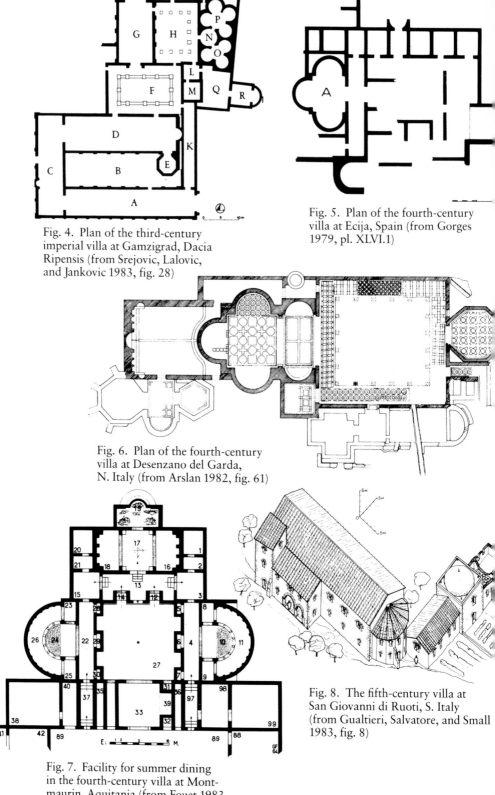

Fig. 4. Plan of the third-century imperial villa at Gamzigrad, Dacia Ripensis (from Srejovic, Lalovic, and Jankovic 1983, fig. 28)

Fig. 5. Plan of the fourth-century villa at Ecija, Spain (from Gorges 1979, pl. XLVI.1)

Fig. 6. Plan of the fourth-century villa at Desenzano del Garda, N. Italy (from Arslan 1982, fig. 61)

Fig. 7. Facility for summer dining in the fourth-century villa at Montmaurin, Aquitania (from Fouet 1983, fig. 23)

Fig. 8. The fifth-century villa at San Giovanni di Ruoti, S. Italy (from Gualtieri, Salvatore, and Small 1983, fig. 8)